DK COLLECTOR'S GUIDES

COSTUME JEWELRY

Miriam Haskell pendant necklace and earrings
of amber glass stones and beads. *1940s*
N: 17½ in (45 cm) circ; E: 2 in (5 cm) long **$130–190** **RITZ**

DK COLLECTOR'S GUIDES

COSTUME JEWELRY

JUDITH MILLER

with John Wainwright

Photography by Graham Rae

DK PUBLISHING

LONDON, NEW YORK,
MELBOURNE, MUNICH AND DELHI

A joint production from **DK** and
THE PRICE GUIDE COMPANY

Dorling Kindersley Limited
Project Editor Paula Regan
Project Art Editor Kelly Meyer
Assistant Designer Anna Plucinska
Senior Editors Caroline Hunt, Angela Wilkes,
Amber Tokeley
Senior Art Editor Mandy Earey
Managing Editor Julie Oughton
Managing Art Editor Heather McCarry
Art Director Carole Ash
Category Publisher Jackie Douglas
Production Joanna Bull, Rita Sinha
DTP Designer Mike Grigoletti
US Editor Christine Heilman

The Price Guide Company Limited
Publishing Manager Julie Brooke
Digital Image Coordinator Cara Miller
Editorial Assistants Megan Watson,
Sara Sturgess

While every care has been taken in the
compilation of this guide, neither the authors
nor the publishers accept any liability for any
financial or other loss incurred by reliance
placed on the information contained in
DK Collector's Guides: Costume Jewelry.

First American edition, 2003
04 05 10 9 8 7 6 5 4 3 2

Published in the United States by
DK Publishing, Inc.
375 Hudson Street
New York, New York 10014

Penguin Group

The Price Guide Company (UK) Ltd
Studio 21, Waterside
44–48 Wharf Road
London N1 7UX
info@thepriceguidecompany.com

Copyright © 2003 Judith Miller and
Dorling Kindersley Limited

All rights reserved under International and
Pan-American Copyright Conventions. No part
of this publication may be reproduced, stored in a
retrieval system, or transmitted in any form or by
any means, electronic, mechanical, photocopying,
recording, or otherwise without the prior permission of the copyright owner. Published in Great
Britain by Dorling Kindersley Limited.

Library of Congress Cataloging-in-Publication Data

Miller, Judith.
Collector's guides: costume jewelry / Judith Miller
with John Wainwright.
p. cm.
Includes index.
ISBN 0-7894-9642-9 (alk. paper)
1. Costume Jewelry--Collectors and collecting--
Catalogs. I. Wainwright, John. II. Title.
NK4890.C67M55 2003
688'.2'075 --dc21
2003051626

Color reproduction by Colourscan, Singapore
Printed and bound by SNP Leefung, China

Discover more at
www.dk.com

Contents

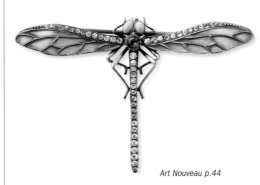

Art Nouveau p.44

Designer profiles 54

Fahrner p.73

A-Z of designers and makers 134

Bakelite p.159

Gallery of unsigned pieces 214

Unsigned necklace p.217

Appendices and index 236

Maison Gripoix p.91

How to use this book

DK Collector's Guides: Costume Jewelry is divided into four main sections: the story of costume jewelry, detailing the changing styles of costume jewelry from ancient times to the present day; designer profiles, focusing on the life and career of 20 major costume jewelry designers; an A–Z of designers and makers, with information and representative sample pieces; and a gallery of unsigned pieces, divided into necklaces, bracelets, bangles, pins, and earrings.

Designer Information
Gives a fascinating insight into the life and career of the costume jewelry designer. Also highlights the particular characteristics of his or her jewelry and offers advice on what styles, motifs, or limited editions are best to collect.

Biography
Provides an at-a-glance history of the designer's career. Significant events are listed, such as birth and death dates, the creation and closure of costume jewelry companies, when key design staff was hired, and the year popular lines were brought out.

Feature Box
Details a particular person or event that influenced the profiled designer, or a material or style central to his or her costume jewelry designs.

Further Features Bar
Indicates the influences and inspirations behind the costume jewelry. It may also highlight important commissions—often from famous clients—that had a positive effect on the designer's career.

ABBREVIATIONS:
The following abbreviations are used in the captions:

B = bracelet or bangle
E = earrings
N = necklace
P = pin
Pd = pendant

circ = circumference
NPA = no price available

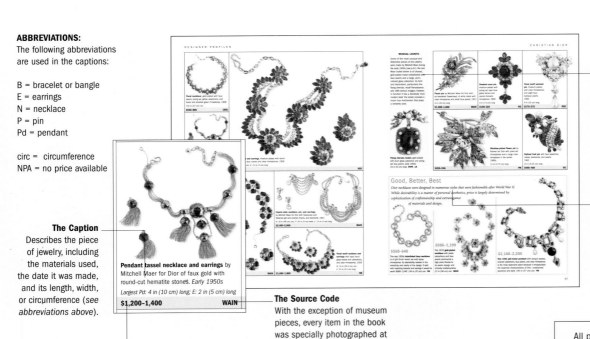

Mini Feature Box
Highlights a particular motif, style, material, or technique used by the designer. It explains why that piece or type of jewelry is so collectible and includes advice on how much you can expect to pay.

Good, Better, Best
This feature compares three specially selected pieces of jewelry—all of the same type and by the same designer. It explains why certain characteristics make each piece more or less desirable to costume jewelry collectors.

The Caption
Describes the piece of jewelry, including the materials used, the date it was made, and its length, width, or circumference (*see abbreviations above*).

Pendant tassel necklace and earrings by Mitchell Maer for Dior of faux gold with round-cut hematite stones. *Early 1950s*
Largest Pd: 4 in (10 cm) long; E: 2 in (5 cm) long
$1,200–1,400   WAIN

The Price Guide
All prices are shown in ranges to give you a ball-park figure of what you should expect to pay for a similar piece.

The Source Code
With the exception of museum pieces, every item in the book was specially photographed at an auction house, dealer, antiques market, or private collection. Each source is credited here by code and can be checked against the Key to Dealer Codes on pp.246–247.

All prices shown are in US$. Please refer to: *http://money.cnn.com/ markets/currencies/* for latest Canadian $ conversion rates.

Foreword

Costume jewelry appeals to me on so many levels: it is undeniably beautiful to look at, it reflects the fashions of the era it was produced in, and the quality of workmanship and materials used are often as good as or better than those used in "real" or precious jewelry. What is even more exciting to those of us who are dazzled by all that diamanté is that costume jewelry was meant to be affordable, and was therefore often produced in large quantities, so there are plenty of examples out there just waiting for a collector to find. And, perhaps even more importantly, it's a collection that you can wear, and it will always attract compliments and admiring glances!

In the last few years the market for costume jewelry has started to grow, and so I believe the time is right for a comprehensive full-color guide that tells collectors more than simply who made a piece and when, what it is made of, and how much it costs. So, in addition to all this vital information, *DK Collector's Guides: Costume Jewelry* also explains what makes one piece more collectible than another and provides tips on what to look for when buying. Plus, we have researched the history of the designers and manufacturers—not just the major ones but many smaller and lesser-known names whose pieces are only now starting to become collectible. We also look at how costume jewelry developed over the years to take in new technologies and materials.

Costume jewelry collections take many different themes. Some people are faithful to a particular designer or era; others tailor their collections to include only flowers, figures or fruit, birds, beasts, or bugs. We have reflected this by including many unsigned pieces, which are collectible simply because they are wonderful to look at—not because they have a famous name stamped on the back.

If you already collect costume jewelry, I hope this book will add to the joy it brings you. And to new collectors, all I can say is beware—all that glitters may not be gold, but it certainly can be addictive!

Robert Goossens, p.199

Judith Miller.

7

Introduction

Costume jewelry is essentially a 20th-century term for jewelry made from non-precious materials, such as imitation gemstones and faux pearls, set in silver or inexpensive base metals. In fact, however, early costume jewelry dates back thousands of years and many pieces incorporate semi-precious stones. Costume jewelry was often produced in large quantities, with pieces designed to go with each new season's outfits. Much of it was unsigned and was never intended to last for a long time, or represent a financial investment, like fine jewelry. However, despite the inexpensive materials used, much costume jewelry is just as beautiful and as highly crafted as its precious counterpart, and it is now considered highly collectible.

Suffragette jewelry, p.38

WHY COLLECT COSTUME JEWELRY?

Not only is costume jewelry beautiful in its own right, it is often more innovative in design than precious jewelry, which in many case relies on the intrinsic value of the materials used for desirability. In fact, the best reason for collecting costume jewelry is so that you can wear the pieces yourself. Since new jewelry designs were produced every season, it is also a fascinating reflection of changing fashions and social history, from the early 19th century through every decade to the present. Although most pieces are affordable, some are now highly sought-after and difficult to find, all of which adds to the excitement and pleasure of collecting. As designers are constantly creating new pieces, costume jewelry is a collecting field with a future, and its popularity is reflected in the fact that more and more pieces are commanding high prices.

HOW TO GET STARTED

The best way to find out more about costume jewelry is to do some thorough background research before buying. Books, decorative arts museums, and exhibition catalogs are a good starting point, as are costume jewelry websites. Visiting specialist dealers will give you an opportunity to see a wide variety of pieces at first hand. Pick them up so that you can take a closer look and feel how much they weigh. Dealers are always happy to talk to enthusiasts, so ask questions about the background and history of the pieces you like. All of this will help you to become familiar with different periods and styles of jewelry and to recognize the characteristics of particular designers and makers.

WHERE AND WHAT TO BUY

When buying pieces to collect, good condition is of paramount importance. Specialist dealers and auction houses are the most reliable sources of good-quality costume jewelry and will provide a receipt and information about the age of each piece and its maker, if known. For less expensive pieces and bargains, it is fun to dig through old jewelry at rummage sales, antique markets, and vintage clothes shops. There is also a vast selection of costume jewelry available on the Internet.

You can build up a jewelry collection that simply complements your own wardrobe. Alternatively, you can collect pieces from a particular period or designer, collect just one type of jewelry such as pins, or go for a subject-themed collection. Examine each piece carefully with a magnifying glass before buying, to check for defects and make sure that any clasps and other fastenings work properly.

FAKES AND FORGERIES

As costume jewelry has risen in value, forgeries have become more common, particularly at the upper end of the market. Some pieces, such as Trifari's Jelly Belly pins and Eisenberg Originals, have been widely forged and often have a fake maker's mark. Until your eye is sufficiently well trained, it is wise to buy pieces in the mid- and lower price ranges and to avoid buying expensive pieces from non-specialists. Building up a relationship with a reputable specialist dealer is the best way to avoid expensive mistakes.

CARE AND REPAIR

Costume jewelry is fragile and should be looked after with care if you want it to last. Do not let it come into contact with soap, face creams, scents, or hairspray, and store pieces flat in individual boxes, wrapped in acid-free paper. Clean your jewelry with cotton swabs or a soft toothbrush and a little distilled water, making sure it doesn't sink into the settings. Pat each piece dry and use a jeweler's cloth to clean metal settings.

The best way to repair costume jewelry is to take it to a specialist, but it's expensive. You can replace lost stones in less valuable pieces by buying replacements from gem wholesalers and art and craft shops, then using jeweler's cement to glue them back in place.

Chanel, p.56

The story of costume jewelry

From ancient cultures to the present day

The term "costume jewelry" wasn't actually coined until the 1920s, but the concept is in fact as old as our most ancient civilizations. From as far back as pre-Christian Mesopotamia, via ancient Egypt to the Roman Empire, and from the Middle Ages and the Renaissance right up to today, people have always derived great pleasure from adorning themselves with decorative artifacts. Such artifacts, although undoubtedly beautiful, are not, however, in themselves necessarily valuable, unlike precious jewelry.

The story of costume jewelry is a fascinating reflection of social history. It lies partly in the constant quest for the new: for amazing new materials and the most modern methods of manufacture. Above all, however, it is the story of the never-ending and tantalizing search for the new in both fashion and style.

An ancient art form

As trade routes began to link different parts of the world, so various cultures started to influence and build upon each other's jewelry styles. New materials were discovered and exploited, and jewelry design became increasingly complex and sophisticated.

A PRIMITIVE DESIRE

The desire for self-embellishment stretches back to our most ancient cultures, when people first began transforming the natural objects around them into decorative pieces to wear. Gradually, numerous styles and forms of ornament were established that not only inspired later civilizations, but which also still resonate today. By around 3,000 BC, trade routes had already linked North Africa, Europe, and the Near and Middle East, and the transmission of jewelry styles, forms, and manufacturing techniques began in earnest.

The Sumerians in Mesopotamia (now Iraq) were widely admired as jewelers, and had mastered many techniques still in use today. In particular, they discovered and exploited the potential of gold, which became prized not only for its rarity and aesthetic qualities, but also for its malleability. Silver, lapis lazuli, and red cornelian were other typical components of Sumerian jewelry.

The Egyptians absorbed the Sumerians' skills, and went on to develop their own distinctive style, which has enjoyed numerous revivals over the centuries, most notably in the 1920s. The Egyptians concentrated on graphic designs that

mirrored their hieroglyphics and were also heavily influenced by African styles. They also used precious metals, especially gold, as well as precious and semi-precious gemstones, faience, and pearls from the Nile River.

Egyptian style was later absorbed by the Phoenicians, who also helped to cross-pollinate jewelry styles through their huge trading empire, which stretched across the Mediterranean to Spain. By around 500 BC, these styles had filtered through to the Etruscans in Tuscany and Umbria. Expanding on the skills of the Egyptians and Phoenicians, their jewelry already displayed tremendous technical expertise: in particular, they refined the technique of granulation—the soldering of tiny grains of metal onto a metal surface.

CLASSICAL STYLES

By 350 BC, when ancient Greek culture dominated the Middle and Near East, jewelry design had become remarkably uniform. Gold was in relatively plentiful supply, and the Greeks exploited it to produce fine, intricate filigree work fashioned, for example, into sprays of flowers often inlaid with colorful enamels. Emeralds and pearls also became increasingly popular and new motifs were introduced, such as the reef knot, crescent shapes, and gods such as Eros. However, it was the introduction of different colors through the inlay of stones and colored glass that made Greek jewelry particularly distinctive.

Greek style later gave way to Roman, although the latter retained certain aspects including the Greek preference for emeralds, pearls, and sapphires. Filigree work, however, was abandoned in favor of smooth, stark, bold pieces, and Christian motifs began to appear as Christianity spread. Other popular Roman jewelry motifs were scrolling acanthus leaves and key patterns, some of which were inspired by Greek prototypes.

A WEALTH OF RESOURCES

By the time the Roman empire was declining, in around the 4th century AD, jewelers had access to a wealth of natural resources. Gold was being mined throughout Europe and Africa; ivory was imported from India and Africa; pearls had been discovered in the Red Sea and off the Indian coast; and a variety of gemstones including emeralds, amber, lapis lazuli, garnets, and onyx had all been added to the design palette.

By the 6th century AD, the jewelers of the Byzantine Empire, and particularly Constantinople, were fully exploiting this wealth of materials. The most innovative technique of this early Byzantine period was *opus interrasile* metalwork, in which gold sheet was pierced using tiny chisels. Earlier styles were also reworked, notably those emanating from Persia

and India. Precious stones were used with increasing frequency and jewelry design generally became more complex. Other new techniques included damascening, in which a soft metal such as silver or gold is inlaid into a hard base metal, and gold cloisonné enamel.

Byzantine and medieval European jewelry styles overlapped, with the Crusaders bringing back a host of influences and earlier styles from North Africa and the Middle East. Generally, Medieval jewelry featured precious stones set in gold or silver and inscriptions were popular. Above all, Christian iconography really came to the fore, and numerous Christian motifs, most notably the cross, were employed.

OLD WORLD, NEW WORLD

While Byzantine and Christian styles and motifs continued to be produced throughout the Renaissance, which spread across Europe from the 14th to the early 17th century, this period was essentially characterized by the rediscovery of classicism and, in particular, Greek and Roman styles of jewelry. At the same time, Spain's activities in the New World in the 15th century resulted in a treasure trove of gold, silver, and precious gemstones flooding into Europe. Consequently, fashionable jewelry became increasingly ostentatious, desirable and, most significantly, the preserve of the super-affluent. With a growing and increasingly fashion-conscious European population, the need to find convincing and cheaper substitutes for precious materials was now pressing.

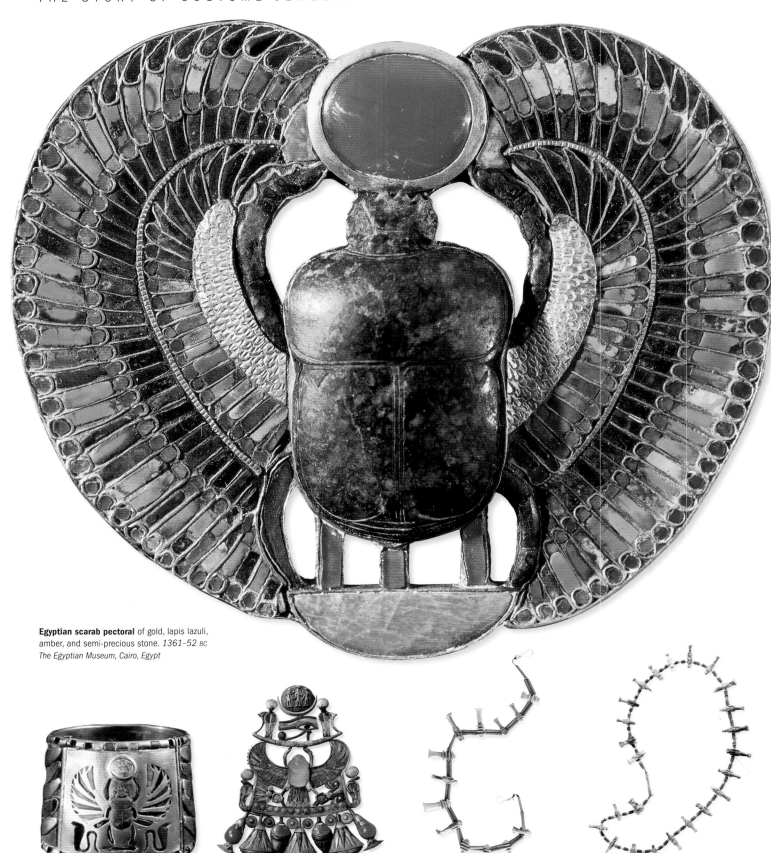

Egyptian scarab pectoral of gold, lapis lazuli, amber, and semi-precious stone. *1361–52 BC*
The Egyptian Museum, Cairo, Egypt

Egyptian scarab anklet of gold, lapis lazuli, and cornelian. *1070–945 BC*
The Egyptian Museum, Cairo, Egypt

Egyptian bird-scarab pectoral of gold, paste, and semi-precious stones. *c.1370–52 BC*
The Egyptian Museum, Cairo, Egypt

Egyptian necklace with blue and turquoise faience beads and amulets. *c.500 BC*
14 in (35.5 cm) long **$1,600–2,100 ANA**

Egyptian necklace with gold and blue faience beads and turquoise amulets. *c.500 BC*
18 in (45.75 cm) long **$1,600–2,400 ANA**

Phoenician earrings cut from sheet gold in the form of an ankh. *600–500 BC* *The British Museum, London*

Mesopotamian necklace, bracelet, and earrings from ancient Assyria. *c.2200–350 BC* *The British Museum, London*

Mesopotamian child's diadem of gold, lapis lazuli, and cornelian. *c.2500–2300 BC* *The British Museum, London*

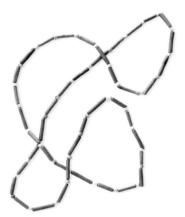

Egyptian necklace with gold and tubular brown faience beads. *c.1800 BC* 15½ in (40 cm) long **$1,000–1,300 ANA**

The beauty of natural forms...

From the earliest times, people have adorned themselves to enhance looks, signal status, ward off evil, and celebrate the beauty of the natural forms around them. The first jewelry was fashioned from bone, shell, and feathers. Later, clay, natural glass, precious metals, and gemstones were used. Meanwhile, various civilizations from the Sumerians to the Etruscans gradually built on each other's manufacturing methods and style influences. Traders, particularly the Phoenicians, transported both raw materials and jewelry around their extensive routes, which helped to spread these techniques and styles. The most enduring of these came from the ancient Egyptians.

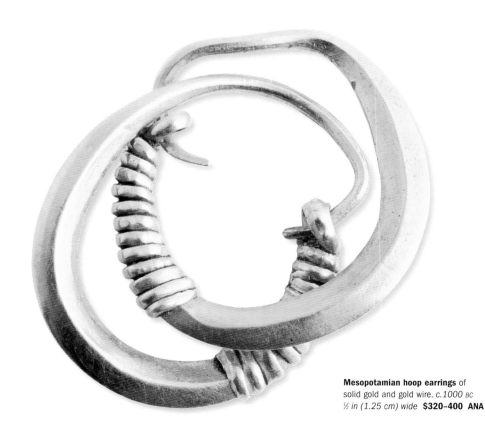

Mesopotamian hoop earrings of solid gold and gold wire. *c.1000 BC* ½ in (1.25 cm) wide **$320–400 ANA**

Greek ring made of gold and set with a precious or semi-precious stone. *330–27 BC*
The British Museum, London

Creations for gods and mortals...

Ancient Greek jewelry was worn to enhance a woman's beauty and to demonstrate wealth. It was given as a gift at births and weddings, and precious pieces were often buried with their owner. Although few such pieces have survived, lists of treasures unearthed from the Parthenon and the sanctuary of Apollo at Delos reveal that the ancient Greeks also dedicated jewelry to their gods. The Greek style was delicate: intricate filigree work was made into flowers, spirals, and waves, often infilled with enamel and set with garnets, emeralds, and pearls. Before long, however, a starker, bolder Roman taste was in the ascendant.

Greek necklace made of gold. *c.200 BC*
The British Museum, London

Greek head-wreath made of gold. From the Dardanelles. *400–300 BC*
The British Museum, London

Roman bronze wheel pin with remnants of inlaid polychrome enamels. *AD c.200.* *2¾ in (7 cm) wide* **$720–800 ANA**

Reflections of Empire...

The Roman Empire produced a style of ornamentation that was bold, striking, and in some respects utilitarian. Filigree work was abandoned in favor of starker, burnished gold pieces, although certain aspects of Greek style were absorbed, including a liking for precious stones. As Christianity started to spread through the Empire, Christian motifs such as the cross and lotus flower appeared. Byzantine jewelry represents a continuation of the Greco-Roman tradition, but it evolved its own unique style as it swiftly adapted to new tastes: solid gold jewelry fell out of fashion, to be replaced by delicate gold leaf work.

Roman solid gold cloak pin in the shape of the Christian cross. *AD c.100–200* *2½ in (6.25 cm) long* **$32,000–42,000 LNXG**

Late Roman–Byzantine gold earrings with sapphires and low-grade pearls. *AD c.400–500* *2¼ in (5.75 cm) long* **$2,100–2,700 LNXG**

Byzantine bronze cross with incised figure of Jesus. *AD c.900* *4 in (10 cm) long* **$720–800 ANA**

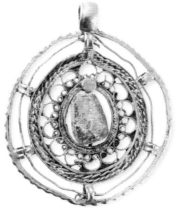

Byzantine filigree gold wire pendant with colored glass stone center. *AD c.500–600* *1½ in (4 cm) long* **$5,300–6,400 LNXG**

Roman solid gold ring with a carved blue agate cameo of a female bust. *AD c.100–200* *½ in (1.25 cm) wide* **$5,300–6,400 LNXG**

English ring pin of punched ornament inlaid with bands of niello. *1200s*
The British Museum, London

Emblems of wealth...

Medieval royalty, noblemen, and even rich merchants invariably kept a store of precious and semi-precious stones, and it was they who supplied the costly raw materials to the goldsmith when jewelry was commissioned. There was no gender distinction in the wearing of jewelry, although women's pieces tended to be more complex and varied. Brooches were especially popular, although girdles and cloak clasps, chains and collars, circlets and chaplets were also worn by both sexes. Cloisonné—enamel with a gold ground—was popular and favored motifs included stylized dragon heads.

Medallion collar of gold set with pearls and jewels with filigree and enamel. *1100s*
The Kremlin Museum, Moscow, Russia

Jeweled disc pin of gold with garnets and pieces of shell. *AD 400–900*
The Ashmolean Museum, Oxford, England

Kingston pin *AD 500–600*
City of Liverpool Museum, Merseyside, England

Renaissance splendor...

Spain's activities in the New World in the 15th century led to vast hoards of gold, silver, and gemstones flooding into Europe. Medieval austerity gave way to ostentation as the royal courts found themselves awash with flamboyant jewelry. A new fashion was set for jewels of incredible size and profusion. Greco-Roman styles were rediscovered, and miniatures came into vogue in the 17th century after French goldsmiths, led by Jean Toutin, developed a way of painting them in enamel on gold.

Renaissance cat pendant with natural baroque pearl. *1450–1600*
S.J. Philips Antique Dealers, London

Italian Renaissance earrings of gold with flower and cherub motifs. *1450–1600*
Location unknown

Enameled pendant of gold with rubies, emeralds, and diamonds. *Late 1500s*
The British Museum, London

Early imitations

As the 18th century got underway, a thriving costume jewelry trade began to develop in Europe. Pastes and metals were improving steadily, along with production techniques, and faux jewelry was becoming increasingly desirable.

A FASHION FOR FAKES

Eighteenth-century Europe witnessed the emergence of an increasingly well-off middle class for whom this was a new and exciting period of affluence. Clothes and jewelry became more extravagant, and gemstones decorated everything from sword hilts to hair ornaments. There was a passion for large set jewels, especially diamonds, and good fakes inevitably became increasingly sought-after.

Gablonz in Bohemia (now the Czech Republic) started producing high-quality paste stones, and a thriving costume jewelry business began to develop in Europe. The advent of machine cutting allowed the production of large numbers of glass stones of regular size and quality, and jewelry became more affordable. Other techniques also improved. Like precious gems of the time, glass and paste were foil-backed to increase brilliance and luster. Ironically, the craftsmanship was sometimes finer on the paste settings than on precious stones, and they were also more innovatively cut and faceted. All these factors made costume jewelry ever more desirable.

As daytime and evening fashions became more defined, so did jewelry, with daytime jewelry becoming significantly more restrained. Diamonds remained the gem of choice for after dark, but convincing substitutes remained elusive: Bohemian stones were not hard enough to withstand the required cutting process. One alternative was rock crystal, a naturally occurring colorless quartz. A seam near Bristol, England, provided a plentiful supply, sometimes known as Bristows or Bristol stones; others came from France, Spain, and Portugal. Then a Frenchman, Georges Frédéric Stras, began exploring the potential of a glass developed by Englishman George Ravenscroft. It proved hard enough to use as a diamond substitute, and Stras went on to produce such spectacular paste jewelry that he established it as a remarkable creation in its own right.

A BOOM INDUSTRY

In London, top quality paste was often sold alongside precious jewels, while in France, working with paste became such a boom industry that by the 1760s, over 300 jewelers and designers belonged to the guild of faux jewelers. For the first time, jewelers could chose from a vast range of precious and non-precious materials to work with, and design started to become significant.

Despite the 18th-century passion for diamonds and diamond lookalikes, gold remained highly valued. The first convincing gold substitute was pinchbeck, named after its creator, Christopher Pinchbeck. It combined well with paste, and ladies often had their favorite gold pieces reproduced in pinchbeck to take with them on their travels. It was later used as an affordable alternative to gold during Queen Victoria's reign (1837–1901), especially for pins. Gold and pinchbeck chains were worn by both sexes. The châtelaine also came back into style: this was an arrangement of chains and clasps to which various useful items, from thimbles to perfume bottles, were attached by a clip and worn around the waist.

THEMES FROM NATURE

Many 18th-century pieces of costume jewelry typically incorporated both large and small stones and often reflected a theme from nature, such as flowers or insects. Parures—matching sets of four or more pieces—became fashionable, and there was also a craze for wearing bow brooches. These mimicked dress trends in which costumes were covered with large silk bows, and jewelers worked hard to imitate in paste jewelry the fall of fabric. Men were equally fond of jewelry, and cravat pins and shoe buckles were particularly popular: apparently, you could tell a man's social standing by the quality of his buckles.

From about 1760 onward, mechanized cutting techniques gave rise to a fashion for jewelry made from cut steel—a hard, durable alloy of iron and carbon, which had previously been used for swords. Steel was also used as a setting for cameos, and ornate shoe buckles of steel, tin, and paste became an essential part of fashionable dress. Another popular innovation of this period was *en tremblant* jewelry, in which paste stones set on steel springs trembled and shimmered when the wearer moved.

MYRIAD INFLUENCES

The second half of the 18th century was the era of the Grand Tour, when people flocked to see the great archaeological discoveries at Pompeii and Herculaneum. This gave rise to a neoclassical movement in which jewelry forms and decorative imagery were inspired by Etruscan, Greek, and Roman prototypes.

At the same time, a backlash began against the extravagant indulgences that had so dominated the courts of Europe. In the past, jewelry had been a clear indicator of social standing, but the success of the paste trade resulted in the blurring of these markers.

The desire for social equality really exploded at the end of the 1780s with the French Revolution. French jewelers soon found themselves out of work, since flashy jewels were considered suspect and people were encouraged to give up their wealth and jewels for the cause.

However, such austerity was relatively short-lived. Ostentatious fashions reemerged with the advent of the Napoleonic era and the regency of the extravagant George IV in England.

Floral motif pin in gilt metal set with
rings of faux diamond pastes. *c.1780*
1¾ in (4.5 cm) wide **$900–1,000 CSAY**

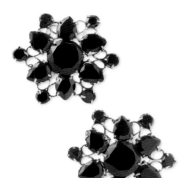

Floral motif earrings with gold wire and round- and pear-cut French jet glass stones. *c.1720. 1½ in (4 cm) wide* **$950–1,300 CSAY**

All the sparkle of a real jewel...

A plentiful supply of "gemstones" made from high-quality paste and glass sparked a frenzy of creativity among jewelry designers in the 18th and early 19th centuries. For the first time, they could experiment in a way that would have been too risky with precious gems. Exciting new designs developed, as well as new cutting and setting techniques. It was the beginning of an era in which jewelry was appreciated for its design and craftsmanship rather than the intrinsic value of the materials used. Ever growing numbers of people could now afford to wear eye-catching "aristocratic" jewelry, and it was becoming increasingly difficult to tell the real from the fake.

Floral cross pin with round- and navette-cut emerald pastes in gold metal. *c.1820 1½ in (4 cm) wide* **$720–880 CSAY**

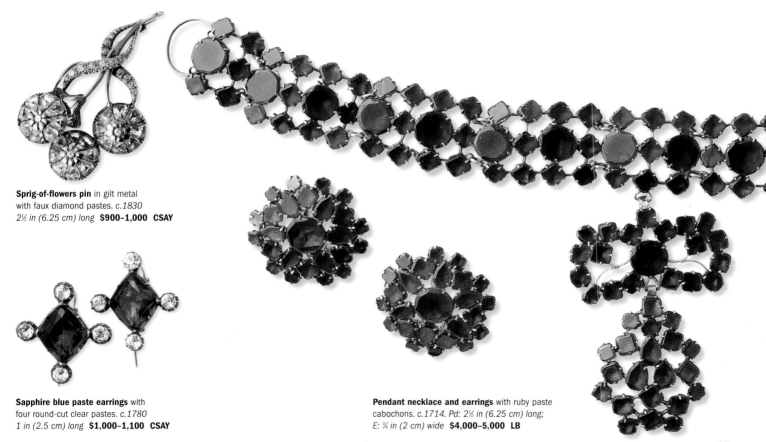

Sprig-of-flowers pin in gilt metal with faux diamond pastes. *c.1830 2½ in (6.25 cm) long* **$900–1,000 CSAY**

Sapphire blue paste earrings with four round-cut clear pastes. *c.1780 1 in (2.5 cm) long* **$1,000–1,100 CSAY**

Pendant necklace and earrings with ruby paste cabochons. *c.1714. Pd: 2½ in (6.25 cm) long; E: ¾ in (2 cm) wide* **$4,000–5,000 LB**

All that glitters is not gold...

Highway robbery was a significant problem in the 18th century. So wealthy people took the precaution of having their favorite pieces of jewelry copied in paste and pinchbeck, for use when traveling. Pinchbeck was the first really successful gold substitute. True pinchbeck was only made by Christopher Pinchbeck and his son until the 1830s, when the term passed into general usage to describe any quality gilt metal. Made from an alloy of zinc and copper, it was highly malleable and had a warm, burnished appearance. Unlike real gold, however, it was relatively lightweight.

Feather-motif pin in pinchbeck with emerald green paste cabochons. *c.1830* *2½ in (5 cm) long* **$320–480 MARA**

Butterfly pin in pinchbeck with a body and head of French jet. *c.1860* *3 in (7.5 cm) wide* **$800–960 CSAY**

Shield pin in pinchbeck with floral motifs, tassels, and green paste cabochons. *c.1830* *2⅜ in (6 cm) long* **$320–480 MARA**

If used in minute quantities, real gold was reasonably affordable. Jewelry inlaid with tiny flakes of the precious metal, known as piqué, was particularly popular.

Multiple-pendant necklace and earrings with inlaid gold and silver piqué. *c.1850*
N: 14½ in (37 cm) circ; E: ⅜ in (1 cm) long
$6,400–8,000 CSAY

Pendant earrings in pinchbeck with prong-set emerald green pastes. *c.1830*
1½ in (4 cm) long **$320–480 MARA**

Drop chain brooch in pinchbeck with clear and emerald green pastes. *c.1830*
1¾ in (4.5 cm) long **$160–320 MARA**

Oval link bracelet in genuine pinchbeck with barrel clasp. *c.1770. 7 in (18 cm) long*
$560–640 RBRG

Oval link necklace in genuine pinchbeck with barrel clasp. *c.1770. 37½ in (96 cm) long*
$1,900–2,200 RBRG

Floral, fruit, and foliate-motif pin of cut steel. *c.1840. 1¾ in (4.5 cm) wide* **$480–560 CSAY**

Pendant hoop earrings of cut steel. *c.1780 2 in (5 cm) long* **$800–960 CSAY**

Steely style...

Although cut steel jewelry made an appearance in the 17th century, it provided new inspiration in the 18th century when it became a fashionable alternative to diamonds. The blue-gray steel was either pierced or carved into faceted studs that were attached to a steel backplate. It was used in a wide range of jewelry, but most notably buckles, buttons, necklaces, bracelets, tiaras, and châtelaines. The wearing of cut steel jewelry was certainly not confined to those unable to afford precious alternatives: Empress Josephine of France had cut steel jewelry in her collection. Fashionable for most of the 19th century, it enjoyed a small but notable revival in the 1940s.

Cut steel provided a less expensive alternative to the more traditional gold or silver settings for cameos.

Wedgwood brooch with a white on blue carved cameo in a cut steel frame. *c.1770 2¾ in (7 cm) long* **$1,400–1,600 RBRG**

Pearl drop necklace of cut steel with a red velvet tie. *c.1830 17 in (44 cm) circ* **$950–1,100 CSAY**

Pendant necklace of cut steel with mother-of-pearl cabochons, by Munsy & Co. of Cambridge, UK. *c.1785. Pd: 3 in (7.5 cm) long* **$1,800–2,100 CSAY**

Cut steel tiara with a four-prong tortoiseshell comb. *c.1800 6¼ in (14 cm) wide* **$900–1,000 CSAY**

Floral motif bracelet of cut steel riveted to brass. *c.1825. 6¾ in (17 cm) long* **$320–480 MARA**

Georgian-style earrings of cut steel with Venetian glass cabochon centers. *c.1910 1⅛ in (3 cm) wide* **$80–160 MARA**

Butterfly pin of cut steel riveted to brass. *c.1825. 1½ in (4 cm) wide* **$160–260 MARA**

A time of change

The 19th century saw the Machine Age grind into high gear, and its impact on costume jewelry was profound. Mass production ensured that ordinary people could now afford to buy jewelry, and a constant desire for novelty led to a proliferation of styles.

A FASHION FOR MOURNING

When the young Victoria became queen of England in 1837, jewelry styles were romantic and patriotic. The new queen adored jewelry and was to become something of a style-setter. Victorian paste and glass were steadily improving, and colors were becoming ever more realistic. Industrialization, better production techniques, and social change all contributed to the rising popularity of faux jewelry.

Two developments characterize the costume jewelry of this era: quantity and variety. Mass production lowered costs and made it available to all, while constantly changing fashions led to an extraordinary profusion of styles.

Ancient European and Asian influences continued to feed through and, in the 1830s, the discovery of ancient Etruscan jewelry in Italy inspired a craze for an archaeological style. This often featured Etruscan-type filigree work and granulation. Arm bracelets, amulets, and Roman coin jewelry were all popular by the mid-19th century—as were mosaic jewelry and enamel pieces featuring scenes from classical antiquity.

For the first time since the Renaissance, religious jewelry became widely popular. Christian motifs, notably crosses, were common, many of them made in Berlin ironwork. Other fashionable motifs echoed medieval Gothic designs such as trefoils or quatrefoils, and were often used in large belt buckles that drew attention to fashionably tiny waists.

Mourning jewelry, a peculiarly Victorian phenomenon, also made its appearance. Known as *memento mori*, or "reminder of death," pieces were often engraved with macabre symbols such as a skull and crossbones and worn alongside grander paste jewels. After the death of Victoria's consort, Prince Albert, the fashion for mourning jewelry really took off. Black mourning jewels were made from materials such as jet, onyx, enamel, and vulcanite. Hairwork jewelry, comprising bracelets or necklaces of woven hair (sometimes human, but more often horse), was also popular in this context.

AN AGE OF SENTIMENT

Sentimental jewelry was very much a signature theme of the Victorian era. A lock of hair or a loved one's portrait were often incorporated into a locket or brooch, inscriptions were etched on to the back of settings, and motifs used that symbolized love or affection. Some dated back to ancient Rome, such as clasped hands denoting friendship or faith. Often the choice of stones held a secret message of love or affection. For example, rubies, emeralds, garnets, amethysts, rubies again, and diamonds, or their paste equivalents, spelt out the word "R-E-G-A-R-D." Men's jewelry, however, became increasingly discreet, although rings, and the newly invented cravat pins, showed great originality and were often highly personalized.

Oriental themes began influencing jewelry design in the 1850s and 60s, when, after centuries of isolation, Japanese wares were displayed at the Great Exhibition of 1851 in London. Flora and fauna themes were also typical of the time, reflecting the Victorians' interest in nature. Organic materials became fashionable, and there were also bizarre curiosities such as stuffed hummingbirds mounted on pins, and bracelets or necklaces hung with real, brightly colored insects.

Gold continued to be imitated, and in the latter half of the century, an alloy called Abyssinian gold became particularly popular. In the United States, where diamonds were not imported until the 1850s, costume jewelry was genuinely appreciated for its decorative qualities rather than its monetary value. Much of it was inexpensively produced by plating base metals with a thin layer of gold or silver.

A BACKLASH AGAINST INDUSTRIALIZATION

As the 19th century progressed, mass production resulted in a lowering of costume jewelry standards. In Europe, there was a backlash against industrialization, which gave rise to the Arts and Crafts movement. Led in England by William Morris and John Ruskin, it favored simple handmade designs based on indigenous

floral, ancient Celtic, and Medieval designs. These were created using traditional manual methods of craftsmanship, rather than machine-made and mass-produced. Silver was the metal of choice, together with uncut and cabochon-cut stones.

Interestingly, in Great Britain and the United States, many Arts and Crafts jewelers were women—a development echoed in the late 19th and early 20th centuries in the appearance of suffragette jewelry. Incorporating green, white, and violet-colored stones, the jewelry spelled out the aspiration: "Give Women the Vote."

END-OF-CENTURY TRENDS

Other notable end-of-century trends include fashions for Italian art jewelry, and a revival of *en tremblant* jewelry, in which spring-loaded floral or figural motifs—especially insects—acquired an additional lively presence through the movement of the wearer. Newly discovered gemstones also made their appearance, notably vivid green garnets from Siberia, golden tiger's eyes from Africa, black opals from Australia, and sapphires from Kashmir. Inevitably, all were soon copied in paste.

As the 19th-century drew to a close, society had undergone extraordinary change, largely due to industrialization and a growing, moneyed middle class. However, the emergence of Art Nouveau—a new art for a new century—the exploitation of plastics, and the advent of *couture* design were about to change things even further.

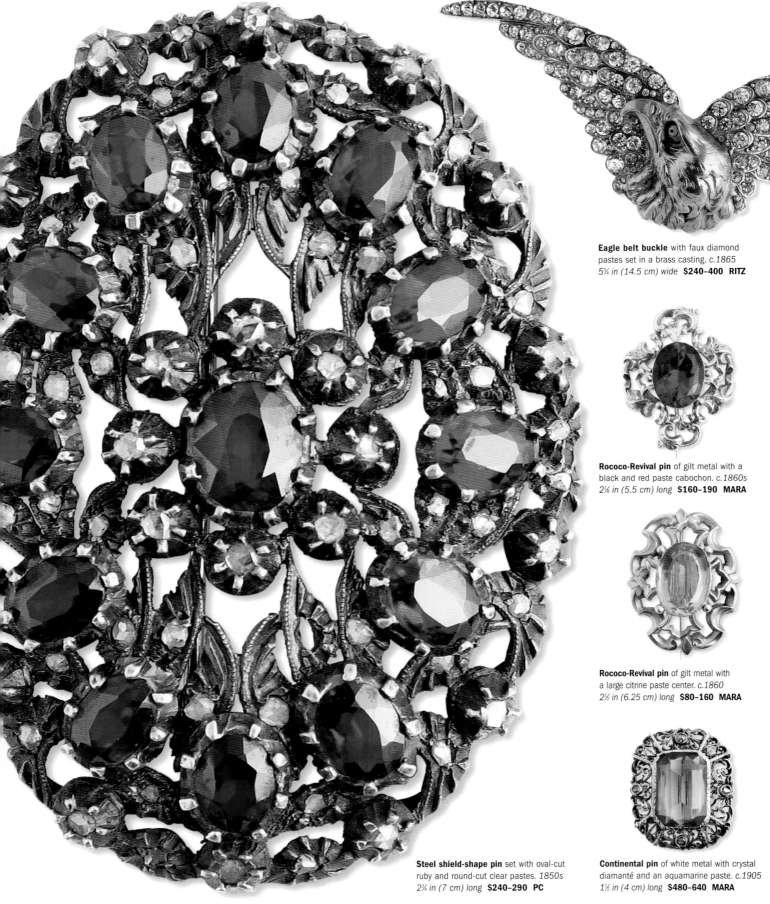

Eagle belt buckle with faux diamond pastes set in a brass casting. *c.1865* *5¾ in (14.5 cm) wide* **$240–400 RITZ**

Rococo-Revival pin of gilt metal with a black and red paste cabochon. *c.1860s* *2⅛ in (5.5 cm) long* **$160–190 MARA**

Rococo-Revival pin of gilt metal with a large citrine paste center. *c.1860* *2½ in (6.25 cm) long* **$80–160 MARA**

Continental pin of white metal with crystal diamanté and an aquamarine paste. *c.1905* *1½ in (4 cm) long* **$480–640 MARA**

Steel shield-shape pin set with oval-cut ruby and round-cut clear pastes. *1850s* *2¾ in (7 cm) long* **$240–290 PC**

Vauxhall glass bee pin and earrings with ruby and turquoise glass and gilt metal. *1870s. P: 1½ in (4 cm) long; E: 1⅛ in (3 cm) long* **$560–880 LYNH**

Romance and realism

The Victorian era saw a steady improvement in the quality of paste and glass, with costume jewelry design and techniques getting better and better. By 1830, open settings were being used for both precious and faux stones. These allowed more light to pass through the stones, enhancing their sparkle. "Gemstone" colors were becoming more realistic and, at the same time, fantasy colors were being introduced. In keeping with Victorian sentiment, different gemstones became associated with particular birthdates, and superstition held that wearing the appropriate birthstone brought good luck.

Vauxhall glass flower pin with clear navette petals. *1850s. Flower: 2 in (5 cm) long* **$160–210 LYNH**

Vauxhall glass was popular for much of the 19th century. Its name comes from a mirror glassworks in Vauxhall, London, owned by the Duke of Buckingham. Vauxhall glass was easy to cut, foil, and set, and it was often a burgundy-red color. Early Vauxhall glass is rare and valuable.

Early Vauxhall glass crown pin with ruby and dark amethyst glass stones and gold pin. *c.1890. 1½ in (4 cm) long* **$290–350 CSAY**

Berlin ironwork ring of gilt metal
with inscribed band of iron. *c.1914*
¼ in (0.75 cm) wide **$640–800 CSAY**

Berlin ironwork floral motif earrings
with gilt highlights. *c.1820s*
2¼ in (6 cm) long **$1,600–1,900 CSAY**

Berlin ironwork necklace with alternating
"S" scroll and cross motifs. *c.1810*
37 in (95 cm) long **$2,800–3,200 RBRG**

A Gothic austerity...

Berlin ironwork came about after a drop in demand for Prussian cast-iron products inspired armorers to experiment in the production of decorative wares. The trade was boosted around 1813 when Prussians who donated their gold jewelry to the Napoleonic campaign funds were given a gift of ironwork. Fashioned from linked cast iron panels, and often featuring delicate fretwork, Berlin ironwork was frequently used for the Gothic Revival jewelry styles popular from the 1820s. It symbolized constancy and durability, and its black austerity also made it suitable for mourning jewelry.

Berlin ironwork bracelets with floral
motifs and V-spring clasps. *c.1880*
7½ in (19 cm) long **$160–190 PC**

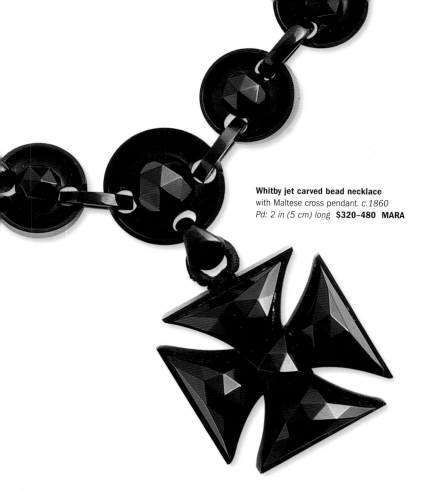

Whitby jet carved bead necklace
with Maltese cross pendant. *c.1860*
Pd: 2 in (5 cm) long **$320–480 MARA**

That old black magic...

The fashion for jewelry made of black jet—a fossilized pine similar to coal—began in the 1850s when Queen Victoria wore it while mourning a cousin. There were large natural jet deposits in Whitby, England, which soon became a busy industrial center for jet jewelry. Mourning jewelry really took off after the death of Prince Albert in 1861, and both jet and Berlin cast iron made ideal materials for this type of jewelry. By the end of the 19th century, jet imitations were being produced from hardened rubber or "vulcanite," and a shiny black glass called French jet.

Whitby jet pendant with carved Egyptian
pharaoh motif. *c.1900. 2½ in (6.5 cm) long*
$160–320 MARA

Unsigned earrings with jet cabochons
in filigree gold-plated metal. *c.1880*
1⅜ in (3.5 cm) long **$130–160 PC**

Whitby jet pin and pendant earrings
with angel coral cameos. *c.1900*
P & E: 2 in (5 cm) long **$480–640 MARA**

Twin-hearts-and-bow pin in gilt metal with diamond and emerald pastes. *c.1880* ¾ *in (2 cm) wide* **$240–320 LYNH**

The language of love...

Love and sentimentalism are both hallmarks of Victorian jewelry. Hearts, cupids, and lovebirds were common romantic motifs, while anchors symbolized hope, and serpents, especially those with their tails in their mouths, represented eternal love. A romantic "language of flowers" developed and was mirrored in jewelry with the use of appropriately colored gemstones that became coded tokens of love and affection. Jewelry was often inscribed with loving messages, and another popular device was to spell out a loved one's name using the names of the stones used in the setting.

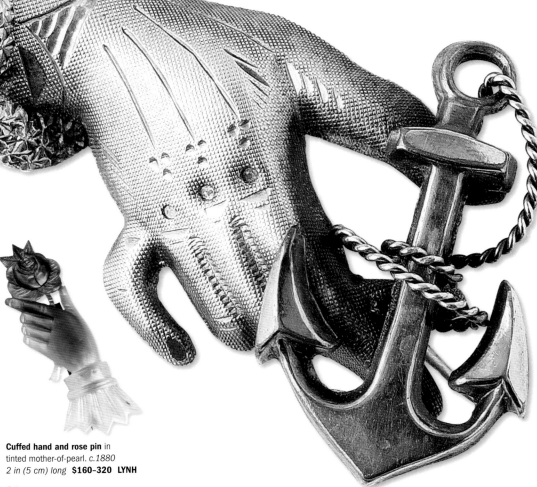

Cuffed hand and anchor pin cast in silver and bronze. *c.1880s. 1½ in (4 cm) wide* **$160–320 LYNH**

Cuffed hand and rose pin in tinted mother-of-pearl. *c.1880* *2 in (5 cm) long* **$160–320 LYNH**

"Regard" pin with faux rubies, emerald, garnet, amethyst, and diamond. *c.1860* 1¾ *in (4.5 cm) wide* **$400–560 CSAY**

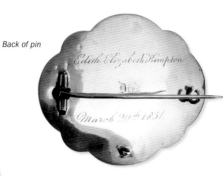

Back of pin

Commemorative pin with gold frame, black enamel, and hair over chalcedony. *c.1850* 2¼ in (5.75 cm) wide **$240–320 MARA**

Early commemorative pin with paste border and "J.W." initials in woven hair. *c.1800* 1¾ in (4.5 cm) long **$600–960 CSAY**

A lost art...

Around the 1840s, jewelry made from human hair became incredibly popular. Called "hairwork," it is now virtually a lost art. Tightly woven lengths were arranged into a pattern, glued into place, and mounted in pinchbeck or other metals. Miniature paintings were also made into pieces such as pins, using ground hair as the coloring agent for the paint. The leading makers were Forrer in London and Lemonier and Charleux in Paris. Hairwork also became a popular hobby among Victorian ladies, who made jewelry or framed hair pictures as a token of love or friendship, or for mourning.

Woven horsehair bracelet with gilt metal clasp engraved with a floral motif. *c.1840* 6¾ in (17.5 cm) circ **$160–320 MARA**

Gold pin with a lock of hair and enamel flowers over chalcedony. *c.1850* 2⅛ in (5.5 cm) long **$240–320 MARA**

Pendant hoop earrings of black and red tortoiseshell with bands of gold inlay. *c.1880* 1¾ in (4.5 cm) long **$1,200–1,600 LYNH**

Crescent moon tortoiseshell pin with inlaid gold and silver floral motifs. *1880s* 1½ in (3.75 cm) long **$640–720 LYNH**

Hand and flower love token pin in mother-of-pearl. *c.1900. 2 in (5 cm) long*
$160–320 LYNH

Kingfisher pin of carved horn with a pearlized finish. *c.1900. 3 in (7.5 cm) long*
$120–240 LYNH

Winged insect pin carved from horn. *c.1900*
3¾ in (9.5 cm) wide **$130–320 LYNH**

Pendant hoop tortoiseshell earrings with inlaid gold floral and foliate motifs. *1880s*
1¾ in (4.5 cm) long **$1,200–1,600 LYNH**

Culled from nature...

The Victorians had an insatiable thirst for novelty, and this era witnessed a proliferation of costume jewelry styles. Organic materials such as tortoiseshell, bone, ivory, coral, and the teeth and claws of tigers became highly fashionable, although their roots can be traced back to ethnic jewelry. Building on the Victorians' interest in nature, flora and fauna were also popular decorative themes. Other influences came from the discoveries of 19th-century explorers, early tourists, and the British Empire.

Jewelry made from nuts was fashionable in the 19th century. Often carved by sailors on long sea voyages, such pieces are generally referred to as "Mariner's Art."

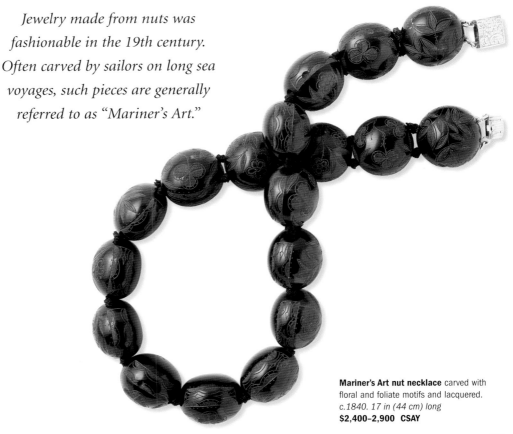

Mariner's Art nut necklace carved with floral and foliate motifs and lacquered. *c.1840. 17 in (44 cm) long*
$2,400–2,900 CSAY

Silver pendant necklace with green, white, and violet pastes. *c.1900*
Pd: 1⅜ in (3.5 cm) long **$400–480 LYNH**

Votes for women...

Suffragette jewelry was the Victorian equivalent of a modern-day political button or T-shirt. Pins and pendants were especially popular and featured green, white, and violet stones. These were the suffragette colors, with their initials standing for "Give Women the Vote." Pieces of suffragette jewelry could be worn as a quiet, understated way of showing support for the movement. Suffragette jewelry is sometimes confused with royal memorabilia, since green, white, and violet were also the royal colors. Violet was Queen Alexandra's favorite color, while the green echoed the Prince of Wales's preferred stone, peridot.

Pendant necklace with green, white, and violet pastes and faux pearls. *c.1900*
Pd: 2⅛ in (5.5 cm) long **$400–560 LYNH**

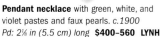

Basket of flowers pendant necklace with green, white, and violet pastes. *c.1900*
Pd: 1⅜ in (3.5 cm) long **$400–560 LYNH**

Gold chain necklace with multiple
fluorescent green moth pendants. *c.1900*
Pds: ¾ in (2 cm) long **$400–720 LYNH**

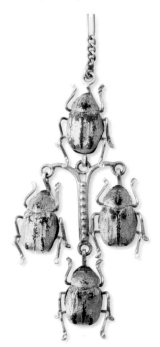

Gold twin-pendant necklace, with two
quartets of fluorescent blue beetles. *c.1900*
Pds: 1½ in (4 cm) long **$1,200–1,900 LYNH**

Necklace detail

The beauty of bugs...

The Victorian craze for insect jewelry was sparked by a love of the bizarre
and an ongoing fascination with natural history, heightened, no doubt, by the
theories of Charles Darwin. Jewelry was fashioned using real insects, which
were often imported as curiosities from far-flung corners of the British Empire.
Often extraordinarily vibrant in color and comparatively large, these lacquered
and mounted insects still have the power to amaze and even shock today. Given
their fragility, few examples have survived, and even those in pristine condition
are almost impossible to value with any degree of certainty.

A coming of age

During the first half of the 20th century, costume jewelry finally came into its own. Thanks to couturiers such as Coco Chanel, it became fashion-led, selling at every price range. At times, it was even regarded as more desirable than precious jewelry.

TWO DISTINCT STYLES

In the early years of the 20th century, costume jewelry was caught between two distinct styles: a desire to keep things as they were, and a yearning for the new, sensual lines of Art Nouveau and plique-à-jour jewelry.

The flowing curves of Art Nouveau supposedly echoed the desire for female emancipation, and role models such as actress Sarah Bernhardt (1844–1923) had a tremendous influence on jewelry design; cut-price copies of her pieces flew off the shelves.

More conventional motifs included floral baskets and bows. Light colors became popular, which revived an interest in diamonds and pearls, along with platinum in fine jewelry. Costume jewelry jumped on the bandwagon, using silver as an obvious substitute for platinum, along with imitation and cultured pearls.

The rarity value and extraordinarily high prices commanded by real pearls—an American skyscraper once exchanged hands for the price of a pearl necklace—increased the need to find convincing substitutes. These came in the form of cultured pearls from Mikimoto Pearls in Japan, who began production in the 1890s.

Genuine diamonds were often combined with synthetic stones, and the best ones, especially faux emeralds, were hard to distinguish from the real thing.

During the 1920s and 30s, Czechoslovakia produced its own distinctive costume jewelry made from crystal stones and beads. Daniel Swarovski (*see p.203*) made the finest paste stones, and his firm is still in production today.

Other popular styles in the 1920s and 30s included an Egyptian Revival, and the Indian-inspired "fruit salad" jewelry, but this period is probably most strongly identified with Art Deco. The geometric forms drew their inspiration from Cubism, and although pre-war figural subjects such as flower baskets still appeared, these were highly stylized rather than naturalistic.

ART DECO TECHNIQUES

Square stones were sometimes "calibré-cut" to follow the exact outline of an irregularly shaped design. These cuts were used for invisible settings, where gems were drilled from the back and mounted edge to edge on invisible rods to create a seamless surface. Careful stone matching and setting techniques became vital. Bracelets were a key Art Deco accessory, and several were often worn on each arm. Dress clips were also in vogue.

One of the most popular synthetic materials for jewelry between 1920 and 1940 was Bakelite, favored for its malleable qualities and bright colors. It could be worked on a lathe and lent itself to Art Deco styling.

By the mid-1930s, costume jewelry really came into its own, and its new-found confidence was reflected in bigger and chunkier designs. Instead of simply imitating precious jewelry, it was evolving its own fashion-led, mass-market identity, and it sold at every price range.

Fashion designers such as Schiaparelli (*see pp.108–111*) and Chanel (*see pp.56–59*) had a great impact during this era, and Coco Chanel was the first to use costume jewelry to create the finishing touch to her overall look. Faux jewelry was now more stylish than its precious equivalent.

THE AMERICAN INFLUENCE

French couturiers opened the doors to costume jewelry, but Americans produced and wore more of it than anyone else. After World War I, the United States became fully industrialized, and by 1930 it was ready to produce costume jewelry on a scale impossible in war-ravaged Europe. For the first time, women had a huge choice of constantly changing fashions that offered both style and quality, and costume jewelry was an ideal way to accessorize and personalize a mass-produced outfit.

Hollywood also had a huge influence on fashion at this time, and whenever a star's jewelry made an impact on the silver screen, factories rushed to reproduce it in costume copies. Trifari's success was based on the firm's ability to reproduce brilliant copies of precious contemporary pieces, and by the mid-30s they were producing cocktail jewelry inspired by Hollywood (*see pp.118–129*).

A welter of historical "costume" movies gave rise to an American "antique" style of jewelry. Antique motifs

such as bows and lockets were revived along with châtelaines, which now took the form of paired pins attached to either side of a jacket or sweater by a chain.

Around the late 1930s, there was a vogue for enamel flower brooches in pastel colors. Also, the Art Deco style was reworked into a dramatic retro style popularized by actresses such as Joan Crawford. Large and solid, it combined free-form swirls with geometric shapes. Retro costume jewelry was usually set in gold-plated metal dominated by a single, large, plainly cut stone or cabochon—a contrast to the small, fancy cut stone designs of Art Deco. It could also be worn day-into-evening—a boon to the new breed of working women.

A SUBSTITUTION FOR SILVER

Due to restrictions on raw materials during World War II, manufacturers had to improvise, and they did so with tremendous success. Materials such as Bakelite and Lucite came into their own, but the most significant change was the substitution of sterling silver for the various base metals. By 1942, silver was the only metal that was allowed for costume jewelry. By then, most American costume jewelry metal was made of vermeil (gold-plated) sterling silver. Coro's 1940 vermeil pieces are particularly collectible (*see pp.68–71*).

Cocktail costume jewelry became a useful tool for cheering up the austere, wartime look, and it became so popular that US sales had tripled by 1945. The industry was now well placed to take advantage of the coming post-war boom.

An illuminating style...

Meaning "window of light," the plique-à-jour enameling technique came into fashion in the late 19th century and is closely associated with Art Nouveau style. Translucent enamels are fused to span across a network of open-backed metal cells, allowing the light to shine through and illuminate it. The effect is similar to stained glass. More technically complex and fragile than other enamelwork, plique-à-jour jewelry is highly prized by today's collectors. Masters of the art include Fernand Thesmar, Gustave Gaudernack, and René Lalique, although many pieces are of unknown origin.

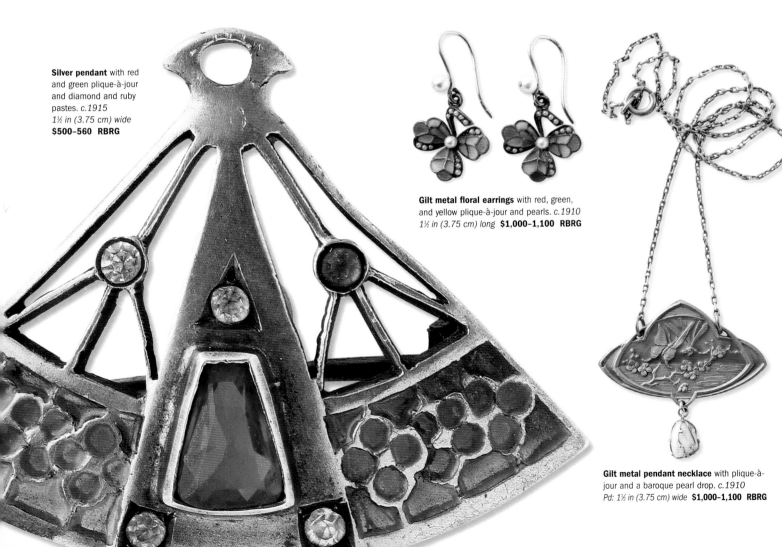

Silver pendant with red and green plique-à-jour and diamond and ruby pastes. *c.1915*
1½ in (3.75 cm) wide
$500–560 RBRG

Gilt metal floral earrings with red, green, and yellow plique-à-jour and pearls. *c.1910*
1½ in (3.75 cm) long **$1,000–1,100 RBRG**

Gilt metal pendant necklace with plique-à-jour and a baroque pearl drop. *c.1910*
Pd: 1½ in (3.75 cm) wide **$1,000–1,100 RBRG**

French silver hanging basket pin with "fruit salads" and crystal diamanté. *Early 1920s 1½ in (3.75 cm) wide* **$200–240 CRIS**

Inspired by the Tree of Life...

The exotic designs and colors of the Indian Moghul "Tree of Life" jewels inspired the hugely popular Cartier-designed precious pieces of the 1920s and 30s. Instead of the stones being faceted, they were carved to resemble flowers, fruit, and leaves. They were then inlaid into swathes of tiny, faceted diamonds to form stylized Art Deco designs, notably baskets and vases, in platinum settings. Cartier began the trend, but other companies, including Van Cleef and Arpels and Trifari, followed suit and produced similar designs—precious and faux—dubbed "fruit salads" or "tutti-fruttis."

French silver pot-of-flowers pin with "fruit salads" and crystal diamanté. *Early 1920s 1¾ in (4.5 cm) long* **$200–240 CRIS**

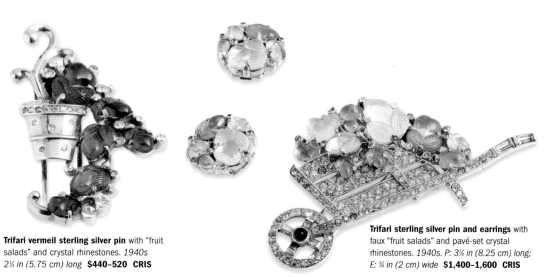

Trifari vermeil sterling silver pin with "fruit salads" and crystal rhinestones. *1940s 2¼ in (5.75 cm) long* **$440–520 CRIS**

Trifari sterling silver pin and earrings with faux "fruit salads" and pavé-set crystal rhinestones. *1940s. P: 3¼ in (8.25 cm) long; E: ¾ in (2 cm) wide* **$1,400–1,600 CRIS**

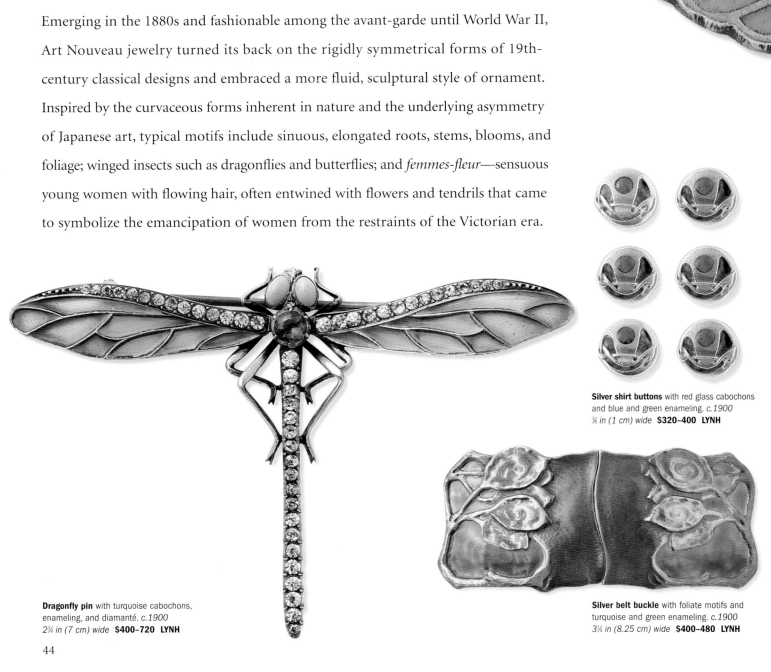

Fluid and sculptural...

Emerging in the 1880s and fashionable among the avant-garde until World War II, Art Nouveau jewelry turned its back on the rigidly symmetrical forms of 19th-century classical designs and embraced a more fluid, sculptural style of ornament. Inspired by the curvaceous forms inherent in nature and the underlying asymmetry of Japanese art, typical motifs include sinuous, elongated roots, stems, blooms, and foliage; winged insects such as dragonflies and butterflies; and *femmes-fleur*—sensuous young women with flowing hair, often entwined with flowers and tendrils that came to symbolize the emancipation of women from the restraints of the Victorian era.

Silver shirt buttons with red glass cabochons and blue and green enameling. *c.1900*
⅜ in (1 cm) wide **$320–400 LYNH**

Dragonfly pin with turquoise cabochons, enameling, and diamanté. *c.1900*
2¾ in (7 cm) wide **$400–720 LYNH**

Silver belt buckle with foliate motifs and turquoise and green enameling. *c.1900*
3¼ in (8.25 cm) wide **$400–480 LYNH**

Silver scarab pin with turquoise, purple, green, blue, and red enamel. *1920s*
1½ in (4 cm) wide **$250–350 MARA**

Pharaoh heads bracelet in gold-tone metal with turquoise glass stones. *1920s*
7 in (18 cm) circ **$100–160 MARA**

Egypt revisited...

The discovery of Tutankhamen's tomb in 1922 provoked a craze for ancient Egyptian styles of ornament that endured well into the 1930s. There had been earlier Egyptian revivals, in the late 18th and mid-19th centuries, but this one had far greater popular appeal—a phenomenon fueled by newsreel footage of archaeological digs and numerous Hollywood biblical epics. Typical motifs employed in Egyptian Revival jewelry include scarabs, snakes, pyramids, palm trees, hieroglyphs, and sphinxes— the latter with the body of a lion and the head of a pharaoh, ram, hawk, or falcon.

Pyramids necklace, bracelet, and earrings of gilt metal with enamel. *c.1930*
Pds: 2 in (5 cm) long; B: 6¼ in (16 cm) long; E: 1¾ in (4.5 cm) long **$240–320 CRIS**

English glass necklace with triangular and shield-shaped blue faceted glass stones. *Late 1920s* *15½ in (40 cm) long* **$100–160 ECLEC**

French shield-shaped pendant of blue enamel with clear crystal rhinestones. *1930s* *2¼ in (5.75 cm) long* **$800–900 TR**

Fahrner silver bar pin with an aquamarine glass stone. *1930s. 2 in (5 cm) wide* **$650–700 TR**

English silver pin with a ruby red paste and clear crystal rhinestones. *1930s* *2 in (5 cm) wide* **$240–320 RG**

French engraved silver bracelet with a large emerald green paste. *1930s* *1¾ in (4.5 cm) wide* **$1,000–1,100 TR**

American sterling silver bracelet with engraved floral motifs. *Late 1920s* 7½ in (19 cm) long **$200–300 JJ**

A bold new age...

Fashionable during the 1920s and 30s, the Art Deco style reflected the new feeling of optimism and excitement that gradually emerged after the privations of World War I. Its abstract and geometric shapes and often bold color combinations were inspired by the early 20th century art movements of Cubism and Futurism. Recently discovered Egyptian and Aztec styles also had an influence, along with the streamlined forms of Machine Age products such as the automobile. All of these marked a radical departure from the organic forms and sinuous sensuality of pre-war Art Nouveau imagery.

English bracelet of red Bakelite and chromed steel. *Late 1920s* 7½ in (19 cm) circ **$190–210 RITZ**

English sterling silver necklace with clear crystal rhinestones. *1930s* Pd: 1½ in (3.75 cm) long **$560–640 RG**

English geometric form necklace with alternating silver and Bakelite. *Late 1920s* 14¾ in (38 cm) circ **$220–260 RITZ**

English necklace with silver chain and yellow and black Bakelite pendant. *Late 1920s* Pd: 2 in (5 cm) wide **$220–260 RITZ**

A brave new world

Since World War II, costume jewelry has grown steadily more popular, and it is now part of mainstream fashion. Quality varies, but a host of new materials, styles, and techniques have evolved to take us forward in the 21st century.

FROM NEW LOOK TO HOLLYWOOD

The post-war period in the United States was a boom time of prosperity and optimism. Dior's New Look in France offered a welcome return to elegance and luxury after the streamlined austerity of the war, and costume jewelry was well made, feminine, and showy. The removal of wartime restrictions on Czech and Austrian pastes resulted in a trend for huge, vividly colored stones that were unashamedly fake.

Meanwhile, a parallel trend had started for more subdued, realistic pieces, largely due to the post-war resurrection of the Paris fine jewelry trade. Hollywood continued to be a major trendsetter, and a vogue for cocktail parties inspired a craze for quirky "conversation piece" jewelry. Figural pins also became popular, especially those made in plastic, since it lent itself to more complex shapes.

CHEAPER TECHNIQUES

By the end of the 1940s, base metals were becoming available again and new electroplating techniques were developed, including Trifari's "trifanium," a matte gold known as Russian gold plating (*see pp.118–129*). Soon, the growing demand for costume jewelry prompted a search for new production methods, and this led to machine stamping. Also, the prong-setting of stones by hand was often replaced by the faster, cheaper method of glue setting. However, these techniques adversely affected quality, and pieces by designers such as Miriam Haskell, who retained handmade techniques and produced limited editions, remain the most collectible.

ANYTHING GOES

During the 1950s and 60s, Op and Pop Art were influential, with artists such as Andy Warhol fueling the inspirational fire. The 1960s "anything goes" youth culture resulted in jewelry that was larger and more over-the-top than ever. This was the time when the twin cults of image and celebrity really started to take root, so visual impact became increasingly important. Styles were fun and young, with a bold use of plastics and strong, unsaturated colors.

Acrylic jewelry came of age in the 1960s, when it was used either on its own for the bold, chunky rings and bangles that were a hallmark of the period, or as decorative features on necklaces and earrings. Substantial yet lightweight, acrylic could be colored and textured or left smooth, so it was ideal for the designs of the time.

The fantasy pastes of the previous decade were now given an extra psychedelic edge. Black metal became a new and popular foil for the resulting acid colors, and white and green metals were also used, along with colorful enamel pieces. A hugely experimental era, the 1960s churned out a bewildering diversity of "looks," from flower power, ethnic, and gypsy to various retro revivals. The first moon missions also inspired a Space Age look, with costume jewelry producing plain metal, plastic, or metal and enamel in geometric shapes.

American designer Kenneth J. Lane (*see pp.84–85*) was one of the few who managed to harness the many diverse strands of 1960s influences into an integrated and original style. His love of bold, photogenic jewelry perfectly mirrored the times. He also produced a successful "Jackie O" line based on Jackie Onassis's celebrated sense of style.

However, the vast majority of jewelry from the 1960s was designed to be "throwaway." As a result, it quickly fell out of fashion and only the big, signed pieces with a strong period flavor have stood the test of time.

BACK TO NATURE

The pendulum swung yet again in the 1970s with a return to handmade values and ethnic jewelry. Natural materials such as wood and feathers, as well as American Indian silver and turquoise, were widely worn, although the popularity of brightly colored enamel, used for flower pins, bangles, and necklaces, continued from the 1960s.

Glitz and glamour burst back on to the scene in the 1980s, creating another boom for costume jewelry. This was the "Dynasty" era when even the gaudiest glitter was flaunted in daytime. In line with the 1980s devotion to designer labels, the Chanel "CC" logo was stamped on everything from belt buckles to earrings.

In response to consumer demand, costume jewelers started making reproduction Victorian, Edwardian, and Art Deco pieces. These designers combined the best from the past with a clutch of exciting new ideas and materials. Imaginative combinations of papier-mâché, glass, mirrors, wood, and rhinestones resulted in a new genre of craft costume jewelry.

MILLENNIUM STYLE

By the mid-1990s, the approach of the new millennium inspired another nostalgic craze for retro and vintage, and numerous costume jewelry companies such as Ciro and Fior started producing a range of traditional styles. Beads came back in, especially those made in Murano glass. Recently, in contrast to this harking back to the past, new styles and materials have also filtered through. Designers such as Dinny Hall (*see p.155*) in Britain have produced ultra-modern, sculptural shapes in innovative materials; in the US, Robert Lee Morris has created organic forms that have been described as "jewelry without gems."

The potential of costume jewelry as a collectible continues to increase steadily. Although some modern and contemporary pieces are cheaply made, the better pieces should rise in price over the coming decades and are likely to be good investments.

Murano glass necklace with alternating oval clear and opaque blue glass beads. *c.1920s 33 in (85 cm) long* **$350–380 RBRG**

The glory of glass...

In the 20th and early 21st centuries, most costume jewelry has been created from various combinations of metals, alloys, faux pearls, enamels, plastics and, above all, faceted rhinestones. However, pieces made from colored glass beads have been a popular alternative, especially since the 1920s. Strung into necklaces and bracelets, the finest beads have come from Murano in Venice and from the Czech Republic. Produced in diverse colors, textures, and degrees of opacity and translucency, the beads lend themselves particularly well to popular fruit and foliate designs.

Multicolor glass necklace with pale green and blue, red, black, lilac, and coffee glass beads. *c.1930s 15¼ in (39 cm) long* **$60–100 ECLEC**

Wheat motif necklace with green, red, turquoise, black, and beige glass beads. *c.1930s. 17 in (44 cm) long* **$60–100 ECLEC**

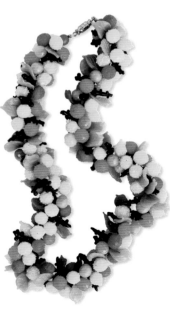

Fruit garland necklace with poured glass leaves and glass bead fruits. *c.1930s 16¼ in (42 cm) long* **$60–100 ECLEC**

Zulu earplugs made from wood and Perspex with chrome studs. *1960s. 2½ in (6.25 cm) wide* **$160–200 (per pair) EL**

All things ethnic...

A backlash against much of the cheap, throwaway costume jewelry of the 1960s created a desire for purer designs and traditional standards of craftsmanship. As a result, consumers started turning to ethnic jewelry. Authentic tribal necklaces, bangles, and earrings imported from Africa and Asia, and Western-made copies, became particularly fashionable, while in the United States, American Indian jewelry also came into vogue. Made from materials such as beaten metal, stones, earthenware beads, bone, wood, and feathers, these pieces were the height of fashion throughout the 1970s.

Bead necklace with alternating smooth black and carved red composite beads. *c.1970s. 14½ in (37 cm) long* **$50–70 PC**

Leaf motif earrings in hand-beaten white metal with wire wraps. *c.1960s 2½ in (6.5 cm) long* **$100–130 PC**

Austrian lariat necklace with woven ropes of jet and white glass beads. *c.1950s 44 in (110 cm) long* **$380–420 CRIS**

Some African necklaces made in the 20th century were made with reclaimed stones first used in tribal jewelry hundreds or thousands of years ago.

Amazonite necklace made with 1,000–200-year-old polished stones from Mauritania and Niger. *c.1900 20 in (51 cm) circ* **$1,900–2,200 PC**

Anoush Waddington "Autumn" necklace
in blue and red nylon with silver fastening.
c.2002. 3½ in (9 cm) wide **$1,100–1,300 LCG**

Kathie Murphy pendant earrings in
resin set with blue threads. *c.2002*
2¼ in (5.75 cm) long **$140–160 LCG**

Jane Adam bangle in abstract pattern of
anodized polychrome aluminum. *c.2001*
3 in (7.5 cm) wide **$260–300 LCG**

Gail Klevan bangle in semi-translucent
yellow acrylic with colored inclusions.
c.2002. 4 in (10 cm) wide **$140–160 LCG**

Carla Edwards bangle of pinkish-red
resin with layered wire inclusions. *c.2001*
4¼ in (10.75 cm) wide **$220–260 LCG**

Anoush Waddington "Autumn" ring in silver and blue and red nylon. *c.2002* *3½ in (9 cm) long* **$340–380 LCG**

On the cutting edge...

While the forms and imagery employed by late-20th- and early-21st-century jewelry designers have rarely been new, their presentation and the materials they are made from have often pushed creative boundaries. Significant trends have included the use of colored, rather than plain, aluminum, and the fashioning of abstract or naturalistic patterns from materials such as cotton and wire set in semi-translucent resins. More unusual and even startling examples have been the multiple-medium pieces in which expensive precious metals such as gold or silver have been combined with inexpensive colorful plastics such as polypropylene.

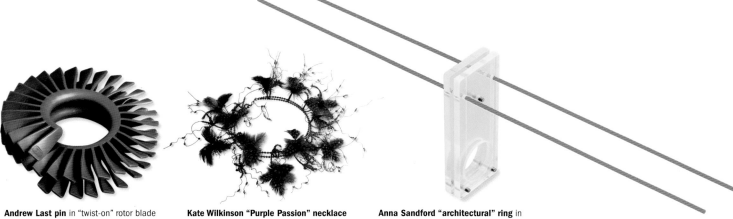

Andrew Last pin in "twist-on" rotor blade form of purple aluminum. *c.2000* *2 in (5 cm) wide* **$180–210 LCG**

Kate Wilkinson "Purple Passion" necklace in feathers, glass beads, and steel wire. *c.2002* *6 in (15.25 cm) wide* **$1,000–1,100 LCG**

Anna Sandford "architectural" ring in translucent yellow and opaque red acrylic. *c.2001. 8¾ in (22.25 cm) long* **$110–130 LCG**

Designer profiles

Major 20th- and 21st-century costume jewelry designers

Everyone who collects costume jewelry, or is simply interested in it, has their own favorite designers and makers, so describing some designers as "better" than others will always be subject to debate. Nevertheless, there are some outstanding 20th- and early-21st-century designers and makers who have figured more prominently than others, and who have acquired a standing beyond personal preference.

Of the 20 leading designers featured over the following pages, some are most admired for their innovative style or influential design, others for their high standards of craftsmanship, and some for the sheer diversity of their output. In most cases, the beautiful and highly collectible jewelry created by these designers displays all of these desirable qualities.

Chanel

One of the legendary stars of French *couture*, Coco Chanel was the first designer to incorporate costume jewelry into her fashion philosophy.

COCO CHANEL
1883–1971

1883 Born Gabrielle Bonheur Chanel in Saumur, France

1909 Chanel begins designing hats and opens a millinery shop in Paris

1914–16 Opens houses of couture in Paris, Deauville, and Biarritz

1923 Chanel No. 5 perfume is introduced

1931 Chanel works with movie producer Goldwyn in Hollywood, dressing stars such as Katherine Hepburn, Grace Kelly, and Elizabeth Taylor

1939 Chanel loses her fashion house at the start of World War II

1945 Exiled to Switzerland for her love affair with a Nazi officer

1954 Reopens her salon and presents her "comeback" collection

1960 Robert Goossens becomes Chief Designer for Chanel

1971 Chanel dies in Paris at the age of 88

1983 Karl Lagerfeld becomes director of the House of Chanel

A RENOWNED TRENDSETTER

Credited by Christian Dior for revolutionizing fashion "with a black pullover and ten rows of pearls," Gabrielle "Coco" Chanel was a renowned trendsetter. She created the little black dress, sportswear, the cardigan suit, beach pyjamas, costume jewelry, and even perfumes. Her staggering success ensured that her designs were copied worldwide.

Inspired by a desire for practical, comfortable clothes in easy-fitting fabrics, such as wool jersey—a complete departure from the corseted restraints of the past—Chanel's innovative style was hugely influential in the 1920s and 30s.

Her first shop opened in Paris in 1914, with the financial backing of her wealthy lover, Boy Capel. Concealing her age and humble origins, Chanel reinvented herself, launching into a world of high fashion and big business. By the 1920s, she was one of the leading Parisian designers.

Chanel then cleverly opened a boutique in her Paris salon dedicated to accessories and jewelry. Instead of copying fine jewelry trends, her designs complemented the simple lines and colors of her clothes, adding a personal "finishing touch." This novel approach catapulted costume jewelry into a fashion-led market.

Above: "Bijoux de Fleurs" orchid pin in shades of pink and red enameled pot metal with smoky brown crystal rhinestones. *1940s. 3 in (7.5 cm) wide* **$960–1,100 CRIS**

ORIGINAL BOXES

Chanel jewelry was, and still is, sold packaged in a box bearing the company name. The individual pieces of parures and demi-parures are all boxed separately. When early Chanel jewelry comes back on to the market, it usually does so without its original box. If a piece still has its box, the value of the jewelry can be increased by up to 30 percent.

Floral necklace and earrings by Maison Gripoix for Chanel with gold-plated links and poured glass petals. *c.1930. N: 15 in (38 cm) wide; E: ¾ in (2 cm) wide* **$1,500–1,800 CRIS**

Floral motif necklace and earrings shown left in their original brown paper-covered cardboard Chanel boxes, lined with the original tissue paper.

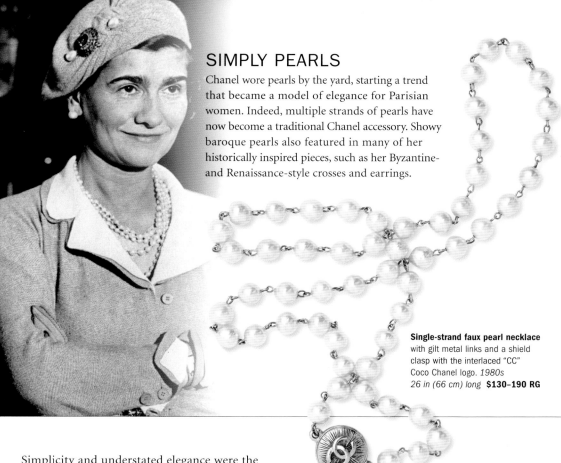

SIMPLY PEARLS

Chanel wore pearls by the yard, starting a trend that became a model of elegance for Parisian women. Indeed, multiple strands of pearls have now become a traditional Chanel accessory. Showy baroque pearls also featured in many of her historically inspired pieces, such as her Byzantine- and Renaissance-style crosses and earrings.

Single-strand faux pearl necklace with gilt metal links and a shield clasp with the interlaced "CC" Coco Chanel logo. *1980s* *26 in (66 cm) long* **$130–190 RG**

Simplicity and understated elegance were the hallmarks of Chanel's design style, and she often mixed faux with fine jewelry. She was known for her ropes of faux pearls and gold-tone chains, "poured glass" jewelry by Maison Gripoix, and Maltese Cross cuffs designed by Verdura.

"If you want to start a collection, start with a brooch because you will find most use for it. It can be pinned on a suit lapel, collar or pocket, on a hat, belt, or evening gown."

Coco Chanel

POST-WAR COMEBACK

After the war, Chanel worked with Parisian designer Robert Goossens (*see p.199*), and throughout the 1960s they produced dramatic rosary-style necklaces with long chains decorated with pearls and beads; *pâte-de-verre* eagles copied from Anglo-Saxon belt buckles; and huge Maltese cross brooches decorated with glass cabochons of green and red, Chanel's signature color combination.

Chanel continued building her vast empire until her death in 1971. Seven years later, Christie's auctioned her costume jewelry, fetching prices comparable to those of precious gems and gold. The company continued to produce Chanel collections that were faithful reissues of her style until 1983, when Karl Lagerfeld took over as director, with a brief to reinterpret and modernize. Like that of his legendary predecessor, Lagerfield's jewelry became an essential part of a distinctive new Chanel look.

INFLUENCES

Chanel's wealthy lovers are credited with influencing her taste in jewelry. However, she drew inspiration from many things: historical jewelry, stained glass windows, Russian icons, Byzantine mosaics, animals, and even the Venetian Republic.

BYZANTINE

The Byzantine jewels in the Treasury of St. Mark's, Venice, influenced Chanel's jewelry. She substituted *pâte-de-verre* and gilt for the cabochon stones and antique gold settings, as in these floral earrings of gold-plated metal with green poured glass, pavé-set clear rhinestone petals, and red glass cabochon centers. *1980s* *1½ in (4 cm) wide* **$440–480 SUM**

EXOTIC

Much of Chanel's jewelry is reminiscent of the cultures of India, Persia, and Egypt. She used carved glass beads in Moghul-style designs, such as this necklace with carved ruby glass beads and emerald glass stones encased in filigree metal with ruby glass cabochon highlights. *1950s. 16½ in (42 cm) long* **$2,900–3,200 WAIN**

Multiple pendant necklace with faux
pearls, blue, red, and green poured glass beads
(some carved) and clear crystal rhinestones. *c.1970*

Longest Pd: 4 in (10.5 cm) long

$2,900–3,500 SUM

Symmetrical pendant-pin with green
and blue glass stones and faux pearls
in gold-plated settings. *1950s*

3¼ in (8.25 cm) long

$400–480 RITZ

Oval pendant-pin with red and green
glass stones, faux pearls, and clear
crystal rhinestones in gilt metal settings.
1930s

3¾ in (9.5 cm) long

$450–510 RITZ

Rare Mr. Punch pin with trembler
head, in white, red, and black
enameled lead, and with pavé-set
rhinestones. *1920s*

2⅜ in (6 cm) high

$2,400–2,900 BY

Exotic oval pin with red, green, and blue glass cabochons, faux pearls,
and round and baguette clear crystal rhinestones. *c.1970*

2¾ in (7 cm) wide

$640–800 SUM

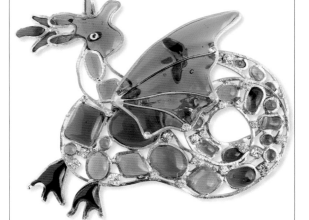

Fiery dragon pin by Maison Gripoix for Chanel, with a gold-plated
wire frame set with green, red, and black poured glass. *1940s*

4 in (10.5 cm) wide

$400–480 RITZ

Good, Better, Best

The prices of these three Chanel pins diverge widely because of their ages, subject matter, and varying complexities of design and craftsmanship.

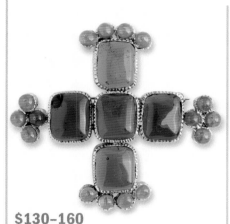

$130–160

This **Maltese Cross pin** features green, red, and pink poured glass cabochons set in gilt metal. Although one of Chanel's signature motifs, crosses in general are not popular with contemporary collectors. *1990s. 2½ in (6.5 cm) long* **PC**

$420–640

This **floral bow pin** has green, blue, and red poured glass, pink and amethyst glass beads, crystal rhinestones, and faux pearls set in gilt metal. It is rarer and more complex than the Maltese Cross pin. *1930s. 2½ in (6.5 cm) long* **BY**

$1,500–1,700

This **stylized floral pin** features green, red, blue, and black poured glass beads and stones, faux baroque pearls, and pavé-set clear crystal rhinestones. Older and rarer than the floral bow pin, it is the most striking and complex in design of the three. *1920s. 4 in (10.5 cm) high* **BY**

Rare peacock pin with turquoise, aquamarine, and red poured glass feathers and pavé-set clear crystal rhinestones. *1930s*
5½ in (14 cm) long

$2,700–3,700 **BY**

Unsigned heart pin and earrings of poured glass with red and clear crystal rhinestones and faux pearls. *1920s*
P: 3¼ in (8.25 cm) long; E: 1 in (2.5 cm) long

$320–400 **CRIS**

Chunky pendant earrings of antiqued, stamped gilt metal with faux pearls and green glass cabochons and drops. *1970s*
3¾ in (9.5 cm) long

$400–480 **SUM**

ENAMELED LEAD

In the late 1920s and early 30s, Chanel retailed a series of pins made from enameled cast lead with crystal rhinestone highlights. The majority were creature pins, notably frogs and cats, although some were "novelty" subjects. It is generally assumed that they were made in France, but many were actually of American manufacture. The enameling and the rhinestones (often pavé-set) are invariably of high quality. All too rare nowadays, these pins change hands for considerable sums of money.

Rare frog pin with green, black, and red enamel on a lead casting, and with pavé-set clear crystal rhinestone webbed feet and eyes. *1927*
2⅜ in (6 cm) long **$2,400–3,200 CRIS**

Christian Dior

The great dictator of European and American style, Christian Dior dominated the world of fashion with his glamorous and striking designs during the late 1940s and 50s.

CHRISTIAN DIOR
1905–57

1905 Born in Normandy, France

1938–41 Works for Parisian couturiers Robert Piguet and Lucien Lelong

1946 Opens Maison Dior in Avenue Montaigne, Paris

1947 Introduces glamorous postwar "New Look" in first collection

1947–57 Twice-yearly collections of clothing and jewelry plus licensing establishes Dior as a global brand

POSTWAR GLAMOUR

Born in Normandy in 1905, Christian Dior began his career in fashion in the mid-1930s, selling sketches of hats and dresses to Parisian couturiers. Following wartime service in southern France, he returned to Paris in 1941 and gained considerable experience working for leading designer Lucien Lelong. In 1946 he established Maison Dior with the financial backing of textile manufacturer Marcel Boussac. A year later, his first *haute couture* collection— the "New Look" (*see below*)—marked a sensational departure from the austerity of the war-torn 1940s. Not only did it help to reestablish Paris as the center of world fashion, it also set the tone for the more prosperous decades that followed.

Unlike many of his contemporaries, who accessorized their clothing with unobtrusive, "off-the-peg" jewelry for fear it would detract from their costume, Dior designed jewelry as an integral part of his collections. Although early designs were almost exclusively *couture* pieces made for particular outfits or individual clients— notably Hollywood actresses Marilyn Monroe and Bette Davis—his later pieces were produced under license in far greater numbers for sale through exclusive retail outlets. These included pieces conceived in his spirit by the House of Dior over the decades following his sudden

Above: Textured gilt metal earrings with irregularly shaped faux jade cabochons and clear rhinestone highlights. *1967 1 in (2.5 cm) wide* **$80–100 ROX**

1957 Dior dies suddenly and protégé Yves Saint Laurent becomes head designer

1960 Mark Bohan becomes head designer

1987 Maison Dior bought by Louis-Vuitton-Moët-Hennessy Group

1989 Gianfranco Ferré becomes head designer

1996 John Galliano becomes head designer

Indian-style pendant necklace of gilt metal with faux pearls, lapis beads, teardrop cabochons, and clear rhinestones. *1970. N: 16 in (40.5 cm) circ; Pd: 3½ in (9 cm) drop* **$400–480 RG**

THE "NEW LOOK"

Introduced in February 1947, Christian Dior's "New Look" was characterized by an extravagant use of fabric, dropped hemlines, exaggerated and softened curves, and a sense of formality enhanced by high heels, stockings, hats, gloves, and costume jewelry. In a postwar Europe where food, fabrics, and other essentials were still in short supply—and in some cases still rationed—such an extravagant use of materials was highly controversial. However, despite some initial and vehement protests, this glamorous and overtly feminine look took root and set the style for women's fashions well into the 1960s.

A 1955 black crepe cocktail dress by Dior is accessorized with an Ottoman bonnet and an opulent faux pearl necklace and earrings.

MITCHELL MAER

Having moved to London in the late 1930s, American-born Mitchell Maer established a metal castings and costume jewelry company known initially as "Metalplastics," and later as "Mitchell Maer,". In 1952 Christian Dior licensed Maer to make jewelry for the Dior collections, and for the next four years he produced some of Dior's most innovative and distinctive designs. His floral and unicorn pins in paricular (*see below and right*) are much sought- after by current collectors.

Stylized floral pin by Mitchell Maer for Dior of rhodium-plated metal with clear rhinestones and a central faux pearl. *Mid-1950s. 2¾ in (7 cm) wide* **$130–190 RG**

Unicorn pin by Mitchell Maer for Dior of rhodium-plated metal with pavé-set clear rhinestones. *Mid-1950s 2½ in (6.25 cm) long* **$110–160 RG**

GLAMOUR

The opulence of the groundbreaking "New Look" collection of 1947 was sustained by Maison Dior during the late 1950s and 60s. Presented as an essential component of costume, rather than simply an accessory, Dior jewelry continued to push fashion beyond the privations of World War II into a more affluent and optimistic age.

ORIENTAL

Oriental influence is clearly evident in this sumptuous Dior outfit originally shown in *Vogue* in November 1961. The velvet jacket is embellished with sable cuffs and iridescent and gilt beads. Characteristically, the outfit is further elaborated with stunning costume jewelry—faux pearl earrings and an extravagant multi-chain necklace of gilt and faux pearls.

MIDDLE EASTERN

Ancient Middle Eastern styles provide much of the inspiration for this elaborate Dior pendant necklace from the late 1950s. Designed to be worn with a strapless evening gown, it comprises a shower of gilt chains encrusted with fine-quality rhinestones that extend across the shoulders and down the back of the wearer.

death in 1957. It is these pieces that collectors are most likely to encounter today.

Maison Dior's concern that costume jewelry sold under the Dior brand should mirror the quality of its clothing design is reflected in the reputation of the companies and individual designers commissioned to produce the pieces. They include Henry Schreiner (*see p.165*) and Kramer (*see p.178*) in the United Stares; Mitchell Maer in England (*see above*); Henkel & Grosse in Germany (from 1955); Josette Gripoix in France (*see pp.90–93*) and, most recently, Robert Goossens (*see p.199*). The list of innovative designers who headed the company after Christian Dior's death is equally impressive: from Yves Saint Laurent, via Mark Bohan and Gianfranco Ferré, to *enfant terrible* John Galliano.

CLASSICAL AND MODERN

Stylistically, Dior jewelry draws inspiration from a wide range of historical styles. Yet pieces are never simply reproduced. Characteristically, they are given a modern twist by the incorporation of unusual pastes and stones—the color and figuring of which are often deliberately artificial and invariably visually striking. Chief among these are the iridescent, polychromatic *aurora borealis* rhinestones that Dior developed with Swarovski (*see p.203*) in 1955.

Apart from unusual components and a diverse range of historical forms, Dior jewelry is also characterized by an extensive use of floral motifs—a reflection of Christian Dior's personal love of gardens and the French countryside. Wild flowers, roses, and, especially, lily of the valley are recurring designs—the latter having virtually acquired the status of signature motif for Dior. In addition, some equally sought-after figural pieces—including fish, circus animals, and unicorn pins—have been produced. Collectors should note that most Dior pieces are signed and dated.

Rare *en tremblant* flower pin designed by Mitchell Maer for Dior of gilt metal with aquamarine and clear rhinestones. *1951. 4 in (10 cm) long* **$1,400–1,800 WAIN**

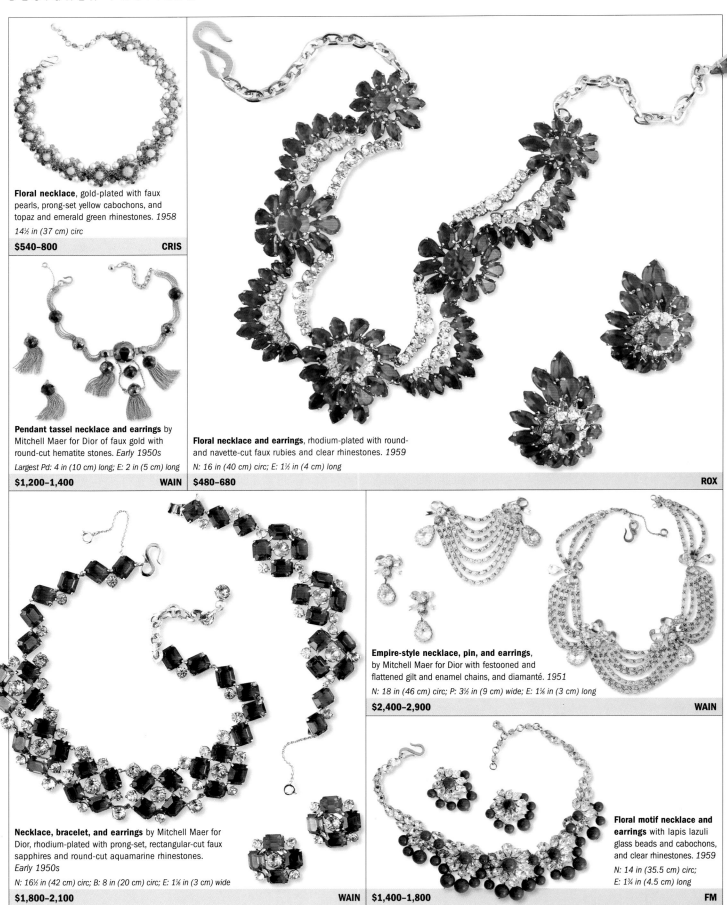

Floral necklace, gold-plated with faux pearls, prong-set yellow cabochons, and topaz and emerald green rhinestones. *1958*

14½ in (37 cm) circ

$540–800   **CRIS**

Pendant tassel necklace and earrings by Mitchell Maer for Dior of faux gold with round-cut hematite stones. *Early 1950s*

Largest Pd: 4 in (10 cm) long; E: 2 in (5 cm) long

$1,200–1,400   **WAIN**

Floral necklace and earrings, rhodium-plated with round- and navette-cut faux rubies and clear rhinestones. *1959*

N: 16 in (40 cm) circ; E: 1½ in (4 cm) long

$480–680   **ROX**

Necklace, bracelet, and earrings by Mitchell Maer for Dior, rhodium-plated with prong-set, rectangular-cut faux sapphires and round-cut aquamarine rhinestones. *Early 1950s*

N: 16½ in (42 cm) circ; B: 8 in (20 cm) circ; E: 1⅛ in (3 cm) wide

$1,800–2,100   **WAIN**

Empire-style necklace, pin, and earrings, by Mitchell Maer for Dior with festooned and flattened gilt and enamel chains, and diamanté. *1951*

N: 18 in (46 cm) circ; P: 3½ in (9 cm) wide; E: 1⅛ in (3 cm) long

$2,400–2,900   **WAIN**

Floral motif necklace and earrings with lapis lazuli glass beads and cabochons, and clear rhinestones. *1959*

N: 14 in (35.5 cm) circ; E: 1¾ in (4.5 cm) long

$1,400–1,800   **FM**

MUSICAL LOCKETS

Some of the most unusual and distinctive pieces of Dior jewelry were made by Mitchell Maer during the early 1950s (*see p.61*). The rare Maer locket below is of chased, gold-plated metal embellished with faux pearls and a large, plum-colored glass cabochon. Its form and decoration, particularly the flying cherubs, recall Renaissance and 18th-century imagery. However, in function it has a decidedly more modern twist: the locket conceals a music box mechanism that plays a romantic tune.

Flying cherubs locket, gold-plated with plum glass cabochon and prong-set faux pearls. *Early 1950s* 2⅜ in (6 cm) long **$NPA LB**

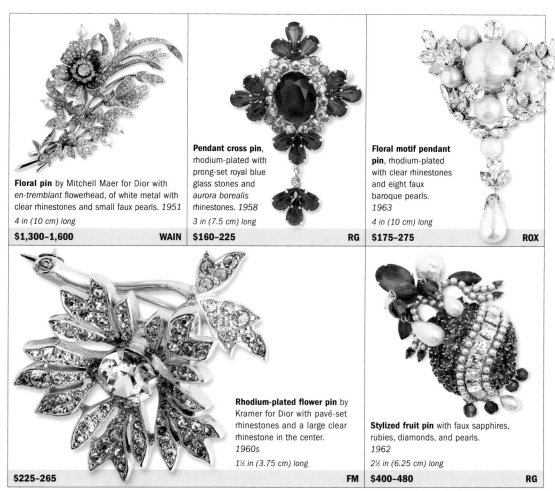

Floral pin by Mitchell Maer for Dior with *en-tremblant* flowerhead, of white metal with clear rhinestones and small faux pearls. *1951* 4 in (10 cm) long

$1,300–1,600   WAIN

Pendant cross pin, rhodium-plated with prong-set royal blue glass stones and *aurora borealis* rhinestones. *1958* 3 in (7.5 cm) long

$160–225   RG

Floral motif pendant pin, rhodium-plated with clear rhinestones and eight faux baroque pearls. *1963* 4 in (10 cm) long

$175–275   ROX

Rhodium-plated flower pin by Kramer for Dior with pavé-set rhinestones and a large clear rhinestone in the center. *1960s* 1½ in (3.75 cm) long

$225–265   FM

Stylized fruit pin with faux sapphires, rubies, diamonds, and pearls. *1962* 2½ in (6.25 cm) long

$400–480   RG

Good, Better, Best

Dior necklaces were designed in numerous styles that were fashionable after World War II. While desirability is a matter of personal aesthetics, price is largely determined by sophistication of craftsmanship and extravagance of materials and design.

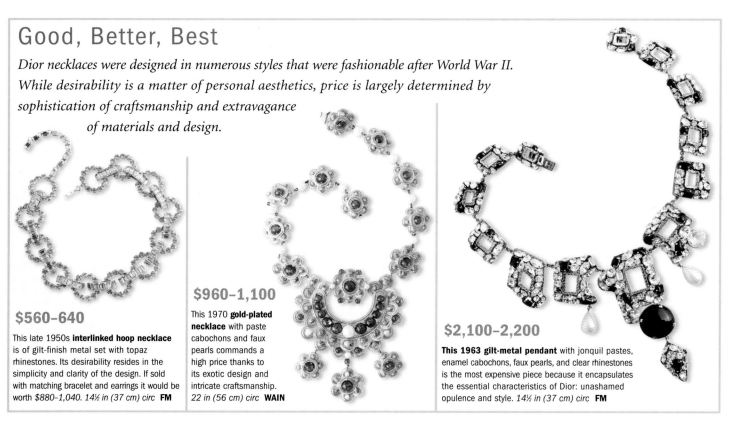

$560–640

This late 1950s **interlinked hoop necklace** is of gilt-finish metal set with topaz rhinestones. Its desirability resides in the simplicity and clarity of the design. If sold with matching bracelet and earrings it would be worth *$880–1,040. 14½ in (37 cm) circ* **FM**

$960–1,100

This 1970 **gold-plated necklace** with paste cabochons and faux pearls commands a high price thanks to its exotic design and intricate craftsmanship. *22 in (56 cm) circ* **WAIN**

$2,100–2,200

This 1963 gilt-metal pendant with jonquil pastes, enamel cabochons, faux pearls, and clear rhinestones is the most expensive piece because it encapsulates the essential characteristics of Dior: unashamed opulence and style. *14½ in (37 cm) circ* **FM**

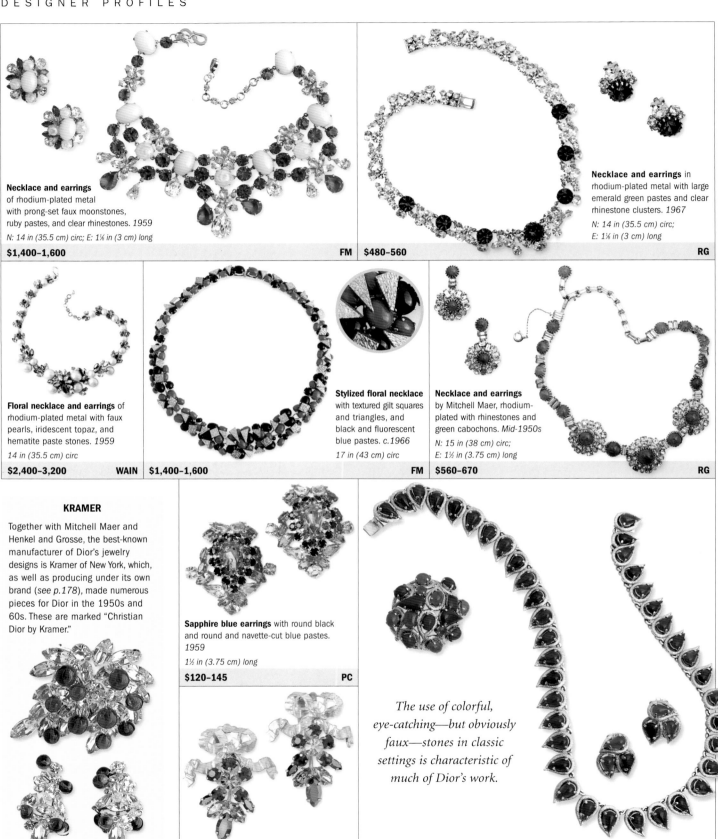

Necklace and earrings of rhodium-plated metal with prong-set faux moonstones, ruby pastes, and clear rhinestones. *1959*

N: 14 in (35.5 cm) circ; E: 1⅛ in (3 cm) long

$1,400–1,600   **FM**

Necklace and earrings in rhodium-plated metal with large emerald green pastes and clear rhinestone clusters. *1967*

N: 14 in (35.5 cm) circ; E: 1⅛ in (3 cm) long

$480–560   **RG**

Floral necklace and earrings of rhodium-plated metal with faux pearls, iridescent topaz, and hematite paste stones. *1959*

14 in (35.5 cm) circ

$2,400–3,200   **WAIN**

$1,400–1,600   **FM**

Stylized floral necklace with textured gilt squares and triangles, and black and fluorescent blue pastes. *c.1966*

17 in (43 cm) circ

Necklace and earrings by Mitchell Maer, rhodium-plated with rhinestones and green cabochons. *Mid-1950s*

N: 15 in (38 cm) circ; E: 1½ in (3.75 cm) long

$560–670   **RG**

KRAMER

Together with Mitchell Maer and Henkel and Grosse, the best-known manufacturer of Dior's jewelry designs is Kramer of New York, which, as well as producing under its own brand (*see p.178*), made numerous pieces for Dior in the 1950s and 60s. These are marked "Christian Dior by Kramer."

Sapphire blue earrings with round black and round and navette-cut blue pastes. *1959*

1½ in (3.75 cm) long

$120–145   **PC**

Pin and earrings by Kramer, rhodium-plated with blue glass and clear rhinestones. *Late 1950s.* P: 2 in (5 cm) long; E: 1½ in (3.75 cm) long $670–770   **CRIS**

Gilt bow earrings with prong-set round and navette ruby red and emerald green rhinestones. *1959*

1½ in (3.75 cm) long

$70–95   **PC**

The use of colorful, eye-catching—but obviously faux—stones in classic settings is characteristic of much of Dior's work.

Necklace, pin, and earrings demi-parure of gilt metal with prong-set faux emerald and lapis teardrops. *1966*

N: 17 in (43 cm) circ; P: 1¾ in (4.5 cm) wide; E: 1 in (2.5 cm) long

$480–560   **RG**

Necklace, bracelet, and earrings by Kramer for Dior, rhodium-plated with white enamel discs and clear rhinestone highlights. *1960s*
N: 14 in (35.5 cm) circ; B: 7 in (17.75 cm) circ; E: ½ in (1.25 cm) long

$210–290   ROX

Rare heart-clover pin of sterling silver with teardrop fuchsia pastes and clear round rhinestones. *1959*
2½ in (6.25 cm) long

$1,600–1,800   WAIN

White metal pin by Henkel and Grosse for Dior set with emerald, topaz, and clear rhinestone baguettes, and a faux pearl. *1962*
2¾ in (7 cm) long

$400–450   WAIN

Rare circus seal pin with jade and emerald green cabochons on gilt metal with a faux pearl ball. *1966*
3 in (8 cm) long

$175–275   ROX

Two faux coral plastic expandable bracelets by Henkel and Grosse of Pforzheim for Dior. *1967*
2½ in (6.25 cm) circ

$225–270   WAIN

Gilt metal fish pin with green, blue, and black molded glass scales, pavé-set clear rhinestones, and black glass cabochon eyes. *1968*
3¼ in (8.25 cm) long

$610–670   WAIN

Heart-shaped pin with oval, round, and navette aquamarine, chalcedony, pale green, and fuchsia pink prong-set pastes. *1960s*
2¾ in (7 cm) wide

$190–240   RG

In ancient Egypt, the Eye of Horus was an amulet of protection, and during the French and American Revolutions, eye motifs symbolized enlightenment.

White metal pin by Henkel and Grosse for Dior with faux pearls and clear rhinestones. *1960*
3 in (7.5 cm) long

$530–610   WAIN

"Eye"pin, rhodium-plated with a sapphire blue cabochon, rings of faux pearls, blue and clear rhinestones, and six faux pearl drops. *Late 1950s*
2⅜ in (6 cm) wide

$350–385   CRIS

COPPOLA E TOPPO
late 1940s–1986

Late 1940s Bruno Coppola and his sister Lyda Toppo found Coppola e Toppo in Milan. Its early pieces are marked with the name of their pet dog, "Mikey"

1950s In addition to producing its own designs, marked "Made in Italy by Coppola e Toppo," it also produces jewelry for Dior, Balenciaga, and Schiaparelli

1960s The company's own designs, especially its beaded necklaces and bracelets, become increasingly sought-after. Coppola e Toppo is also commissioned to produce ranges for leading Italian designers Pucci and Valentino

1972 It is absorbed by a large Italian company, which continues production of Coppola e Toppo jewelry

1986 Production ceases

Coppola e Toppo

Much of the work Coppola e Toppo did for Italian and French fashion houses may be consigned to anonymity, but the sumptuous compositions it produced in its own name brought much-deserved recognition and acclaim.

FROM BEHIND THE SCENES

Brother and sister jewelry designers Bruno Coppola and Lyda Toppo formed the Coppola e Toppo company in the late 1940s in Milan, Italy. Impressed with samples of its work, the Paris-based fashion houses of Dior and Balenciaga utilized Coppola e Toppo's design talents behind the scenes for a number of catwalk and retail line pieces—an important, albeit sporadic arrangement it maintained for the next ten years. In contrast, the 1950s commission it received from Elsa Schiaparelli (*see pp.108–111*) to make a line of faux coral bead jewelry, entitled "Bijoux Voyages," proved both lucrative and high-profile. Further commissions from Italian couturiers such as Pucci and Valentino (*see opposite*), enabled Coppola e Toppo to substantially increase the number of pieces released under its own trademark, "Made in Italy by Coppola e Toppo."

EXTRAVAGANCE AND INNOVATION

Part of the explanation for Coppola e Toppo's rise to prominence from the late 1950s to the early 70s lies in the fact that this period saw the epicenter of fashion switch from Paris to Milan, Coppola e Toppo's base. However, its success was ultimately guaranteed by its innovative multiple strands of crystal, Murano glass, and plastic beads (*see below*). This "swinging sixties" style suddenly made diamanté and faux pearl jewelry seem decidedly "old hat." Numerous collectors, prepared to pay increasingly high prices for Coppola e Toppo's pieces, would still agree.

Above: Multiple strand necklace with gilt metal clasps, baroque pearls, and clear glass beads. *1950s* 13¾ in (35 cm) circ **$2,600–2,900 FM**

BEAUTIFUL BEADS

Although Coppola e Toppo produced many pieces incorporating materials such as gilt metal, silver, faux pearls, and crystal rhinestones, these were usually used as accents or highlights within extravagant compositions dominated by colorful beads. Whether Venetian glass, Austrian crystal, or plastic, beads were combined by Coppola e Toppo in striking combinations that captured all the glamour and spirit of late-1950s and 60s Italian *dolce vita*.

Stylized floral motif necklace with dark blue, pale green, and turquoise glass beads. *Early 1960s* 28½ in (72.5 cm) circ **$2,200–2,400 FM**

Multiple-strand necklace with pink and cranberry red plastic beads, and a gilt metal clasp embellished with glass beads. *1960s* 3 in (7.5 cm) circ **$1,100–1,300 SUM**

Multiple-strand necklace with red glass beads, finished with gilt metal and red bead clasps. *1960s*

26 in (66 cm) circ

$80–1,000　　　　　　　**ROX**

Four-strand necklace of lava stone beads, and ornaments of gilt metal, beads, and faux pearls. *1960s*

19½ in (49.5 cm) circ

$1,100–1,300　　　　　　**FM**

VALENTINO

Coppola e Toppo received numerous commissions from eminent fashion houses (*see opposite*), but some of the most prestigious were from the Italian couturier Valentino. The stunning gilt metal and sapphire blue and clear diamanté pendant necklace shown here was designed for a Valentino line in 1970. At this time Valentino was generally recognized as the "King of Fashion" with a celebrity client list that included Jacqueline Kennedy and Hollywood stars such as Elizabeth Taylor.

Pendant necklace and earrings, designed for Valentino, with blue and clear Swarovski crystals set in gilt metal. *1970. N: 13 in (33 cm) circ; E: 1 in (2.5 cm) wide* **$2,900–3,200 WAIN**

Bow motif necklace with five strands of turquoise, mauve, and black glass beads, with matching earrings. *1960s*

N: 13 in (33 cm) circ; Pd: 1½ in (3.75 cm) wide; E: 1 in (2.5 cm) wide

$2,100–2,200　　　　　　　**FM**

Multiple-strand necklace of faux pearls and clear glass beads, and beaded gilt metal clasps. *1950s*

2¼ in (5.75 cm) wide

$375–575　　　　　　　**ROX**

Beaded choker with blue, red, amber, and clear Bohemian crystal beads and beaded clasps. *1950s*

2 in (5 cm) wide

$720–800　　　　　　**WAIN**

Four-strand necklace of black and clear plastic beads, and a black-beaded oval clasp. *1960s*

19½ in (49.5 cm) circ

$800–960　　　　　　　**FM**

Multiple-strand necklace of amber, topaz, and citrine colored crystal beads. *1960s*

2½ in (6.25 cm) wide

$1,200–1,400　　　　　**SUM**

Gilt metal clasp necklace with strands and pendants of clear crystal, and citrine and green plastic stones. *1960s*

2½ in (6.25 cm) wide

$640–800　　　　　　　**SUM**

CORO AND COROCRAFT
1901–79

1901 The firm of Cohn and Rosenberger is founded in New York City by businessmen Emanuel Cohn and Carl Rosenberger

1919 The "Coro" mark is used for the first time

1924 Adolph Katz joins the company as Design Director

1929 Cohn and Rosenberger open their own factory in Rhode Island and rapidly become the largest costume jewelry manufacturer in the United States

1931 Adolph Katz patents the interlocking catch mechanism for Coro Duettes

1937 "Coro Craft" (later "Corocraft") mark introduced for top-end designs

1943 The company is incorporated as Coro, Inc.

1944 The "Vendome" mark is introduced and the full, up-market Vendome line is launched in 1953

1957 The Richton International Corporation purchases Coro

1979 Production ceases (although continues at Coro Inc. Canada until the mid-1990s)

Coro and Corocraft

At the height of production in the 1930s and 40s, the Coro company employed nearly 3,500 staff. A prolific output meant that they covered most styles and price points, from 50-cent pieces sold at "five-and-dime stores" to jewelry worth hundreds of dollars.

PRODIGIOUS OUTPUT

Although not officially incorporated as Coro, Inc. until 1943, Coro effectively came into existence as Cohn and Rosenberger in 1901. Founded by businessmen Emanuel Cohn and Carl Rosenberger as an accessories boutique in New York City, it outsourced much of its costume jewelry from independent designers and makers until 1929, when it opened a large factory in Providence, Rhode Island. Thereafter, under the design and sales directorships of, respectively, Adolph Katz (*see below*) and Royal Marcher, the company expanded rapidly. By the mid-1930s, with retail stores in most American cities and manufacturing plants established in Great Britain and Canada, it was well on the way to becoming the largest costume jewelry manufacturer in the world.

Cohn and Rosenberger's, and subsequently Coro's, commercial success can be attributed to various factors. Not least was its employment of highly talented designers such as Katz, Gene Verecchio, Robert Geissman, Massa Raimond, François, Oscar Placco, and Albert Weiss (*see pp.132–133*). Underpinning it all, however, was the sheer volume and diversity of its output, which catered to most income brackets using a number of brands of different quality and varying price.

Above: Corocraft bunch-of-grapes pin with prong-set faux moonstone, and chalcedony glass stones, and sterling silver leaves. *1940s. 3 in (7.5 cm) long* **$290–350 CRIS**

ADOLPH KATZ

Appointed Coro Design Director in 1924, Adolph Katz made an enormous contribution to the success of the company. In addition to selecting designs, he also created numerous pieces and mechanisms himself. He is most admired for his exquisite *en tremblant* floral pins and Coro Duettes. Equally sought-after, however, are his diverse static figurals, such as Jelly Bellies and animal subjects, and various other whimsical designs.

Corocraft fish pin designed by Adolph Katz. The head, tail, and fins in sterling silver with enameling, crystal rhinestones, and cabochons; the "belly" is of semi-translucent white Lucite. *1940s. 2¾ in (7 cm) long* **$440–480 RG**

Coro horse-head pin and earrings of gold-tone metal with aquamarine rhinestone eyes, pink rhinestone ears, red enameled flowers, and green enameled leaves. *c.1960. P: 2 in (5 cm) long; E: 1 in (2.5 cm) long* **$195–225 ABIJ**

MARKS OF QUALITY

For the most part, pieces marked "Coro" are of good quality and originally targeted the middle and lower sections of the market. Nearly all fashionable styles were covered, employing imagery ranging from patriotic motifs, to floral and foliate, to figural. Double-pin Coro Duettes are much sought-after and have become a collecting field in their own right (*see pp.186–187*). Of their upmarket brands, Coro Craft is the best known. It embraces equally diverse subjects, but the pieces are made in more expensive materials, such as sterling silver and European crystal rhinestones. (Its equally impressive Vendome line became a subsidiary company in 1953 [*see pp.130–131*]).

Sometimes innovative, sometimes commercial imitations of other companies' popular designs, Coro and Corocraft pieces appeal to as broad a spectrum of collectors today as they did to their original consumers.

Coro floral bracelet and earrings with white plastic petals and gold-tone metal centers with pale green and blue and clear crystal rhinestones. Mid-*1950s*. *B: 6 in (15.25 cm) circ; E: 1½ in (3.75 cm) wide* **$50–60 MILLB**

Coro's "Diadem Jewels," promoted by a 1947 magazine advertisement, which bore their top-line "Coro Craft with Pegasus" branding. The sense of refined luxury is typical of Coro designs and advertising in the immediate aftermath of World War II.

Good, Better, Best

Materials used and current appreciation of particular styles ultimately determines the price of these Coro pins.

$20–30

Made in the late 1950s, this inexpensive **starburst pin** is a simple but well-defined radiating design made from brightly polished, lightweight gold-tone metal with a center of clear and ruby rhinestones. *2¼ in (5.75 cm) wide* **MILLB**

$30–40

This is a late-1950s **Space Age motif pin**. It commands a slightly higher price than the starburst pin because the body of the pin, which radiates out from a pearlescent metallic cabochon, is cast from a heavier white metal with a more sophisticated finish. *2¼ in (5.75 cm) wide* **MILLB**

$55–75

Made in about 1950, this **floral pin** is a more traditional motif than the other examples (*see left and above*), which makes it more appealing to a broad range of collectors. However, its higher price is also influenced by the fact that it is cast from vermeil sterling silver, which lends it both physical substance and a pleasing antique gold-tone finish. It is also enhanced by the incorporation of good-quality, clear crystal rhinestones of Austrian or Czechoslovakian origin. *2 in (5 cm) wide* **MILLB**

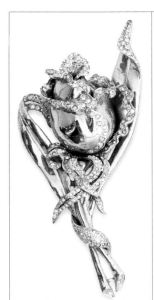

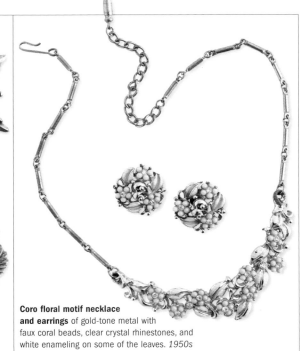

Corocraft floral pin in vermeil sterling silver with pavé-set clear crystal rhinestones. *1940s*

2¾ in (7 cm) long

| $320–400 | RG |

Coro Victorian-style love token pin of gold-tone metal casting in the form of a hand proffering a rose. *1950s*

2½ in (6.25 cm) long

| $45–50 | JJ |

Badge and shield pin with matching earrings in gold-tone metal; the shields with white and red enameling. *1940s*

P: 2 in (5 cm) wide; E: 1 in (2.5 cm) long

| $45–65 | ABIJ |

Coro floral motif necklace and earrings of gold-tone metal with faux coral beads, clear crystal rhinestones, and white enameling on some of the leaves. *1950s*

N: 16 in (40.5 cm) circ; E: 1 in (2.5 cm) wide

| $75–100 | MILLB |

Many of the pieces in Coro's upmarket Corocraft line were produced in high-quality sterling and vermeil sterling silver.

Corocraft pin of scrolling forms and stylized floral motif in vermeil sterling silver set with ruby red glass cabochons and round-cut clear crystal rhinestones. *Mid-1940s*

3¼ in (8.25 cm) wide

| $190–240 | CRIS |

Corocraft bracelet of gold-plated metal with ruby and emerald crystal cabochons, pavé-set clear crystal rhinestones, and green enameled leaves. *1940s*

3 in (7.5 cm) wide

$400–480   **CRIS**

Corocraft rose pin in sterling and vermeil sterling silver with clear crystal rhinestone highlights. *1940s*

2½ in (6.25 cm) long

$320–400   **RG**

COLORED LUCITE

Together with many other costume jewelry manufacturers, Coro enthusiastically adopted the "plastic" Lucite after it was developed by the Du Pont company in 1937. Like Trifari (*see pp.118–129*), Coro employed Lucite primarily in its translucent white form for its Jelly Belly figural pins. However, since it came in varying degrees of opacity and a wide range of colors, it also proved to be a very effective substitute for various rock-forming minerals, such as moonstone and chalcedony, often used in precious jewelry.

Coro basket-of-fruits pin of white metal with clear crystal rhinestones and pale blue and moonglow Lucite cabochons. *c.1940.* 1 in (2.5 cm) long **$45–55 JJ**

Coro bracelet with silver-tone metal links and leaves and jonquil-colored crystal rhinestones. *1950s*

7 in (17.75 cm) long

$40–50   **MILLB**

Coro floral motif earrings of antiqued goldwash metal with faux baroque pearls and red crystal rhinestones. *1950s*

1¼ in (3.25 cm) long

$45–55   **MILLB**

Coro American Indian chief earrings in pewter-tone white metal castings. *c.1960*

1 in (2.5 cm) long

$45–50   **MILLB**

Coro floral motif earrings in gold-tone metal with pink, aquamarine, and citrine crystal navettes. *c.1945*

1 in (2.5 cm) long

$25–35   **MILLB**

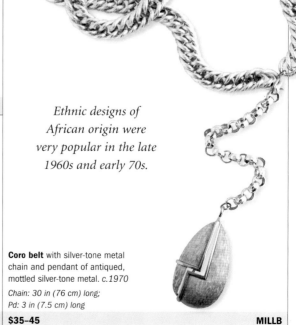

Ethnic designs of African origin were very popular in the late 1960s and early 70s.

Coro floral earrings with pale pink plastic petals and *aurora borealis* crystal rhinestone centers. *c.1955*

2½ in (6.25 cm) long

$25–35   **MILLB**

Coro châtelaine pin with a pair of ballerinas of gold-tone metal castings linked by a a twin-strand gilt metal chain. *Late 1940s*

Ballerinas: 2½ in (6.25 cm) long; Chains: 6 in (15.25 cm) long

$110–125   **JJ**

Coro belt with silver-tone metal chain and pendant of antiqued, mottled silver-tone metal. *c.1970*

Chain: 30 in (76 cm) long;
Pd: 3 in (7.5 cm) long

$35–45   **MILLB**

FAHRNER
1855–1979

1855 Georg Seeger and Theodor Fahrner, Sr. open a jewelry factory in Pforzheim, Germany

c.1883 Theodor Fahrner, Jr. takes over the running of the company

1900 Fahrner jewelry wins silver medal at Paris World's Fair

1901 The "TF" trademark is introduced and Fahrner begins exporting to Great Britain via Murrle Bennet & Co.

1910 Introduction of the "Fahrner Schmuck" trademark

1919 Theodor Fahrner, Jr. dies. The company is sold to Gustav Braendle and becomes Gustav Braendle-Theodor Fahrner Nachf

1979 Production ceases

Fahrner

A spectacularly successful blend of art and industry, Fahrner's exquisite, and often semi-precious, Art Nouveau and Art Deco jewelry commands understandably high prices—provided it bears the company stamp.

ARTISTIC DESIGNS

Founded in Pforzheim, Germany, in 1855, and run by Theodor Fahrner, Jr. from about 1883 onwards, the Fahrner company was one of the most successful European jewelry manufacturers of the late 19th and early 20th centuries. Sold in 1919 to Gustav Braendle and renamed Gustave Braendle–Theodor Fahrner Nachf, the company continued to thrive well into the 1950s and remained in production until 1979.

Prior to the mid-1920s Fahrner was known for its Art Nouveau, Arts and Crafts, and Celtic Revival jewelry. Designed by eminent German artists and industrially produced in limited runs, many pieces were exported via other companies, such as Murrle Bennet & Co. in England. Subsequently, Fahrner

was acclaimed for its striking geometric designs, which encapsulated the spirit of the Jazz Age and Art Deco movement.

MATERIALS AND MARKS

While Fahrner believed that the true worth of any piece lay in its artistic merits, rather than the value of the materials used, the company often incorporated semi-precious stones and pearls into its designs. Understandably, this is reflected in the high prices Fahrner jewelry now commands. However, the absence of a Fahrner stamp detracts by anything up to 75 percent from the value of a marked equivalent.

Above: Art Deco pin in silver and marcasite with black onyx and coral cabochons. *c.1929. 3¼ in (8.25 cm) long* **$2,000–3,000 TR**

Art Deco pin of pierced silver casting with pale blue matte enamel and lapis and amethyst cabochons. *1930s 2 in (5 cm) long* **$1,000–1,400 TR**

Fahrner Schmuck 1929 advertisement in *Die Dame* for a range of jewelry by Gustav Braendle-Theodor Fahrner Nachf. The "Fahrner Schmuck" trademark was registered in May 1910.

Art Deco pin of gilded silver with an amazonite bar and two faceted blue glass triangles. *1927*

2⅛ in (5.5 cm) wide

$1,300–1,800   TR

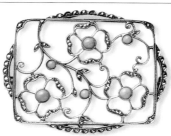

Floral motif pin in silver and matte rock crystal with turquoise cabochons. *Late 1920s*

1½ in (3.75 cm) long

$1,500–2,000   TR

Art Deco gilt metal pendant with turquoise matte enamel and cabochons and a large pink quartz stone. *1930s*

2 in (5 cm) long

$2,200–2,700   TR

Pendant earrings in silver, marcasite, onyx, and coral. *Late 1920s*

2 in (5 cm) long

$2,000–2,500   TR

Pierced ivory pin in silver with blue enamel, pearls, and an emerald glass cabochon. *Late 1920s*

2¼ in (5.75 cm) long

$700–800   TR

Floral motif bar pin in silver with matte black enamel and an aventurine quartz cabochon. *c.1925*

2¾ in (7 cm) long

$800–880   RBRG

Art Deco pin in silver, marcasite, black matte enamel, and hematite. *Late 1920s*

1¾ in (4.5 cm) long

$3,500–4,500   TR

Art Deco pin in silver and marcasite with amazonite bars, blue glass cabochons, and a pink quartz stone. *Late 1920s*

1¾ in (4.5 cm) long

$1,100–1,400   TR

Necklace and bracelet in gold-plated metal with turquoise cabochons. *1930s*

N: 14 in (35.5 cm) long; B: 8 in (20.5 cm) long

$3,500–4,500   TR

Silver and marcasite pendant with green enamel and a green glass cabochon. *1920s*

2 in (5 cm) long

$450–500   TR

Stylized leaf pin in silver and marcasite with a single pearl highlight. *1920s*

1¾ in (4.5 cm) long

$450–500   RBRG

Hattie Carnegie

For almost half a century, petite Austrian-born Hattie Carnegie strode the world of American fashion like a colossus. Innovative and invariably high-quality, her costume jewelry still commands serious attention.

HATTIE CARNEGIE
1886–1956

1886 Born Henrietta Kanengesier in Vienna, Austria

c.1904 Emigrates to the United States and works as milliner's assistant and messenger at Macy's, New York City

1909 Having changed her name to Hattie Carnegie, opens her first shop—Carnegie-Ladies Hatter—in partnership with seamstress Rose Booth

1918 Founds Hattie Carnegie, Inc., launches first full-scale collection, and starts manufacturing high-quality costume jewelry to complement her clothing

1928 Launches Hattie Carnegie Originals ready-to-wear line and over ensuing years substantially expands retail outlets across the United States

1934 Establishes Spectator Sports to wholesale less expensive lines

1956 Hattie Carnegie dies but production of clothing and jewelry continues

1976 Hattie Carnegie, Inc. is acquired by the Chromology American Corp.

ENTREPRENEURIAL SPIRIT

In 1904, at age 18, Henrietta Kanengesier emigrated to the United States from Vienna. On the ship bound for New York, she purportedly asked the name of America's richest man. Her subsequent adoption of the entrepreneurial Andrew Carnegie's surname proved appropriate. From a single shop opened in 1909, Hattie Carnegie went on to found a chain of exclusive fashion boutiques across the United States. At the time of her death in 1956, the sheer size of her empire reflected not only her commercial success, but also the enormous impact she had made on American

fashions. A uniquely American reinterpretation of French *couture*, Carnegie's style was epitomized by her trademark: the "little Carnegie suit." Her jewelry, produced from 1918 onward, attracted an elite clientele, including Tallulah Bankhead, Joan Fontaine, Norma Shearer, and Joan Crawford.

DISTINCTIVE DESIGNS

Commissioned from many designers, Carnegie jewelry was made in numerous styles. Flowers, leaves, and fruit are recurring motifs, while unique imagery is employed in her oriental figure and stylized animal pins (*see opposite*). Favored materials include enamel, faux pearls, rhinestones, and glass beads—often in unusual combinations. Marked "Hattie Carnegie," "Carnegie," or "HC," these fine-quality pieces are as eagerly sought-after today as when they first appeared.

Above: Mask pin of gold-plated casting with faux pearl, turquoise, coral, and diamond highlights. *1950s* *2½ in (6.5 cm) long* **$320–400 CRIS**

Flower pin of gold-tone metal with clear crystal rhinestones. *1950s* *4 in (10 cm) long* **$160–240 CRIS**

Carnegie silk brocade dress accessorized at the rib cage with a large Carnegie pear pin studded with rhinestones. Photograph from a 1961 issue of *Vogue*.

Merman pin with iridescent white enameling, faux pearl drops, and faux ruby, sapphire, and gilt metal highlights. *Mid-1950s*

4⅜ in (11 cm) long

$375–475   **ROX**

Lion head pin with iridescent white enameling, faux pearl drops, and banded faux ruby, emerald, sapphire, and gilt metal highlights. *Late 1950s*

4 in (10 cm) long

$275–375   **ROX**

Pendant leaf motif necklace and earrings of gold-washed metal with faux pearl highlights. *1960s*

N: 17 in (43 cm) circ; E: 1½ in (4 cm) long

$195–200   **JJ**

Three-strand necklace of polychrome Murano glass and Austrian crystal beads. *c.1960*

16 in (40.5 cm) circ

$145–150   **ABIJ**

Antiqued gold-plated earrings with aquamarine glass cabochons encircling dark faux sapphire glass centers. *1950s*

1 in (2.5 cm) wide

$45–50   **MILLB**

STYLIZED ANIMAL PINS

Of all Carnegie's figural pins, the most instantly recognizable are the stylized animal subjects. Mostly of African inspiration, they are made of vibrantly colored Lucite, and include sparkling clear rhinestones, colored beads, and gilt highlights. Diverse species include fish, goats, and—the most sought-after of all—anteaters.

Fish pin of black, green, and yellow Lucite, with gilt metal and clear rhinestone highlights. *1950s*

2 in (5 cm) long

$240–270   **CRIS**

Stylized African anteater pin of turquoise and orange-red Lucite with gilt metal and clear rhinestones. *1950s*

3⅜ in (8.5 cm) long   **$320–350 CRIS**

Pansy pin with large "cabochon" center, of base metal coated with metallic yellow cold enamel. *1970s*

2 in (5 cm) wide

$65–75   **ABIJ**

Stylized goat head pin of orange-red and green Lucite with lapis glass beads and clear rhinestones. *1950s*

3¾ in (9.5 cm) long

$240–290   **CRIS**

HOBÉ
1887–present

1887 The original Hobé Cie is founded in Paris by master goldsmith Jacques Hobé

Early 1920s One of Jacques's three sons, William Hobé, begins selling theatrical costume in the US

Mid 1920s Florence Ziegfeld commissions William Hobé to create costumes and jewelry for his *Ziegfeld Follies* productions on Broadway

c.1927 William Hobé founds the American Hobé Cie jewelry company

1930s Hobé begins selling its retail lines through up-market stores

1950s Hobé designs pieces for many Hollywood stars, including Bette Davis and Ava Gardner

1960s William Hobé's sons Robert and Donald take over the running of the company

1980s William Hobé's grandson James continues production

Hobé

Worn on stage and screen, promoted by Hollywood stars, and sold through up-market retail outlets, Hobé's high-quality pieces lived up to its advertising slogan: "Jewels of Legendary Splendor."

PARISIAN ORIGINS

A son of master goldsmith Jacques Hobé, who had established Hobé Cie in Paris in the late 19th century, William Hobé set up the American Hobé Cie in about 1927 in New York.

Essentially launched on a prestigious commission to produce both costumes and jewelry for the *Ziegfeld Follies* (*see below*), Hobé Cie rapidly expanded to become, together with Joseff of Hollywood (*see pp.78–83*), the major supplier of pieces for theater and film during the 1940s and 50s. This high-profile work, enhanced by postwar advertising campaigns with leading Hollywood actresses and top models, ensured an enthusiastic reception from the public for Hobé's retail lines.

TOP QUALITY

Always relatively expensive, Hobé jewelry was only sold by leading department stores and exclusive boutiques. Apart from the jewelry designed by Lou Vici, who worked for the company from the 1930s to the 70s, all Hobé pieces were designed by members of the Hobé family. They invariably display the same techniques and high standards of craftsmanship found in precious jewelry. The materials—vermeil, platinum, high-quality pastes, and sometimes semi-precious stones—are equally impressive. Of numerous exotic designs, which include reproductions of historical pieces owned by European royalty, Hobé's floral pins (*see opposite*) are among the most sought-after.

Above: Hinged bracelet of gilt metal with crystal rhinestones and faux amethyst pastes. *1970s. 2½ in (6.5 cm) wide* **$170–180 MAC**

Roses-and-heart locket pin in sterling and vermeil sterling silver with metallic faux pearls and white metal tassels. *1940s* *5½ in (14 cm) long* **$500–600 BY**

ZIEGFELD FOLLIES

Hobé's first major commission in the US came in the mid-1920s from the legendary impresario Florence Ziegfeld. In accepting an offer by William Hobé to provide costumes for his spectacular *Ziegfeld Follies* Broadway productions, Florence also asked Hobé to create inexpensive but realistic-looking jewelry to complement the outfits. This successful commission had the effect of substantially enhancing Hobé's profile, and similar orders from other theater companies and Hollywood film studios soon followed.

Miss Angel Forbes of the *Ziegfeld Follies* wearing stylized American Indian jewelry and costume.

Bib necklace, bracelet, pin, and earrings parure in gilt metal with strings of faceted faux topaz and red *aurora borealis* beads with overlaid spherical blue and pink Venetian glass beads. *c.1960*

N and P: 2½ in (6.5 cm) long; B: 6½ in (16.5 cm) circ; E: 1½ in (3.75 cm) wide

$450–500   **BY**

Heart-shaped pin and earrings of filigree gilt metal with clear crystal rhinestones and large, faceted faux sapphire pastes. *1950s*

P: 1½ in (4 cm) long; E: 1⅛ in (3 cm) long

$140–180   **MG**

Antiqued gilt metal earrings with pink and white faux pearls and molded green glass. *1950s*

1¾ in (4.5 cm) long

$105–160   **LB**

Floral bow pin in sterling silver with peridot, rose quartz, jonquil, and amethyst crystal rhinestones. *1940s*

4 in (10 cm) wide

$320–350   **CRIS**

Bracelet and pin with flower, fruit, and bow motifs in vermeil and antiqued vermeil sterling silver. *1940s*

B: 7 in (17.75 cm) circ; P: 2½ in (6.5 cm) wide

$150–200   **BY**

Silver-tone metal earrings with dark and light blue paste cabochons and clear rhinestones. *1960s*

1 in (2.5 cm) wide

$30–40   **TR**

Heart pin in vermeil sterling silver with a large square-cut faux amethyst center. *1940s*

2½ in (6.5 cm) long

$400–450   **CRIS**

FLORAL PINS

Hobé is best known for the exquisite floral pins it produced in the 1940s. Made in antiqued sterling or vermeil sterling silver with pastes or semi-precious stones, the pins are either in the form of floral sprays set in baskets or, as here, bouquets of stemmed blooms entwined with ribbons and bows.

Rose bouquet pin in vermeil with crystal rhinestones. *1940s. 6 in (15.5 cm) wide* **$960–1,120 CRIS**

Unsigned necklace and earrings with rose motifs and bow in vermeil sterling silver, metallic faux pearls, and a white-on-red carved cameo. *1940s*

N: 15½ in (40 cm) circ; Cameo: 1¾ in (4.5 cm) long; E: 1½ in (3.75 cm) wide

$500–600   **BY**

Joseff of Hollywood

EUGENE JOSEFF
1905–48

1905 Born in Chicago

1923–26 Works as a graphic artist in Chicago advertising agency. Designs jewelry in his spare time

1927 Moves to Los Angeles to escape the Great Depression. Starts training as a jewelry designer

1931–35 Some of his early pieces are used in Hollywood films

1935 Opens Sunset Jewelry in Hollywood and founds "Joseff of Hollywood"

1937 Now a leading supplier of costume jewelry to Hollywood film studios, he develops his retail line for sale to the public

1948 Tragically killed in a plane crash

1950s onward Joseff of Hollywood run by his widow, Joan Castle

In 1934 Eugene Joseff criticized the use of historically incorrect jewelry in Hollywood films. Premier costume designer Walter Plunkett responded, "Well, if you're so smart, let's see what you can do!"

FOUNDATIONS OF SUCCESS

Of Austrian heritage, Eugene Joseff was born in Chicago in 1905. Following a spell in advertising, he moved to California in the late 1920s to pursue a passion for jewelry design in one of the few growth industries of the Great Depression: Hollywood. Rapid elevation to leading designer and supplier of costume jewelry to the major studios—which endured beyond his death in 1948 through to the 1960s—was fueled by Joseff's artistic creativity and commercial acumen.

In addition to developing a camera-friendly substitute for gold (*see opposite*), Joseff had the ability to accurately research and simplify specific historical styles of jewelry that immediately conveyed the appropriate period ambience on the "Silver Screen." Together with his wife, Joan Castle, he also adopted a policy of leasing, rather than selling, pieces to the studios for a specific film, and thereby accumulated an archive of nearly three million pieces available for rental. In addition, from 1937 they developed a massively successful line of jewelry for retail to the star-struck public, much of which was copied from, or inspired by, pieces originally designed for the cinema. It is these latter pieces that are the most readily found today.

STAR PROVENANCE

Joseff's jewelry is never nondescript—it always makes a strong visual statement. However, its popularity is most certainly linked to its Hollywood connections. The vast list of films for which Joseff designs were commissioned includes: *A Star is Born* (1936); *The Wizard of Oz* and *Gone With The Wind* (both 1939); *Casablanca* (1942); *Easter Parade* (1949); *Singing in the Rain* (1952); *To Catch a Thief* (1955); *Ben*

Above: Bee pin, Russian gold plated. *1940s* 1½ in (4 cm) wide **$65–80 CRIS**

> "If you want to start a collection, start with a brooch because you will find most use for it. It can be pinned on a suit lapel, collar, or pocket, on a hat, belt, or evening gown."
> *Eugene Joseff*

Dolphin and shell pendant necklace, Russian gold plated with a faux pearl. *1940s* Shell: 1⅛ in (3 cm) long **$370–430 CRIS**

FINE ART

Joseff studied fine art for authentic period motifs. Seashells, as in Botticelli's *The Birth of Venus* (c.1485), recur in classical mythology and feature in some of the jewelry he designed for Roman and Biblical epics.

INSPIRATION

Joseff compiled a substantial collection of rare antiquarian books on costume and jewelry, which provided inspiration and reference for many of his historically authentic designs.

ALL THAT GLITTERS IS NOT GOLD

Joseff's status as Hollywood's leading supplier of costume jewelry was partly founded on his development of a visually effective substitute for gold. Known as Russian gold plating, its semi-matte, copper-gold finish minimized the traditional problem of flare from over-reflective jewelry when filming real gold, or other gold substitutes, under powerful studio lights. It proved a popular material aesthetically, too, and many of Joseff's retail line pieces were also created from this new metal.

Semi-matte Russian gold plating

Crescent moon and cherub pin, Russian gold plated with faux pearl drops. From Joseff's retail line, modeled on a a pin and earrings worn by the actress Virginia Mayo. *1940s. 1½ in (4 cm) long*
$110–160 CRIS

Sun god pin, one of Joseff's most distinctive pieces, is of Russian gold and has clear rhinestone eye tremblers. It is also shown being modeled by the Hollywood actress Pier Angeli. *1940s. 3 in (7.5 cm) wide*
$385–450 CRIS

Hur (1959); *Breakfast at Tiffany's* (1961); *Cleopatra* (1963); and *My Fair Lady* (1964). The list of stars who wore the jewelry is equally impressive, ranging from Greta Garbo, Vivien Leigh, and Grace Kelly, to Clark Gable, Errol Flynn, and Tony Curtis.

Typical objects include pins, bracelets, buckles, necklaces, pendants, and earrings—sometimes produced in parures or demi-parures. Diverse styles include Art Nouveau, Art Deco, 1940s retro, oriental, and Middle-Eastern, as well as astrological, and animal, fish, bird, and insect imagery.

Decoratively, Russian gold pieces are either plain or embellished with faux pearls and clear or colored crystal—the latter hand-cut, rather than pressed, on the best pieces. There are also a number of black, ivory, or red Bakelite examples.

IDENTIFICATION AND CONDITION

Identification is quite straightforward since most pieces are stamped "Joseff" or "Joseff of Hollywood"—exceptions being one-offs made for celebrity clients. However, collectors should note that some of the pieces made in the late 1930s and 40s have been reissued by the Joseff company in recent years to meet increased demand. Recent examples are still very collectible, but you can expect to pay slightly less than you would for an original piece. Bear in mind that much of the attraction of Russian gold jewelry lies in its subtle, semi-matte finish, which acquires a darker, more mellow patina over time. Be wary, therefore, of overly bright examples—usually the result of abrasive polishing, which renders them almost worthless.

Bow motif châtelaine pin of solid and pierced Russian gold, with prong-set rhinestones. *1940s. 2¾ in (7 cm) long*
$240–290 CRIS

EGYPT

Inspiration for the Joseff jewelry worn by Elizabeth Taylor in *Cleopatra* (1963), included pieces found in Tutankhamen's tomb in 1922. These Russian gold coiled snake earrings incorporate red glass cabochons. *1940–65 3⅜ in (8.5 cm) long* **$290–350 CRIS**

ROMANCE

Star motifs featured in the Joseff jewelry worn by Norma Shearer in *Marie Antoinette* (1938). Later they were a hit in Joseff's retail line. These Russian gold star pendants have rhinestone centers. *1940s 2¾ in (7 cm) long* **$130–190 CRIS**

Floral motif pin with aquamarine crystal lozenges and clear rhinestones set in Russian gold plated metal. *1940s*

4⅝ in (11.5 cm) wide

$1,300–1,400 SUM

Russian gold plated tassel pin of Middle-Eastern inspiration. (Also made with a faux silver finish). *1940s*

6½ in (16.5 cm) long

$560–720 SUM

SWARM OF BEES

Joseff's Russian gold plated bee pins were originally made in the 1940s and 50s, but are being reproduced today. Originals range from $40 to $110, depending on size. They are worn either individually or as a small swarm.

Bee pins in various sizes. *Large: 2⅛ in (5.5 cm), medium: 1¾ in (4.5 cm), small: 1 in (2.5 cm) wide* **$40–110 CRIS**

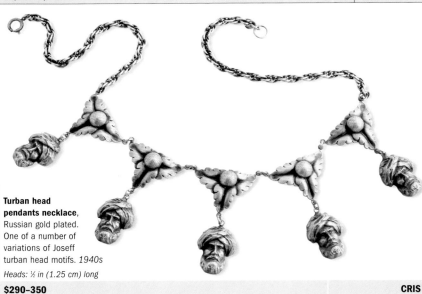

Turban head pendants necklace, Russian gold plated. One of a number of variations of Joseff turban head motifs. *1940s*

Heads: ½ in (1.25 cm) long

$290–350 CRIS

Floral motif pendant necklace and earrings, Russian gold plated with faux topaz and clear rhinestones. *1940s*

Floral pd: 3 in (7.5 cm) wide; E: 2¾ in (7 cm) long

$800–960 SUM

Unusual floral motif necklace and earrings, Russian gold plated with navette-cut ruby and round-cut clear rhinestones. *1940s*

Longest Pd & E: 3½ in (9 cm) long

$1,300–1,400 SUM

Joseff's faux precious stone pieces are particularly desirable to collectors.

Early heart-shaped floral pendant with graduated teardrop and round faux amethysts, and clear rhinestones. *1930s*

2½ in (6.25 cm) long

$180–270 ROX

American eagle and flag pin, Russian gold plated with prong-set ruby, sapphire, and clear colored rhinestones. *1940s*

2¼ in (5.75 cm) wide

$160–240 CRIS

Moon god with ruff pin, Russian gold plated with clear rhinestone eye tremblers. Extremely rare. *1940s*

2½ in (6.25 cm) wide

$430–480 CRIS

Floral pin, Russian gold plated with central ruby red cabochon and navette-cut clear rhinestones. *1940s*

3½ in (9 cm) wide

$400–480 SUM

Crown pin with clear rhinestone finial, Russian gold plated and signed "Joan Castle" (Joseff's wife). *1950s*

2 in (5 cm) wide

$400–480 CRIS

Faux pearl pendant earrings, Russian gold plated, as worn by Grace Kelly in the film *High Society*. Mid-1950s

4 in (10 cm) long

$240–320 SUM

Cherub earrings, Russian gold plated with prong-set round clear rhinestones and inverted teardrop clear rhinestone pendants. *1940s*

1½ in (3.75 cm) long

$190–240 PC

Pendant owl head earrings, Russian gold plated and suspended from a gold-tone faux pearl. *1940s*

2 in (5 cm) long

$225–255 CRIS

Leaf and berry "C-cutter" pin, Russian gold plated and very rare. *1940s*

6⅛ in (15.5 cm) long

$1,000–1,200 CRIS

Swarm of bees châtelaine pin, Russian gold plated with two large and three small bees. *1940s*

Large bees: 2 in (5 cm) long

$370–430 CRIS

Large floral pin with pendant tassel. Russian gold plated with three large pear-cut clear rhinestones. *1940s*

6 in (15 cm) long

$480–560 SUM

Good, Better, Best

In addition to rarity and condition, the price of Joseff pins is primarily determined by subject matter, quality of design, and wearability.

$290–350

A 1940s Russian gold plated **bee and flower pin**. Robustly styled with good attention to detail and a collectible motif. Worth $560–640 if sold with matching earrings.
2¾ in (7 cm) wide **CRIS**

$320–400

A 1940s Russian gold plated **lily of the valley pin**. Rarer than the bee and flower pin (see above) with a more fluid, stylized sense of movement. Ultimately, more feminine and wearable.
3 in (7.5 cm) wide **CRIS**

$900–1,000

A 1940s **Russian gold plated leaf pin** with three hand-cut, aquamarine lead crystal stones in basket settings. Very rare, naturalistic, and displaying exceptional standards of craftsmanship. The largest and most visually striking of the three pieces. *6 in (15 cm) wide* **CRIS**

SIGNS OF THE ZODIAC

Astrology became very fashionable in the United States in the 1930s and 40s. In response, Joseff of Hollywood designed a set of 12 Russian gold plated Signs of the Zodiac pins for his retail line, including Sagittarius, The Archer (*see below*), and Aries, The Ram (*see bottom*).

Zodiac pins. *1940s. 2 in (5 cm) long* **$160–240 CRIS**

Charging bull pin, Russian gold plated with three basket-set, rectangular-cut sapphire, emerald, and red crystals. *1940s*
4 in (10 cm) wide

$160–240   **CRIS**

Pair-of-wolves pin, Russian gold plated with ruby, chalcedony, amber, and sapphire crystal cabochons. *1940s*
2½ in (6.25 cm) long

$160–240   **CRIS**

Insects, animals, and fish are recurring motifs in Joseff's jewelry designs.

Monarch butterfly pin, Russian gold plated with prong-set clear, emerald, and amethyst rhinestones. *1940s*
3½ in (9 cm) long

$385–450   **CRIS**

Châtelaine camel pin, Russian gold plated with ruby, emerald, citrine, jade, and aquamarine crystal cabochons. *1940s*
1⅛ in (3 cm) wide

$385–450   **CRIS**

"Kitty Kat" pin, Russian gold plated with prong-set, navette-cut emerald rhinestone eyes. *1940s*
3 in (7.5 cm) wide

$240–320   **CRIS**

Crab and seashell pin, Russian gold plated with a faux pearl. *1940s*
2 in (5 cm) wide

$120–160   **CRIS**

Pendant earrings of French bulldogs with ruffs, Russian gold plated. *1940s*
2¾ in (7 cm) long

$135–160   **CRIS**

Retro design châtelaine pin, Russian gold plated with square and rectangular basket-set clear crystal stones. *1940s*

4¾ in (12 cm) wide

$880–960 CRIS

Twin-tassel pendant necklace, Russian gold plated with oriental figures. *1940s*

42 in (107 cm) long

$280–320 CRIS

Large, rare scrolling leaf and flower pin, Russian gold plated with basket-set ruby red crystal petals and a central round clear rhinestone. *1940s*

5½ in (14 cm) long

$1,000–1,200 CRIS

Art Deco Egyptian-style earrings, Russian gold plated with ruby red crystal cabochons. *1940s*

2½ in (6.25 cm) long

$120–160 CRIS

Oak-leaf and acorn pendant necklace, Russian gold plated. The original was designed for the actress Carol Lombard. *1940s*

Pd: 3½ in (9 cm) long

$720–800 CRIS

Russian gold plated earrings of butterfly wings and leaf motifs with faceted amethyst crystals. *1940s*

2 in (5 cm) long

$130–190 CRIS

Pendant stars bar pin, Russian gold plated with clear rhinestone centers. *1940s*

4⅜ in (11 cm) wide

$520–600 CRIS

Multiple fish pendant-hoop earrings, Russian gold plated with topaz crystal cabochons. *1940s*

3½ in (9 cm) long

$190–240 CRIS

Fish scatter pins, Russian gold plated with ruby red crystal cabochon eyes. *1940s*

1½ in (4 cm) wide

$40–50 each CRIS

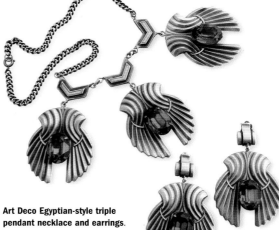

Art Deco Egyptian-style triple pendant necklace and earrings. Russian gold plated with amethyst crystal stones. *1940s*

Pd & E: 3½ in (9 cm) long

$880–960 CRIS

Horse-heads châtelaine pin, Russian gold plated with emerald crystal cabochon eyes and trailing cowboy motifs. *1940s*

Heads: 1 in (2.5 cm) long

$240–290 CRIS

Kenneth Jay Lane

"Wearing costume jewelry is like wearing glass slippers. You can feel like you're going to the ball, even if you're not." (Kenneth Jay Lane's "Cinderella" philosophy, from his autobiography, *Faking It*.)

KENNETH JAY LANE
c.1930–present

c.1930 Born in Detroit, MI

Mid-1950s Begins work in *Vogue*'s art department

Late 1950s–early 60s Designs shoes for Roger Vivier studio at Dior, then shoes and jewelry for Arnold Scaasi

1963 Founds K.J.L. company in New York and soon establishes a clientele that includes first ladies, royalty, and movie stars

Mid-1980s Begins designing jewelry lines for Avon

Late 1990s Begins selling his jewelry on QVC

FOR THE RICH AND NOT-SO-RICH

Detroit-born Kenneth Jay Lane began his illustrious career in the mid-1950s in New York. His work in the art department at *Vogue* was championed by the legendary editor Diana Vreeland, and she featured his designs in the magazine. Lane went on to create shoes for Dior, and shoes and earrings for Arnold Scaasi. After such a prestigious start, 1963 saw the foundation of K.J.L., his enormously successful costume jewelry company. Almost immediately a highly enviable clientele was knocking at the door for his bold and exquisitely made designs.

High-profile admirers included Jackie Kennedy Onassis, Audrey Hepburn, Elizabeth Taylor, Raquel Welch, Ivana Trump, Nancy Reagan, Barbara Bush, and Diana, Princess of Wales. Equally, however, lack of social standing or wealth have been no bar to owning a piece of K.J.L. His prices have always been accessible to most, recently evidenced by the volume sales achieved via the QVC shopping channel.

INVENTIVE STYLING

Always bright, bold, and elegant, Lane's jewelry is characterized by distinctive combinations of materials and by creative, and often witty reworkings of many traditional styles, including Greco-Roman, Egyptian, Medieval and Renaissance, through to Art Deco and Asian (*see below*). His brilliant clear stones are always the best Swarovski crystals, while his colored stones and faux pearls display exceptional depth and luminosity of color. Pieces made up until the late 1970s (the most collectible) are signed "K.J.L"; thereafter they are signed "Kenneth Jay Lane" or "Kenneth Lane."

Above: Big Cat with Indian goddess pendant pin, gold-plated with faux coral, emerald, turquoise, and jet cabochons, and a faux pearl. *1960s. 5⅛ in (13 cm) long* **$475–575 ROX**

Pendant necklace with Buddha and snakes. Gold-plated with faux mother-of-pearl, emerald cabochons, jade, and coral. *1980s. N: 24½ in (62 cm) circ; P: 5½ in (14 cm) long* **$150–170 JJ**

ASIAN INFLUENCE

Motifs and imagery of Asian origin have been recurring themes in the designs of Kenneth Jay Lane. They were particularly prevalent in the late 1960s and early 70s, when Eastern mysticism, religion, and ornament captured the imagination of many travelers. Examples include extravagant Maharajah-style earrings, pins, and pendants of gilt base metal encrusted with faux precious stone cabochons and drops. Favorite figural subjects include snakes, warriors, dancers, gods and goddesses, and religious teachers—most notably Buddha. Lane's 1960s series of "Big Cat" pins also displays his enthusiasm for Asian imagery.

A giant seated stone Buddha in the grounds of a ruined temple at Ayuthaya, Thailand. Buddhism, Hinduism, and other religions of Asian origin have been a rich source of figural imagery for Kenneth Jay Lane's jewelry designs.

"Catwalk" pendant chain necklace of gilt base metal with faux emerald and ruby oval cabochons. *1970s*

N: 29 in (73 cm) circ; Pd: 5¾ in (14.5 cm) long

$300–350   **JJ**

Chain necklace of gold-plated base metal set with four faux deep sapphire oval glass cabochons. *1950s*

25 in (63.5 cm) circ

$70–100   **TR**

Flower earrings of gilt base metal with large French jet cabochon centers encircled by small clear rhinestone highlights. *1970s*

1 in (2.5 cm) long

$35–50   **TR**

Gilt earrings with large pink cabochon centers encircled by small clear rhinestones and faux turquoise cabochons. *1960s*

1 in (2.5 cm) long

$175–200   **TR**

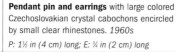

Pendant pin and earrings with large colored Czechoslovakian crystal cabochons encircled by small clear rhinestones. *1960s*

P: 1½ in (4 cm) long; E: ¾ in (2 cm) long

$950–1,000   **TR**

Multiple-pendant "catwalk" necklace of silver-gilt base metal set with clear rhinestones. *Late 1960s*

Longest pd: 7⅞ in (20 cm) long

$950–1,000   **TR**

Faux precious earrings of gilt metal with prong-set faux jade and diamond cabochons above rows of clear rhinestone baguettes. *1970s*

2½ in (6.25 cm) long

$80–120   **ABIJ**

Textured gilt base metal bangle with large faux amber and smaller French jet cabochons. *c.1980*

3¼ in (8.25 cm) wide

$400–450   **TR**

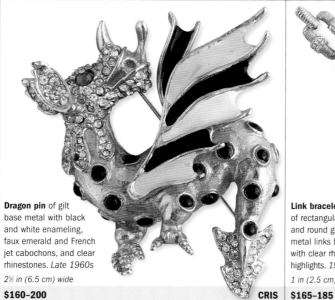

Dragon pin of gilt base metal with black and white enameling, faux emerald and French jet cabochons, and clear rhinestones. *Late 1960s*

2½ in (6.5 cm) wide

$160–200   **CRIS**

Link bracelet of rectangular and round gilt base metal links banded with clear rhinestone highlights. *1970s*

1 in (2.5 cm) wide

$165–185   **TR**

LEA STEIN
1931–present

1931 Born in Paris, France

1957 Having trained as an artist, establishes her own textile design company

1965 Begins designing and making buttons for the fashion industry

1967 Starts making buttons from laminated rhodoid—a process developed by her husband

1969–81 Designs costume jewelry from laminated rhodoid, and experiments with fabric and metallic inclusions to produce variations of texture and color. At the peak of its expansion, the company employs up to 50 people

1981 The company closes and a costume jewelry dealer purchases most of the remaining stock and begins selling Lea Stein pieces in the United States. For the first time, her designs begin to achieve recognition outside France

1988–present Lea Stein returns to designing and making laminated rhodoid costume jewelry. Each year she introduces at least one new and eagerly awaited design

Lea Stein

From the late 1960s to the early 80s, when she first produced her unique rhodoid jewelry, Lea Stein was barely recognized outside France. Recently, however, her work has become international hot property.

INNOVATIVE MATERIAL

Having trained as an artist, and run a textile design company from the late 1950s, Parisian-born Lea Stein began making costume jewelry in 1969. The material she used was superficially similar to Bakelite, but was actually developed by her husband Fernand Steinberger and consisted of laminated layers of colored rhodoid (multiple, bake-bonded sheets of cellulose acetate). This process also allowed for the inclusion of layers of other material—most notably metallic elements and textured fabrics, such as lace. By cutting or shaping the resulting composition into different shapes, Lea Stein was able to produce polychromatic "plastic" jewelry with marked or subtle variations of both color and texture.

The pieces she made from 1969 to 1981 included rings, bangles, and earrings, but mostly pins. Figural subjects ranged from cats, dogs, birds, and insects, to children, portraits, and Joan Crawford and Elvis Presley lookalikes. Other favorite imagery included cars, stars, hats, hearts, rainbows, eyes, and flowers.

BELATED RECOGNITION

Although they sold well in her native France up until the company's demise, Lea Stein's pieces only became appreciated overseas when, in 1981, a dealer bought most of the remaining stock and began selling it in the United States. By the late 1980s, demand from collectors was such that Lea Stein returned to designing her unique rhodoid pins, and has subsequently introduced at least one new instant collectable each year. All pieces are marked "Lea Stein Paris." However, dating specific pieces as "first" or "second" generation isn't always easy, so buying Lea Stein pieces from a reputable dealer is advisable.

Above: "Felix Brothers" cat pin made of red, black, gray, and blue laminated rhodoid. *Late 1980s* 3⅜ in (8.5 cm) long **$130–150 CRIS**

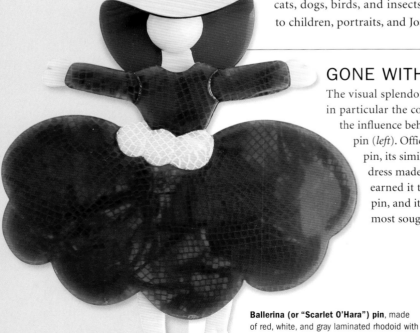

GONE WITH THE WIND

The visual splendor of *Gone With The Wind*, in particular the costumes and jewelry, was the influence behind this beautiful Lea Stein pin (*left*). Officially known as the Ballerina pin, its similarity to Scarlett's infamous dress made from red velvet drapes has earned it the title "Scarlett O'Hara" pin, and it is by far one of Lea Stein's most sought-after pieces.

Ballerina (or "Scarlet O'Hara") pin, made of red, white, and gray laminated rhodoid with lace inclusions. *c.1980. 2½ in (6.5 cm) long* **$130–150 CRIS**

Vivien Leigh as Scarlett O'Hara in *Gone With The Wind*, the movie that was the influence behind Lea Stein's "Ballerina" pin.

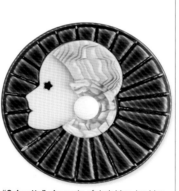

Penguin pin made of red, orange, terra-cotta, black, cream, and faux mother-of-pearl laminated rhodoid. *2001*

3½ in (9 cm) long

$130–150 CRIS

"Black Cat and Ball" pin made of black, gray, and faux mother-of-pearl laminated rhodoid. *Late 1980s*

2¾ in (7 cm) wide

$95–110 CRIS

"Ric the Dog" pin made of blue, gray, brown, and white laminated rhodoid with metallic inclusions. *Late 1980s*

3½ in (9 cm) long

$65–95 CRIS

Indian Chief pin made of blue, black, gray, and white laminated rhodoid with lace inclusions. *Early 1980s*

2⅛ in (5.5 cm) long

$130–150 CRIS

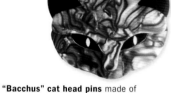

"Buba the Owl" pin made of brown, yellow-ocher, and turquoise laminated rhodoid. *Early 1990s*

2⅜ in (6 cm) long

$65–95 CRIS

"Bacchus" cat head pins made of orange, peach, red, gray, black, and white laminated rhodoid. *Early 1990s*

2⅜ in (6 cm) wide

$65–95 CRIS

Edelweiss flower pin made of red, pink, orange, brown, green, and white laminated rhodoid. *Late 1980s*

3⅜ in (8.5 cm) long

$130–150 CRIS

"Colorette" pin made of dark blue, ice blue, black, and faux pearl laminated rhodoid. *Early 1980s*

2⅛ in (5.5 cm) wide

$95–110 CRIS

Panther pin made of mottled brown and orange laminated rhodoid. *Late 1990s*

4 in (10 cm) wide

$95–110 CRIS

"Egyptian Eye" pin made of red, black, and iridescent white laminated rhodoid. *Late 1970s*

3⅛ in (8 cm) wide

$95–110 CRIS

FOX PINS

Instantly recognizable, Lea Stein's 3-D fox pins have acquired the status of a signature piece. They have been made in numerous colorways and textures, variations of which are produced by fabric or metallic inclusions. No Lea Stein collection is complete without at least one of these fabulous fox pins.

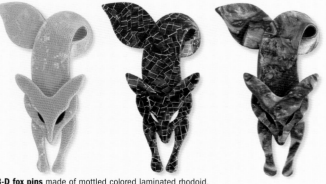

3-D fox pins made of mottled colored laminated rhodoid. *Left: early 1990s; center and right: late 1980s* 4 in (10 cm) long **$65–95 each CRIS**

LISNER
1904–79

1904 D. Lisner and Company founded in New York City

1920s Sells good-quality jewelry marked "Lanvin's Violet"

Mid-1930s Becomes the authorized US agent for Elsa Schiaparelli. The "Lisner" mark, in block letters, is used for the first time on its own pieces

1938 "Lisner" mark in script is introduced

1950s Production at its most prolific

1960s onward Most pieces are marked "Lisner" in block letters together with an elongated "L"

1978 The company merges into the Lisner-Richelieu Corporation

1979 Production ceases

Lisner

In the late 20th century, Lisner jewelry was largely overlooked by collectors. This is no longer the case. Its distinctive designs, especially those from the 1950s and 60s, are becoming increasingly sought-after.

DISTRIBUTOR AND MAKER

The early years of the Lisner company are not well documented. Founded in New York City in 1904, it spent approximately the first three decades of its existence selling jewelry that didn't bear its company name, and distributing jewelry for others. Lisner is best known as the authorized US importer and distributor for Elsa Schiaparelli's Parisian jewelry (*see pp.108–111*) prior to World War II. It began to gain a higher profile in the mid 1930s, following the introduction of the "Lisner" mark on its own designs. However, it took until the 1950s for the pieces most sought-after by today's collectors to emerge.

QUALITY AND VALUE

Colored Lucite, crisply molded into either geometric or organic shapes, is the most prevalent material in Lisner pieces (*see below*). However, clear and colored rhinestones—notably *aurora borealis*—were also used, usually as accents, as were larger, more exotic lava stones. Settings, links, and clasps were mostly chromed or silver-plated, although black japanned metal was also employed in the 1960s. Lisner jewelry was traded for very low sums up until the late 1990s. Subsequently, however, there has been a significant rise in the price of Lisner jewelry as its pieces become increasingly popular with modern collectors.

Above: "C-scroll" pin with green lava stones and *aurora borealis* crystal rhinestones set in silver-plated metal. *Mid-1950s. 2 in (5 cm) wide* **$95–110 CRIS**

ACRYLIC PLASTIC

Many costume jewelry makers enthusiastically adopted DuPont's acrylic plastic, Lucite, when it was launched in 1937. Lisner's extensive and impressive use of colored Lucite, especially in its 1950s and 60s pieces, is only now being fully appreciated by collectors. Much of the attraction lies in the wonderful range of colors and pretty combinations Lisner employed.

Necklace, bracelet, circular pin, and earrings parure of hand-looped silver-plated metal with pink, mauve, blue, and white Lucite heart motifs. *Late 1950s N: 14 in (35.5 cm) circ; B: 7 in (17.75 cm) circ; P: 1½ in (3.75 cm) wide; E: ¾ in (2 cm) wide* **$290–320 CRIS**

Necklace, bracelet, and earrings with silver-plated metal, Lucite, and rhinestones. *1950s*
N: 15¼ in (38.75 cm) circ; B: 7¼ in (18.5 cm) circ; E: 1⅛ in (3 cm) long

$160–200   **CRIS**

Necklace, bracelet, and earrings of gold-plated metal set with navette-cut pink, brown, and amber Lucite leaf motifs. *Late 1950s*
N: 15½ in (40 cm) circ; B: 7½ in (19 cm) circ; E: 1½ in (4 cm) long

$160–200   **CRIS**

Gold-tone metal chain necklace set with Rivoli cabochons and clear crystal rhinestones. *1960s*
16 in (40.5 cm) circ

$160–180   **JJ**

Sprig-of-leaves-and-berries pin in silver-tone metal with prong-set blue *aurora borealis* rhinestones. *1950s*
2 in (5 cm) long

$15–25   **MILLB**

Necklace, bracelet, and earrings of gold-tone metal with Lucite leaf motifs and crystal rhinestone highlights. *Late 1950s*
N: 16½ in (42 cm) circ; B: 7 in (17.75 cm) circ; E: 1½ in (3.75 cm) long

$240–280   **CRIS**

Floral motif bracelet of gold-tone metal with white Lucite petals and clear crystal rhinestone highlights. *1950s*
6⅜ in (17 cm) circ

$25–35   **MILLB**

Leaf motif bracelet of gold-tone metal set with dark and pale green Lucite. *1950s*
6½ in (16.5 cm) circ

$30–65   **ECLEC**

Maison Gripoix

For three generations, Maison Gripoix created *haute couture* jewelry for Chanel, Dior, Yves St. Laurent, and other leading fashion houses. The pieces it produced in its own name are equally impressive.

MAISON GRIPOIX
c.1870–present

1870s Company starts life as a wholesaler of glass buttons and beads

1895 Suzanne Gripoix (above) born in Paris

Mid-1920s Produces costume jewelry for Chanel

1940s Produces pieces for Dior

1980s Produces pieces for YSL

1990s Histoire de Verre line introduced

FROM BUTTONS AND BEADS

Founded in Paris in about 1870, Maison Gripoix's primary business for 30 years was the manufacture and wholesale of glass beads and buttons. However, at the turn of the century, it began to establish a reputation for making costume jewelry, by creating inexpensive copies of the flamboyant Art Nouveau-style pieces worn by the actress Sarah Bernhardt. Soon afterward, it began producing pieces for Piguet, a leading Parisian couturier, and in the mid-1920s, it started working for Chanel (*see pp.56-59*). Other eminent clients followed, such as Worth, Jacques Fath, and Christian Dior (*see pp.60–65*)—the most notable pieces for the latter being those that were worn with his 1940s "New Look" collection (*see p.60*). More recent prestigious clients have included Yves St. Laurent, Balmain, Ungaro, and Guy Laroche.

Throughout this long association with *haute couture*, Gripoix continued to create jewelry in its own name and, from the 1990s, under the Histoire de Verre brand (*see below*). It is known above all for its fabulous *pâte-de-verre* work, produced in both subtle and vibrant colors of varying degrees of translucency and opacity. Provided the pieces are in good condition—fine crazing in the glass is acceptable, but chips are not—they continue to fetch high prices from admiring collectors.

Above: Maison Gripoix flower pin with *pâte-de-verre* leaves and turquoise, emerald, and black glass cabochons in an antiqued gilt metal frame. *1940s. 3¼ in (8.25 cm) long* **$1,000–1,100**

HISTOIRE DE VERRE

In the early 1990s, Josette Gripoix's son Thierry became head of Maison Gripoix. The pieces the company subsequently produced, branded "Histoire de Verre," are dominated by floral, leaf, and fruit imagery. While materials such as faux pearls are sometimes used, *pâte-de-verre* remains Maison Gripoix's signature material. Handcrafted, and highlighted with crystal rhinestones, Histoire de Verre pieces uphold Gripoix's reputation for style and craftsmanship of the highest order.

Histoire de Verre flower pin with a gold-plated brass stem, stamens, and leaf and petal borders, sapphire blue and emerald green *pâte-de-verre* petals and leaves, and clear crystal rhinestone stigmas. *1990s. 3¼ in (8.25 cm) long* **$290–350 CRIS**

Histoire de Verre floral necklace and earrings with amethyst and jonquil *pâte-de-verre* petals and amethyst glass bead centers in gold-plated brass wire frames. *1990s N: 21¼ in (54 cm) circ; E: 2 in (5 cm) wide* **$1,500–1,600 CRIS**

A FAMILY BUSINESS

Maison Gripoix has always been a family-run firm. Born in 1895, Suzanne Gripoix (*shown opposite*)—reverentially known in the jewelry world as "Madame Gripoix"—led the company from the mid-1920s throughout its long associations with Chanel, Dior, and other leading French fashion houses. After World War II, she was assisted by her daughter Josette (*shown right*), who took over the running of the company from Suzanne in 1969 and who was still at the helm in the 1980s.

Histoire de Verre flower necklace and earrings with *pâte-de-verre* petals and cabochon centers encircled by clear crystal rhinestones in gold-plated brass wire frames. *1990s. N: 20⅜ in (51 cm) circ; E: 2¼ in (5.75 cm) wide* **$1,200–1,400 CRIS**

Good, Better, Best

Different materials, color, and complexity of composition determine the desirability of these Histoire de Verre necklaces.

$240–285

Made in the 1990s, this **single-strand faux baroque pearl necklace** has been given an interesting modern twist by having just four—rather than all—of the pearls capped with filigree gilt metal, also employed in the small clasp. *32¼ in (82 cm) circ* **CRIS**

$290–350

This 1990s **leaf and petal necklace** is of red, pink, amethyst, topaz, and amber *pâte-de-verre* set in gilt brass. Since both the imagery and the materials employed are more representative of Gripoix's work than those in the piece on the left, this necklace commands a slightly higher price. *19in (48.25 cm) circ* **CRIS**

$1,000–1,100

The flowers and leaves of this 1990s **floral necklace** are in amethyst, black, and emerald green *pâte-de-verre*, set in gilt metal. Like the leaf and petal necklace shown left, this is a classic and easily recognizable Gripoix design. Its layered composition is complex and its dark, rich palette conveys substance and sophistication. These qualities considerably enhance both the desirability and the value of the piece. *20½ in (51.25 cm) circ* **CRIS**

Flowers and leaves modeled in opaque or, as here, translucent pâte-de-verre are characteristic of Maison Gripoix's jewelry designs.

Maison Gripoix glass flower necklace with amber and topaz *pâte-de-verre* petals set in japanned metal frames, and clear crystal rhinestone stigmas. *c.2001*

Largest flower: 2¾ in (7 cm) wide

$720–800   **RITZ**

Maison Gripoix spray-of-flowers pin with *pâte-de-verre* petals and leaves set in gilt wire, and clear crystal rhinestone highlights. *1980s*

3¼ in (8 cm) wide

$320–385   **RITZ**

Maison Gripoix green flower pin with *pâte-de-verre* petals and leaves set in gilt wire and with a ruby glass center. *c.2001*

2¾ in (7 cm) wide

$320–385   **RITZ**

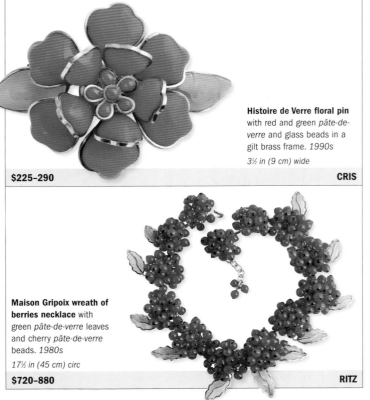

Histoire de Verre floral pin with red and green *pâte-de-verre* and glass beads in a gilt brass frame. *1990s*

3½ in (9 cm) wide

$225–290   **CRIS**

Maison Gripoix wreath of berries necklace with green *pâte-de-verre* leaves and cherry *pâte-de-verre* beads. *1980s*

17½ in (45 cm) circ

$720–880   **RITZ**

PLANT ORNAMENTS

In the 1950s, Maison Gripoix produced decorative plant ornaments made from the same materials—notably *pâte-de-verre*—that it used in its jewelry. Primarily intended as window displays for retailers, the ornaments were set in antiqued gold-tone metal pots or baskets. Most were 5–8 in (12–20 cm) tall, but some larger trees were up to 3 ft (90 cm) high. Fairly scarce, these pieces rarely come on the market.

Maison Gripoix basket of flowers ornament in antiqued gold-tone metal with emerald *pâte-de-verre* leaves and faux baroque pearl drops. *1950s. 6⅜ in (16 cm) high*   **£600–650 CRIS**

L'Atelier de Verre

At the end of the 1990s, four ex-Maison Gripoix workers set up their own small costume jewelry studio: L'Atelier de Verre. For a brief period—until early 2003, when Chanel acquired it—the studio designed and manufactured high-quality costume jewelry in keeping with the spirit and style of Gripoix and Gripoix for Chanel pieces. Marked "L'Atelier de Verre," its refined, mostly floral compositions of *pâte-de-verre*, lustrous faux pearls, shimmering crystal rhinestones, and gilt metal were sold through prestigious outlets such as Neiman Marcus and Saks Fifth Avenue in the United States, Galeries Lafayette in France, and Harrods in England.

L'Atelier de Verre floral pin and earrings, with emerald green *pâte-de-verre* leaves and pavé-set clear crystal rhinestone petals in gilt metal settings. *c.2000*

P: 3 in (7.5 cm) long; E: 2 in (5 cm) long

$1,000–1,400   SUM

L'Atelier de Verre four-strand bracelet with dark amethyst *pâte-de-verre* beads and a *pâte-de-verre* pansy clasp. *c.2000*

8 in (20 cm) long

$400–480   SUM

L'Atelier de Verre flower pin in gold-plated metal with *pâte-de-verre* petals and leaves, and rhinestone stigmas. *c.2000*

2½ in (6.5 cm) long

$400–480   SUM

L'Atelier de Verre green flower earrings with *pâte-de-verre* petals in gold-plated settings, outlined with clear crystal rhinestones. *c.2000*

2⅛ in (5.5 cm) long

$320–400   SUM

L'Atelier de Verre pendant rose necklace with faux pearls and emerald *pâte-de-verre* and mother-of-pearl leaves. *c.2000*

N: 15¼ in (39 cm) circ; Pd: 2¾ in (7 cm) drop

$640–800   SUM

L'Atelier de Verre pendant necklace with faux pearls, *pâte-de-verre* petals, and glass cabochons and rhinestones in the center. *c.2000*

N: 16 in (41 cm) circ; Pd: 2½ in (6.5 cm) long

$400–480   SUM

Late 1910s Marcel Boucher starts work for Cartier, in Paris

1922 Boucher transfers to Cartier's New York workshops

Early 1930s Cartier cuts its workforce and Boucher leaves the company to work with other New York jewelers

1937 Forms his own company, Boucher et Cie in New York

1939 Saks Fifth Avenue places an order for Boucher designs

1949 French designer Sandra Semensohn joins the company and later becomes Boucher's second wife

1965 Boucher dies. Semensohn takes over the company

1972 Boucher et Cie sold to American watch manufacturers Dovorn Industries

Marcel Boucher

French by birth, Marcel Boucher became one of the finest US costume jewelry designers and makers. His superbly crafted and colorful pieces are often mistaken for precious jewelry.

FROM PRECIOUS BEGINNINGS

Marcel Boucher's reputation for producing costume jewelry that was, and still is, often mistaken for "real" jewelry dates from the early stages of his career.

An apprentice model-maker with Cartier in Paris during the late 1910s and early 20s, he was transferred to its New York branch in about 1922 and continued working in fine jewelry until the Wall Street crash of 1929. Fortunately for costume jewelry collectors, the Great Depression of the 1930s forced Boucher to transfer his considerable talents to costume jewelry, a burgeoning industry that employed more affordable materials. After initially designing for Mazer Brothers (*see pp. 96–97*), Boucher felt sufficiently confident to establish his own small company, Boucher et Cie, in 1937. Just two years later, a lucrative order from Saks Fifth Avenue for a run of six innovative, three-dimensional

bird pins gave Boucher the financial boost to substantially expand his operation.

The jewelry produced by Boucher et Cie before Boucher's death in 1965, and up until the early 1970s under the control of his second wife, designer Sandra Semensohn, was of exceptional quality. Often innovative, it is characterized by exquisite metalwork, fabulous rhinestones in hues and cuts that bear a striking resemblance to real gemstones, and wonderfully colorful enameling. Marked either "MB" or" "Marboux" (earlier pieces), or signed "Marcel Boucher" or just "Boucher" (later pieces), most pieces are currently competitively priced—even undervalued. As such, they represent an excellent investment.

Above: Sterling silver earrings with prong-set, emerald crystal cabochons, faux pearls, and pavé-set clear rhinestones. *1940s 1 in (2.5 cm) long* **$90–105 TR**

Retro-style fan-motif clip earrings made from a single casting of bright-finish, gold-tone base metal. *Late 1940s 1 in (2.5 cm) long* **$30–40 CRIS**

"ILLUSION" . . . intriguing new Brooches skillfully designed by Marcel Boucher to drape the material of your dress . . . wear it on your neckline, torso, or suit lapel.
a. Rhodium-plated metal paved with Rhinestones. **$20.00**
b. Scroll textured Gold-plated metal trimmed with Rhinestones. **$10.00**
c. Circlet of white and smoke-grey simulated Pearls and Rhinestones on Rhodium-plated metal. **$10.00** Earrings to match. (not illustrated)

At better stores in U.S. and Canada. For nearest store write marcel Boucher et cie

All designs copyrighted © Boucher   347 Fifth Avenue, New York

Marcel Boucher et Cie's "Illusion" pins are advertised in a 1955 edition of *Vogue*. The pins are made from textured gold- and rhodium-plated metals, crystal rhinestones, and faux pearls.

Necklace, bracelet, and earrings of rhodium-plated metal with prong-set aquamarine and clear crystal rhinestones. *Early 1950s*
N: 14 in (35.5 cm) circ;
B: 7 in (17.75 cm) circ;
E: 1⅛ in (3 cm) long

$800–960   CRIS

Circular floral and bow-motif pin and earrings of rhodium-plated metal with prong-set sapphire blue and pavé-set clear crystal rhinestones. *1950s*
P: 2 in (5 cm) wide; E: 1 in (2.5 cm) wide

$130–145   CRIS

Ballerina pin of rhodium-plated metal with gilt highlights and round-cut and pavé-set clear crystal rhinestones. *c.1950*
2 in (5 cm) long

$160–185   ABIJ

Sheaf-of-wheat pin in silver-plated metal with green enameling and emerald and clear crystal rhinestone highlights. *c.1940*
4¼ in (10.75 cm) long

$320–400   CRIS

Scrolling forms pin in sterling silver with clear crystal rhinestone highlights around a faux ruby paste. *1930s*
2¼ in (5.75 cm) long

$215–265   ABIJ

Gold-plated metal bracelet with ruby, emerald, and sapphire crystal cabochons, edged with clear crystal rhinestones. *1950s*
7 in (17.75 cm) circ

$320–400   CRIS

Floral-motif pin of antiqued silver-tone metal with pale blue round and striated crystal cabochons. *1960s*
2½ in (6.25 cm) long

$80–90   ABIJ

Fruit tree pin with ladder and basket, in rhodium- and gold-plated metal with faux pearls, turquoise paste cabochons, and clear crystal rhinestones. *1950s*
1½ in (3.75 cm) long

$80–95   CRIS

CREATURE PINS

Marcel Boucher designed hugely popular animal pins. Rare examples from the late 1930s and 40s include birds of paradise, praying mantises, and other stylized insects. Produced in greater numbers, his 1950s elephant, poodle, donkey, and kitten pins, like Boucher et Cie's late 60s to early 70s bird and turtle pins, are more commonly found.

Turtle pin of textured gold-tone metal with clear crystal rhinestone highlights. *1970s.* 1½ in (3.75 cm) long **$40–50 JJ**

Bird pin of gold-tone metal with blue enameling and rhinestones. *1970s* 2½ in (6.25 cm) long **$70–80 JJ**

Plant form pin and earrings of gold-plated metal castings with pavé-set clear crystal rhinestones. *1950s*
P: 4 in (10 cm) long;
E: 1½ in (3.75 cm) long

$110–135   CRIS

Mazer Brothers and Jomaz

Made from fine-quality materials, Mazer Brothers and Jomaz jewelry was competitively priced. For current collectors it remains an affordable investment in excellent craftsmanship and interesting design.

JOSEPH AND LOUIS

Mazer Brothers was founded by Joseph and Louis Mazer in New York City in 1927, and rapidly established a reputation for making remarkably good, affordable simulations of precious jewelry. Its early pieces, many of which were designed and made by Marcel Boucher before he established his own company in 1934 (*see p.94*), were mostly classic floral, foliate, or ribbon-and-bow-motif designs, accented with fine "Sea-Maze" faux pearls or the best Austrian crystal rhinestones—the latter often intricately cut in sophisticated settings. The same standard of materials and craftsmanship was also evident in the pieces Mazer produced during the late 1930s and 40s. Usually made from sterling or vermeil sterling silver, these included opulent cocktail necklaces, bracelets, and earrings, as well as a series of Duette pins and crown jewel pins—both of which echoed similar lines produced at that time by Trifari (*see pp.118–129*) and Coro (*see pp.68–71*).

Above: Mazer Bros. bow pin in vermeil sterling silver with clear crystal rhinestones and faux ruby glass cabochons. *1940s. 3 in (7.5 cm) long* **$240–290 RG**

JOSEPH GOES IT ALONE

Mazer Brothers continued making jewelry until 1977. However, in 1946, Joseph Mazer left the company to set up a new and totally separate business, Joseph J. Mazer & Co. This new company produced jewelry until 1981, marked either "Joseph Mazer", "Mazer", or, more commonly, "Jomaz". A testament to the creative skills of designers such as Andre Fleuridas (in the early 1950s) and Adolfo (in the 1970s), its pieces were also of high quality and reasonably priced. Combinations of textured metals (*see opposite*) with pavé-set rhinestones and colorful pastes, were typical of many innovative and unusual compositions—some of which are stylistically similar to those made by Boucher et Cie (*see pp.94–95*).

Advertisement from *Harper's Bazaar*, November 1948, promoting a Mazer Bros. parure of necklace, bracelet, pin, and earrings set with faux emerald, ruby, sapphire, amethyst, aqua, topaz, and clear crystal rhinestones.

Mazer Bros. pendant necklace and earrings of rhodium-plated metal set with clear crystal rhinestones. *1940s
N: 15 in (38 cm) circ;
Pd: 2½ in (6.25 cm) long;
E: 1¾ in (4.5 cm) long*
$240–290 RG

For your most precious hours...shimmering crystals and flickering Magicut* stones of simulated emerald, ruby, crystal, sapphire, amethyst, aqua or topaz...each—hand-set by Mazer to dance with every flash of light like the most precious gems. Necklace $35. Bracelet $30. Pin $30. Earrings $25 pr., at better department stores and jewelers. Plus 20% tax.

Mazer
the Precious Look in fashion jewelry

MAZER BROS INC. 20 W. 33rd St., N. Y. 1

TEXTURED METALS

While silver- and rhodium-plated metal were regularly used in Mazer Bros. and Jomaz jewelry, gold-plating and gold-tone metal alloys also featured. In the 1960s, these often had fashionable textured finishes, in contrast to the smooth gold-plating that had been in vogue during the 1940s and early 50s.

Jomaz gold-tone leaf pin with faux turquoise and lapis stones and clear crystal rhinestone highlights. *1960s*
2¾ in (7 cm) long **$95–130 RG**

Rhodium-plated Mazer Bros. pin set with round- and baguette-cut clear crystal rhinestones. *1930s*
3 in (7.5 cm) long

$190–225   **RG**

Mazer Bros. crown pin of sterling and vermeil sterling silver with amethyst glass cabochons and crystal rhinestones. *1940s*
2¼ in (5.75 cm) long
$400–480   **CRIS**

Mazer Bros. floral bow pin of rhodium-plated metal with prong-set glass stones and clear crystal rhinestones. *1930s*
2¾ in (7 cm) long
$240–320   **RG**

Jomaz chandelier-pendant earrings of gold-plated metal with cranberry glass cabochons and clear crystal rhinestones. *1960s*
2¾ in (7 cm) long
$80–120   **RG**

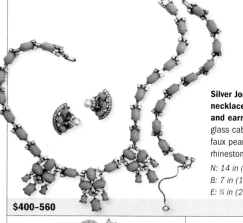

Silver Jomaz necklace, bracelet, and earrings with glass cabochons, faux pearls, and rhinestones. *1960s*
N: 14 in (35 cm) circ;
B: 7 in (18 cm) circ;
E: ¾ in (2 cm) long
$400–560   **RG**

Mazer Bros. gold-plated bangle and earrings with glass cabochons and crystal rhinestones. *1950s*
B: 7½ in (19 cm) circ;
E: 1 in (2.5 cm) wide
$320–400   **CRIS**

Mazer Bros. pendant earrings with leaves pavé-set with crystal rhinestones, and turquoise glass cabochon berries. *Late 1950s*
2 in (5 cm) long
$190–215   **CRIS**

Mazer Bros. caterpillar earrings of rose-gold-plated metal with faux amethyst glass stones and clear crystal rhinestones. *Mid-1950s*
1¼ in (3 cm) long
$95–110   **CRIS**

Jomaz leaf pin and earrings of brushed gold-tone metal with clear crystal rhinestones (some pavé-set). *c.1960*
P: 2 in (5 cm) long; E: 1⅛ in (3 cm) long
$70–80   **ABIJ**

Jomaz pin and earrings of textured, gold-plated metal with faux emerald and lapis glass cabochons and clear crystal rhinestones. *1960s*
P: 3 in (7.5 cm) wide; E: 1 in (2.5 cm) long
$130–190   **RG**

Prong-set faux precious cabochons are often a feature of Jomaz designs.

Miriam Haskell

Together with Coco Chanel and Elsa Schiaparelli, Miriam Haskell elevated the status of costume jewelry to an accessory as prestigious as, and even more fashionable than, its precious equivalent. Her innovative pieces are among the finest ever made.

MIRIAM HASKELL
1899–1981

1899 Born in Cannelton, IN

1924 Moves to New York and opens shop in the McAlpin Hotel

1926 Establishes Miriam Haskell Company with Frank Hess as chief designer

1930s Establishes retail outlets at Saks Fifth Avenue in New York and Harvey Nichols in London

1940s Starts trademarking jewelry

1960 Robert F. Clark becomes chief designer

1970s Larry Vrba becomes chief designer

1981 Miriam Haskell dies

A PIONEER OF FASHION

Miriam Haskell's energetic and hugely successful career from the mid-1920s to the late 1940s introduced new standards of glamor to the world of fashion. Haskell did for the women of the United States what her contemporary Coco Chanel (*see pp.56–59*) had done for the well-dressed ladies of Paris: namely, established costume jewelry as a fashionable and valued art form in its own right. For that alone, costume jewelry collectors of today have much to thank her for.

Born in 1899 to a family of modest means in Cannelton, Indiana, Miriam Haskell moved to New York in 1924 and opened her first costume jewelry shop the same year in the prestigious McAlpin Hotel. Although not a designer herself—she had majored in education at the University of Chicago—her skill lay in spotting the potential in others and in choosing which of their designs should go into production. Recognizing the latent talents of Frank Hess, a window-dresser at Macy's, and appointing him Chief Designer of the Miriam Haskell Company, which she founded in 1926, was her first stroke of genius. Hess, who retained his position until 1960, rapidly established a precedent for stylish and innovative designs, which was maintained subsequently under the aegis of other hugely talented head designers, namely Robert Clark and Peter Raines in the 1960s, Larry Vrba in the 1970s (*see p.180*), and Millie Petronzio from 1980 onward.

Above: Multiple strand bracelet with pink and pearl poured glass beads. *1940s. Clasp: 1½ in (3.75 cm) wide* **$150–250 ROX**

Necklace and earrings by Robert F. Clark with royal blue poured glass cabochons and rose montées and rhinestone baguettes on silvered metal. *c.1965 N: 15½ in (40 cm) circ; E: 1⅛ in (3 cm) wide* **$1,300–1,400 SUM**

Floral necklace and earrings by Miriam Haskell with faux seed pearls and clear rhinestones, advertised in American *Vogue* and *Harper's Bazaar* in October 1958.

FOUNDATIONS OF SUCCESS

Haskell pieces are of innovative design and rarely replicate the classic forms of precious jewelry, which does much to explain why her jewelry has consistently struck a chord with show business (*see opposite*), retail clients, and current collectors alike. Nevertheless, other equally important factors have contributed to its desirability. Haskell's ground-breaking acquisition of a front-of-store retail outlet in Saks Fifth Avenue in New York, and a similar arrangement with Harvey Nichols in London, elevated both her profile and her prestige. The employment of highly skilled emigré European craftsmen during the late 1920s and 30s also ensured that the innovative and often complex designs were executed to the highest standards.

Above all, however, it is the choice and standard of materials used in Haskell jewelry that has proved so compelling. Both Haskell and Hess, and subsequent head designers, regularly traveled abroad to source the best materials. Notable among these are glass beads from Murano; faceted crystals from Austria, including flat-backed rose montées mounted in pierced metal cups (a Haskell favorite); lustrous faux pearls from Japan (*see below*); and, during the restrictions of World War II, wood, feathers, and plastics. Invariably hand-wired, often combined with filigree antiqued gilt metal, and presented in unusual and striking color combinations, Haskell pieces have proved continuously irresistible. However, collectors should note that good condition is very important: missing colored Austrian rhinestones or chipped or eroded faux pearls are hard to replace and therefore detract substantially from the value of a piece.

Floral pin of gilt metal with coral poured glass beads, faux seed and baroque pearls, and clear rose montée highlights. c.1940
4 in (10 cm) long **$1,000–1,200 SUM**

MIRIAM HASKELL

SHOW BUSINESS

Haskell jewelry has often appeared on stage and in film and television. Florenz Ziegfeld bought pieces for his Ziegfield Follies, Lucille Ball often wore Haskell in her TV shows, and in more recent times the company has provided the jewelry for Broadway hits such as The Phantom of the Opera.

JOAN CRAWFORD

Hollywood actress Joan Crawford, seen above wearing a cascading bib necklace with earrings, regularly bought Haskell jewelry from the early 1930s to the late 60s. In 1978, the year after she died, Crawford's extensive collection was sold at auction amid much publicity by the Plaza Art Gallery in New York City.

JAPANESE PEARLS

Of all the high-quality components Haskell's craftsmen employed in her jewelry, it is the faux pearls that have been the most consistently admired. Traditionally, the primary source of fine-quality imitation pearls was Gablonz, in Bohemia (also famed for its Bohemian glass). However, in the late 1930s Japan became an alternative and highly competitive supplier, and one enthusiastically adopted by Haskell after the hiatus of World War II. Multiple immersions in *essence d'orient*, a solution of cellulose, fish scales, and various resins, gave Haskell's Japanese faux seed and baroque pearls—the latter supplied exclusively to her—a deep, lustrous finish unrivaled by European equivalents and highly prized by collectors of her costume jewelry.

Sorting faux pearls at a Japanese factory c.1947. In addition to white pearls, other colors were produced, including champagne, pink, brown, and various shades of gray.

Faux baroque pearls

Edwardian-style pendant necklace with multiple-looped and interlaced strands of baroque pearls; the clasp and head of the pendant encrusted with rings of tiny baroque pearls and rose montées. c.1950. Pd: 4 in (10 cm) long **$2,500–2,800 SUM**

Necklaces

Regardless of style, all Miriam Haskell necklaces are extremely desirable. The best-known are those with single or multiple strands of lustrous faux pearls in shades ranging from white and champagne, through pink and gray, to dark brown. Other examples, with exquisite combinations of high-quality materials such as Murano beads, pressed and poured French glass, seed pearls, and rose montées, are equally admired. Often finished with elaborately decorated clasps, Haskell's necklaces are nothing less than costume jewelry classics.

Floral necklace and earrings with amber and citrine poured glass cabochons, glass oval beads, and rhinestones. *c.1950*
N pd: 2¾ in (7 cm) long; E: 1⅛ in (3 cm) long

$1,800–2,000   **SUM**

Pendant necklace, two pins, and earrings parure with black resin beads and cabochons and square-cut clear rhinestones. *c.1960*
N: 15 in (38 cm) circ; Round P: 3⅛ in (8 cm) wide; Long P: 3¾ in (9.5 cm) long; E: 2 in (5 cm) long

$4,000–4,400   **SUM**

Two-strand faux pearl necklace with floral pendant of glass beads, seed pearls, rose montées, and poured glass leaves. *c.1960*
N: 14 in (35.5 cm) circ; Pd: 3½ in (9 cm) wide

$2,400–2,700   **SUM**

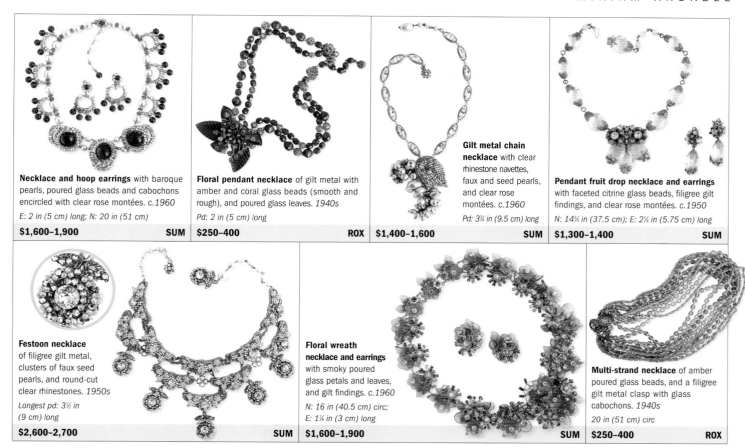

Necklace and hoop earrings with baroque pearls, poured glass beads and cabochons encircled with clear rose montées. *c.1960*

E: 2 in (5 cm) long; N: 20 in (51 cm)

$1,600–1,900 SUM

Floral pendant necklace of gilt metal with amber and coral glass beads (smooth and rough), and poured glass leaves. *1940s*

Pd: 2 in (5 cm) long

$250–400 ROX

Gilt metal chain necklace with clear rhinestone navettes, faux and seed pearls, and clear rose montées. *c.1960*

Pd: 3¾ in (9.5 cm) long

$1,400–1,600 SUM

Pendant fruit drop necklace and earrings with faceted citrine glass beads, filigree gilt findings, and clear rose montées. *c.1950*

N: 14¾ in (37.5 cm); E: 2¼ in (5.75 cm) long

$1,300–1,400 SUM

Festoon necklace of filigree gilt metal, clusters of faux seed pearls, and round-cut clear rhinestones. *1950s*

Longest pd: 3½ in (9 cm) long

$2,600–2,700 SUM

Floral wreath necklace and earrings with smoky poured glass petals and leaves, and gilt findings. *c.1960*

N: 16 in (40.5 cm) circ; E: 1⅛ in (3 cm) long

$1,600–1,900 SUM

Multi-strand necklace of amber poured glass beads, and a filigree gilt metal clasp with glass cabochons. *1940s*

20 in (51 cm) circ

$250–400 ROX

Good, Better, Best

When comparing Haskell necklaces made from similar materials, price difference is mostly determined by the styling and degree of elaboration of features such as clasps and pendants.

$200–300

This 1940s to early 50s **triple-strand necklace** has two strands of faux baroque pearls with a single strand of chalcedony poured glass beads. The color of the glass beads is echoed in the sapphire blue rhinestone in the clasp. *20 in (51 cm) circ* **ROX**

$375–475

This 1940s **flowerhead pendant necklace** has two strands of faux pearls and a pendant of antiqued gilt metal with seed pearls, rose montées, and faux pearl centers. It commands a high price because of its striking pendant. *18 in (45.75 cm) circ* **ROX**

$1,400–1,500

This 1960s **"Shooting Star" necklace** by Robert F. Clark has strands of baroque pearls and a wheat ear pendant of antiqued metal with rose montées and tassels of filigree-capped baroque pearls. Its elaboration and dynamic shape make it the best piece. *18 in (45.75 cm) circ* **WAIN**

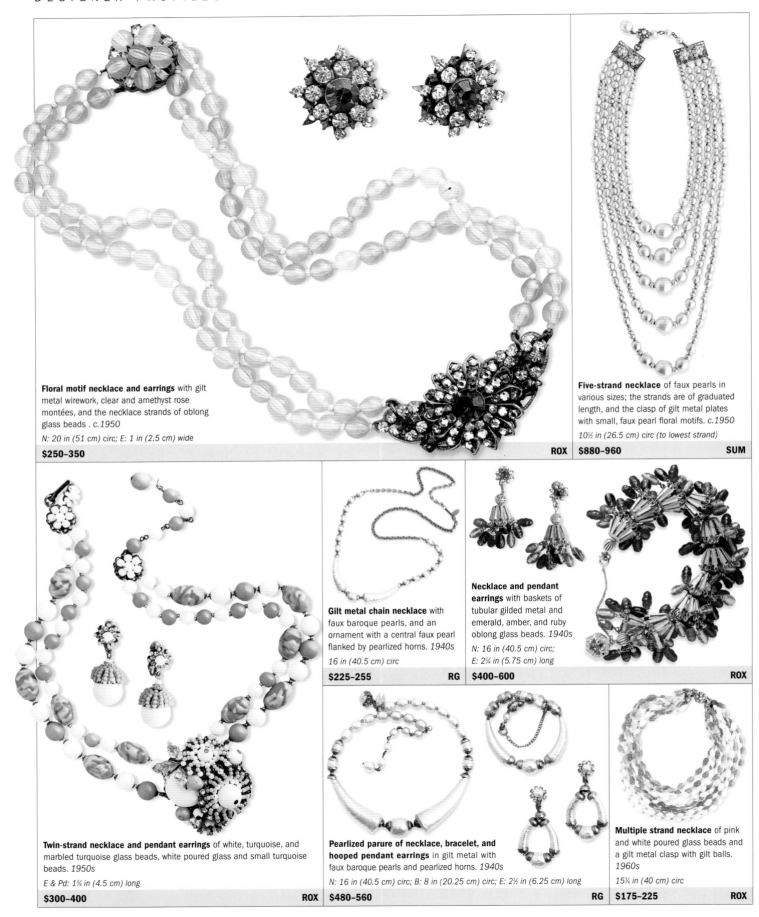

Floral motif necklace and earrings with gilt metal wirework, clear and amethyst rose montées, and the necklace strands of oblong glass beads . c.1950

N: 20 in (51 cm) circ; E: 1 in (2.5 cm) wide

$250–350   **ROX**

Five-strand necklace of faux pearls in various sizes; the strands are of graduated length, and the clasp of gilt metal plates with small, faux pearl floral motifs. c.1950

10½ in (26.5 cm) circ (to lowest strand)

$880–960   **SUM**

Gilt metal chain necklace with faux baroque pearls, and an ornament with a central faux pearl flanked by pearlized horns. 1940s

16 in (40.5 cm) circ

$225–255   **RG**

Necklace and pendant earrings with baskets of tubular gilded metal and emerald, amber, and ruby oblong glass beads. 1940s

N: 16 in (40.5 cm) circ;
E: 2¼ in (5.75 cm) long

$400–600   **ROX**

Twin-strand necklace and pendant earrings of white, turquoise, and marbled turquoise glass beads, white poured glass and small turquoise beads. 1950s

E & Pd: 1¾ in (4.5 cm) long

$300–400   **ROX**

Pearlized parure of necklace, bracelet, and hooped pendant earrings in gilt metal with faux baroque pearls and pearlized horns. 1940s

N: 16 in (40.5 cm) circ; B: 8 in (20.25 cm) circ; E: 2½ in (6.25 cm) long

$480–560   **RG**

Multiple strand necklace of pink and white poured glass beads and a gilt metal clasp with gilt balls. 1960s

15¾ in (40 cm) circ

$175–225   **ROX**

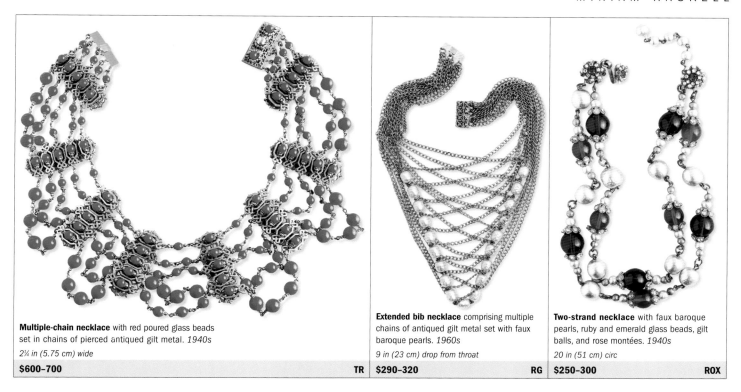

Multiple-chain necklace with red poured glass beads set in chains of pierced antiqued gilt metal. *1940s*

2¼ in (5.75 cm) wide

$600–700   **TR**

Extended bib necklace comprising multiple chains of antiqued gilt metal set with faux baroque pearls. *1960s*

9 in (23 cm) drop from throat

$290–320   **RG**

Two-strand necklace with faux baroque pearls, ruby and emerald glass beads, gilt balls, and rose montées. *1940s*

20 in (51 cm) circ

$250–300   **ROX**

Bracelets

Most Haskell bracelets are of plain and antiqued gilt or silvered metal. Decoration with faux pearls and glass beads and stones is usually colorful, invariably elaborate, and often incorporates delicate filigree work. A matching pin or earrings usually enhances the desirability and price.

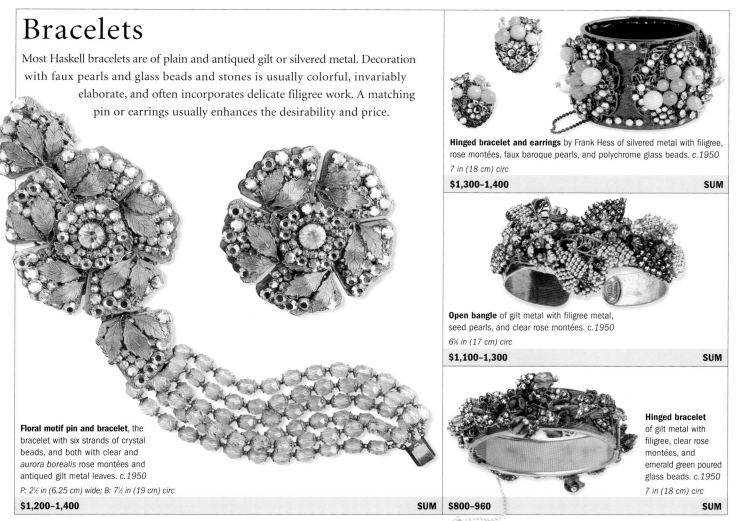

Hinged bracelet and earrings by Frank Hess of silvered metal with filigree, rose montées, faux baroque pearls, and polychrome glass beads. *c.1950*

7 in (18 cm) circ

$1,300–1,400   **SUM**

Open bangle of gilt metal with filigree metal, seed pearls, and clear rose montées. *c.1950*

6⅝ in (17 cm) circ

$1,100–1,300   **SUM**

Floral motif pin and bracelet, the bracelet with six strands of crystal beads, and both with clear and *aurora borealis* rose montées and antiqued gilt metal leaves. *c.1950*

P: 2½ in (6.25 cm) wide; B: 7½ in (19 cm) circ

$1,200–1,400   **SUM**

Hinged bracelet of gilt metal with filigree, clear rose montées, and emerald green poured glass beads. *c.1950*

7 in (18 cm) circ

$800–960   **SUM**

Pins

The majority of Haskell pins are complex compositions of metal, crystal, and paste made to exceptionally high standards of craftsmanship. Floral and foliate subjects and shell motifs are common, and figurals, especially turtles and exotic birds, are also in evidence—either featured prominently or secreted within a design.

Leaves are a recurring motif in Haskell jewelry. Many are highly naturalistic, particularly those in gilt metal, but others, especially in glass, can be quite stylized.

French jet cabochon pin of antiqued gilt metal with rings and clusters of clear rose montées. *1940s*

3⅜ in (8.5 cm) long

$800–960 **SUM**

Floral motif pin with dark amber poured glass petals set under an antiqued gilt metal shell motif, and with five pendants comprising amber and dark amber poured glass beads of various shapes (some capped with filigree gilt metal findings) and finished with textured poured glass amber leaves. *1930s*

6¼ in (16 cm) long

$320–400 **SUM**

Two-tier pendant pin of antiqued gilt metal with clusters of clear rose montées and three faux baroque pearl drops. *c.1950*

3¾ in (9.5 cm) long

$800–960 **SUM**

Floral motif pin of antiqued gilt metal with lavender, amethyst, and moonstone glass cabochons and clear rose montées. *1950s*

4 in (10 cm) long

$720–880 **SUM**

Floral motif pin with ringed clusters of faux seed pearls with faux baroque pearl centers, set in antiqued gilt metal. *1940s*

3¼ in (8.25 cm) long

$200–300 **ROX**

Grapes and leaves pin with rose montées and white poured glass beads in various sizes. *1940s*

3 in (7.5 cm) long

$150–250 **ROX**

Floral and foliate pin with antiqued gilt metal leaves and chained petals, and clear rose montées. *c.1950*

3¾ in (9.5 cm) long

$960–1,100 **SUM**

FILIGREE METAL

Like the beads and faux pearls of the pin below, most decorative components of Haskell jewelry are painstakingly hand-wired to a filigree metal backing. Although ultimately functional, these backings have an aesthetically pleasing architectural quality.

Fruit and floral motif pin with silvered faux "black" baroque and seed pearls on a filigree gilt metal casting. *1950s* 2 in (5 cm) long **$160–225 PC**

A filigree antiqued gilt metal back with horseshoe-shaped signature plaque as used in the 1940s.

Floral pin with pressed glass, glass beads, and rhinestones in fuchsia and shades of pink. *1940s*
2½ in (6.25 cm) long

$275–375 ROX

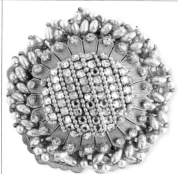

Floral pin of antiqued gilt metal with rings and rows of faux seed and baroque pearls and clear rose montées. *c.1950*
2¼ in (5.75 cm) wide

$625–720 SUM

Floral and foliate pin of antiqued gilt metal with melon-cut emerald beads and clear rose montées. *c.1960*
3 in (7.5 cm) long

$720–800 SUM

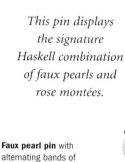

Floral pin of antiqued textured and filigree gilt metal with prong-set blue and green poured glass cabochons. *1940s*
3 in (7.5 cm) long

$125–225 ROX

This pin displays the signature Haskell combination of faux pearls and rose montées.

Faux pearl pin with alternating bands of antiqued gilt metal and small faux baroque pearls, flanked by large baroque pearls and topped with gilt metal leaves and clear rose montées. *c.1960*
3 in (7.5 cm) long

$800–960 SUM

Floral motif stick pin with bird and turtle figures, of antiqued gilt metal with clear crystal beads and rose montées. *c.1960*
3¾ in (9.5 cm) long

$800–960 SUM

Bird of paradise stick pin of antiqued gilt metal with sapphire, emerald, and pink glass beads. *1940s*
3 in (7.5 cm) long

$80–110 SUM

Floral motif stick pin with antiqued gilt metal leaves and faux baroque pearl centers and drop, and three small faux pearl highlights. *1950s*
2¾ in (7 cm) long

$145–190 CRIS

Art Nouveau style floral motif bracelet of antiqued gilt metal bordered with clusters of faux seed pearls. *c.1950*
6¼ in (16 cm) circ

$800–960 SUM

Floral motif pin of filigree antiqued gilt metal studded with faux pearls and clear rose montées. *c.1950*
3¼ in (8.25 cm) wide

$720–880 SUM

Earrings

Haskell earrings were produced in myriad designs, sometimes as part of a demi-parure with matching pin. Mostly floral, foliate, or fruit motifs, all are collectible, although the classic combination of gilt metal, faux pearls, and clear rose montées commands a higher price.

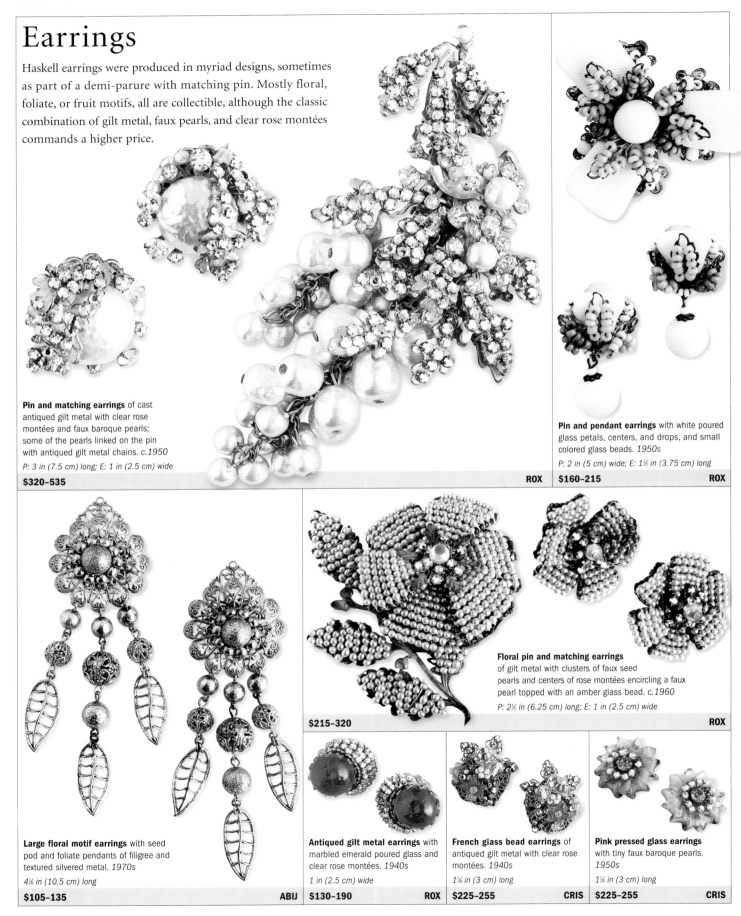

Pin and matching earrings of cast antiqued gilt metal with clear rose montées and faux baroque pearls; some of the pearls linked on the pin with antiqued gilt metal chains. *c.1950*

P: 3 in (7.5 cm) long; E: 1 in (2.5 cm) wide

$320–535   ROX

Pin and pendant earrings with white poured glass petals, centers, and drops, and small colored glass beads. *1950s*

P: 2 in (5 cm) wide; E: 1½ in (3.75 cm) long

$160–215   ROX

Large floral motif earrings with seed pod and foliate pendants of filigree and textured silvered metal. *1970s*

4⅛ in (10.5 cm) long

$105–135   ABIJ

Floral pin and matching earrings of gilt metal with clusters of faux seed pearls and centers of rose montées encircling a faux pearl topped with an amber glass bead. *c.1960*

P: 2½ in (6.25 cm) long; E: 1 in (2.5 cm) wide

$215–320   ROX

Antiqued gilt metal earrings with marbled emerald poured glass and clear rose montées. *1940s*

1 in (2.5 cm) wide

$130–190   ROX

French glass bead earrings of antiqued gilt metal with clear rose montées. *1940s*

1⅛ in (3 cm) long

$225–255   CRIS

Pink pressed glass earrings with tiny faux baroque pearls. *1950s*

1⅛ in (3 cm) long

$225–255   CRIS

Good, Better, Best

The most desirable Haskell earrings and pins are the classic 1940s and 50s designs incorporating signature components. More recent and overtly "modern" examples are currently less expensive but are equally well crafted and worth collecting.

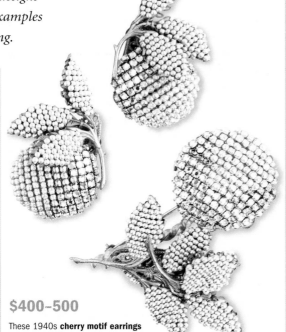

$175–250

These 1960s **fruit and foliate earrings with matching pin** have clusters of seed pearls and metallic colored beads above pewter glass drops; the pin also has five faux baroque pearls. Their modern style and coloring currently commands lower prices than the more classic Haskell designs. *P: 3½ in (9 cm) wide; E: 1¾ in (4.5 cm) long* **ROX**

$270–330

These late 1940s **faux pearl and amber earrings with matching pin** feature hand-wired faux pearls with amber-colored rose montées and poured glass beads. The exotic, variegated coloring of the beads combined with the greater complexity of the composition explains the higher price band. *P: 2½ in (6.25 cm) wide; E: 1 in (2.5 cm) wide* **ROX**

$400–500

These 1940s **cherry motif earrings and matching pin** are considered by current collectors to be a classic example of Haskell design. Antiqued gilt metal, clusters of faux seed pearls, and bands of clear rose montées are all signature Haskell components. The coloring of these pieces is stylized, but in much of their detail they are exquisitely naturalistic. *P: 2¾ in (7 cm) long; E: 2 in (5 cm) long* **ROX**

Floral earrings of antiqued gilt metal with pink poured glass centers, rose montées, and emerald and sapphire rhinestones. *1940s*

1⅛ in (3 cm) long

$125–200	**ROX**

Seed pearl earrings of antiqued gilt metal with centers of rose montées and a faux pearl. *1940s*

1½ in (3.75 cm) long

$150–200	**ROX**

Clear rose montée earrings of antiqued gilt metal with prong-set clear rhinestone centers. *1940s*

1½ in (3.75 cm) long

$180–220	**ROX**

Floral earrings with yellow pressed glass flower heads, sapphire, pink, and clear rhinestones and rose montées. *1940s*

1⅛ in (3 cm) long

$180–220	**ROX**

Antiqued gilt metal earrings with clusters of small faux baroque pearl beads and prong-set clear rhinestones. *c.1950*

2 in (5 cm) long

$400–480	**SUM**

Schiaparelli

In pushing costume jewelry to the cutting edge of fashion, flamboyant couturier Elsa Schiaparelli created a legacy of Surrealist-inspired designs that shocked critics in the 1930s, then became fashion statements, and still receive much admiration today.

ELSA SCHIAPARELLI
1890–1973

1890 Born in Rome, Italy

1920s Establishes her first *maison couture* on the Rue de la Paix in Paris. Becomes a rival of Coco Chanel and befriends Dadaist and Surrealist artists such as Salvador Dali

1936 Introduces "shocking pink" in a collection. This becomes her signature color

1940 Moves to New York to seek refuge from the war

1945 Returns to her fashion house in Paris where future couturiers Hubert de Givenchy and Pierre Cardin train as assistants

1949 Opens a retail ready-to-wear outlet in New York and licenses DeRosa to make her jewelry stamped or tagged "Designed in Paris–Created in America"

1954 Closes her French fashion house and returns to New York to concentrate on costume jewelry designs

Late 1950s Production ceases

1973 Elsa Schiaparelli dies

INSPIRATION
Schiaparelli's main sources of inspiration were the forms of nature and Surrealism, the latter also evident in her love of unusually cut or colored fantasy gemstones.

ROME, NEW YORK, AND PARIS

Born in Rome in 1890, Elsa Schiaparelli moved to New York in the early 20th century to become a scriptwriter. However, her career soon gravitated to her first loves—fashion and the arts—and she established her *maison haute couture* in Paris in the early 1920s. Like her Parisian contemporary Coco Chanel (*see pp. 56–59*), Schiaparelli believed costume jewelry was not only a vital art form in its own right, but also an integral component of costume. Stylistically, however, these often bitter rivals were miles apart.

> *"Fashion is born by small facts, trends, or even politics, never by trying to make little pleats and furbelows, by trinkets, by clothes easy to copy, or by the shortening or lengthening of a skirt."*
>
> Elsa Schiaparelli

In contrast to Chanel's elegant, classic designs, many of Schiaparelli's pieces dating from the 1920s and 30s were unusual and quirky. For example, some incorporated circus imagery and others astrological motifs. Where more natural imagery was employed (*see below*), the floral or faunal subjects were usually either particularly exotic or highly stylized. Bizarre examples include pea-pod pendant necklaces and human eye pins.

Underpinning many of these seemingly light-hearted subjects, however, were the artistic and political philosophies of Dadaism and Surrealism, whose leading exponents were close friends of Schiaparelli and who designed a number of pieces for her (*see opposite below*). The influence of Surrealism on Schiaparelli's work was most evident in her dramatic "Shocking Pink" collection of 1936 (*see opposite above*).

Above: Stylized flower earrings with amber and olivine glass stones encircling *aurora borealis* rhinestones. *c.1950* 1¾ in (4.5 cm) wide **$240–320 SUM**

FORMS OF NATURE

Flora and fauna are recurring themes in Schiaparelli's jewelry. The fantastic sea coral shapes of a glass and rhinestone necklace and bracelet in this 1952 advertisement are typical, as are the foliate forms of this pin and earrings set, made of pale pastel green and pink Lucite, and gold-plated metal. *1950s.* P: 3½ in (9 cm) long; E: 1¾ in (4.5 cm) long **$440–560 PC**

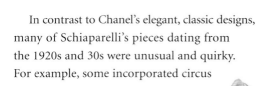

SHOCKING PINK

Elsa Schiaparelli's dramatic injection of "shocking pink" at a time when a black cocktail dress was still *de rigueur* was entirely in keeping with the artistic principles of her Dadaist and Surrealist social set (*see below*). The rapturous reception given to what rapidly became her signature color ensured its translation into the exotic stones used in many pieces of her jewelry, such as this necklace, and also into the hugely successful Shocking perfume and range of cosmetics. As the accompanying advertisement implies, this was Schiaparelli wearing her Surrealist heart on her sleeve.

Lava rock necklace with staggered rows of shocking pink lava stones suspended from a rhinestone studded collar. *c.1940* *15 in (38 cm) circ* **$640–800 CRIS**

Surrealist-style advertisement from *Vogue*, November 1938, promoting Schiaparelli's Shocking range of cosmetics. The torso was purportedly inspired by the actress Mae West.

As ground-breaking as Christian Dior's "New Look" collection after World War II (*see pp.60–63*), Schiaparelli's collection confirmed her ability to both shock and, at the same time, win over even the most conservative critics.

A NEW FOCUS

Having sought refuge from the war in New York, Schiaparelli returned to her fashion house in Paris in 1945 and, in 1949, set up one of the first ready-to-wear *couture* retail outlets back in New York. After selling her business in Paris in 1954—much to the dismay of her assistants Hubert de Givenchy and Pierre Cardin—she returned to New York and to the second major phase of her career. Focusing on costume jewelry, she produced during the course of the 1950s a series of fabulous abstract, floral, and faunal designs characterized by the use of unusual and often very colorful stones and glass. It is these, and her 1940s pieces, that collectors are most likely to come across today (examples from the 1930s being all too rare).

Would-be collectors should note that most early French Schiaparelli pieces are unsigned, although some carry her name in block lettering on a rectangular plate. In contrast, most of the later French and all of the American pieces bear her signature. However, forgeries (and legitimate reproductions from the 1980s) are not unknown. Consequently, purchasing Schiaparelli pieces via a specialist dealer or reputable auction house is strongly advisable.

SURREALISM

The Surrealist artists Salvador Dali (pictured left posing in the village of Port Lligat in Spain in 1951), Jean Cocteau, and Christian Bérard were close friends of Schiaparelli. In addition to designing some pieces for her, their Surrealist concept of art and imagery pervaded her often playful, sometimes shocking designs.

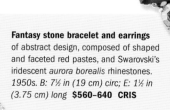

Fantasy stone bracelet and earrings of abstract design, composed of shaped and faceted red pastes, and Swarovski's iridescent *aurora borealis* rhinestones. *1950s. B: 7½ in (19 cm) circ; E: 1½ in (3.75 cm) long* **$560–640 CRIS**

Necklace, bracelet, and earrings with rhodium-plated links, prong-set blue and green glass stones, and *aurora borealis* rhinestones. *1950s*

N: 15 in (38 cm) circ; B: 7⅝ in (19.5 cm) circ; E: 1 in (2.5 cm) long

$1,600–1,900 **CRIS**

Necklace, bracelet, and earrings of gold-plated metal with prong-set smoked topaz and amber crystal stones and beads. *1950s*

N: 16 in (40.5 cm) circ;
B: 9½ in (24 cm) circ;
E: 1½ in (3.75 cm) long

$640–720 **CRIS**

Necklace, bracelet, and earrings with gilt metal links and prong-set glass stones and rhinestones. *1950s*

N: 14½ in (37 cm) circ;
B: 7¼ in (18.5 cm) circ;
E: 1¾ in (4.5 cm) long

$1,400–1,600 **SUM**

Necklace and earrings with gilt metal links, faux pearls, prong-set lilac, amethyst, and dusty pink pastes, and *aurora borealis* rhinestones. *1950s*

N: 14½ in (37 cm) circ; E: 1⅛ in (3 cm) long

$480–620 **SUM**

PERFUME FLACON PINS

Like other couturiers, Schiaparelli produced house perfumes retailed in very distinctive flacons. Miniature examples in the form of lapel pins were also made. As well as the "Success Fou" FLACON below, other rare and collectible examples include a "Sleeping" candlestick (1938), and a "Shocking" torso (see p.109).

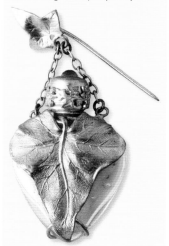

Perfume bottle pin, made for the perfume "Success Fou," in antiqued gilt metal with glass cabochons. *1945* 1¾ in (4.5 cm) high **$1,800–2,100 WAIN**

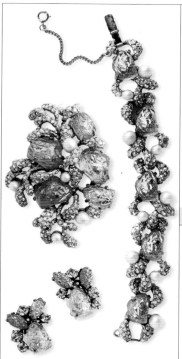

Bracelet, pin, and earrings of textured gilt metal with lava rock stones, faux pearls, and tiny turquoise cabochons. *1950s*
B: 7 in (18 cm) circ; P: 3¼ in (8.25 cm) long; E: 1⅜ in (3.5 cm) long

$1,400–1,600   **SUM**

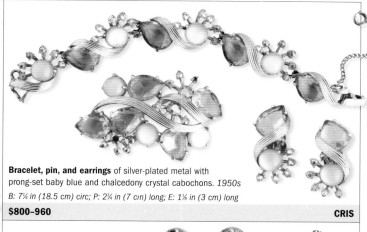

Bracelet, pin, and earrings of silver-plated metal with prong-set baby blue and chalcedony crystal cabochons. *1950s*
B: 7¼ in (18.5 cm) circ; P: 2¾ in (7 cm) long; E: 1⅛ in (3 cm) long

$800–960   **CRIS**

Bracelet and earrings with antiqued gilt metal discs set with faux amethyst glass stones and *aurora borealis* rhinestones. *1950s*
B: 7 in (18 cm) circ; E: 1½ in (3.75 cm) long

$680–760   **CRIS**

Good, Better, Best

Complexities of composition and the size, colors, and cuts of the stones determine the prices of these Schiaparelli bracelets.

$360–440

Made in the 1950s, this is a very pretty and elegant **rhinestone bracelet**. It combines carved white, faux "baby tooth" pearls with prong-set aquamarine and *aurora borealis* rhinestones. 6¼ in (16 cm) long **CRIS**

$520–600

The dense, complex combination of stones in this pretty 1950s **seashell motif bracelet** commands a higher price than the bracelet above. Set with white glass shells, faux pearls, and cabochons. 7 in (18 cm) long **CRIS**

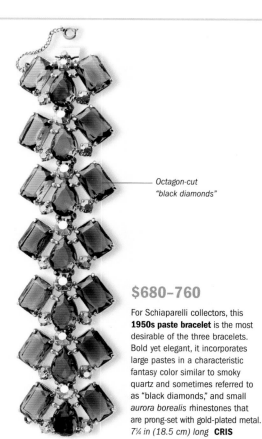

Octagon-cut "black diamonds"

$680–760

For Schiaparelli collectors, this **1950s paste bracelet** is the most desirable of the three bracelets. Bold yet elegant, it incorporates large pastes in a characteristic fantasy color similar to smoky quartz and sometimes referred to as "black diamonds," and small *aurora borealis* rhinestones that are prong-set with gold-plated metal. 7¼ in (18.5 cm) long **CRIS**

Stanley Hagler

Described as "the Picasso of jewelry," American designer Stanley Hagler created pieces that were unique, colorful, seemingly larger than life, and often outrageous.

STANLEY HAGLER
1923–96

1923 Stanley Hagler is born in the United States

Late 1940s Works briefly as a business advisor to Miriam Haskell

Late 1950s Hagler begins creating his own designs. His signature is "Stanley Hagler" until 1983

1968 Hagler wins the Swarovski Design Award for the first time

1979 Mark Mercy joins as a contributing designer

1983 The company relocates to Florida. Signature changes to "Stanley Hagler N.Y.C."

1989 Ian St. Gielar joins as Chief Designer, remaining until 1993

1993 Hagler retires

1996 Stanley Hagler dies. After his death, jewelry continues to be produced under Stanley Hagler & Company

Floral pendant necklace and earrings with faux coral glass beads and cabochons hand-wired to a filigree gold-plated backing. *1980s*
N: 15¾ in (40 cm) circ; E: 1½ in (3.75 cm) wide **$800–960 CRIS**

INSPIRATION
Stanley Hagler followed Miriam Haskell's lead, creating intricately designed handcrafted costume jewelry. Flowers are a recurring motif in his work, as are oriental and figural motifs, such as butterflies. The twice-yearly Fashion Press Week was another major source of inspiration.

DESIGNER TO THE STARS
For a man who apparently launched his jewelry career on a whim, Stanley Hagler was remarkably successful, creating and selling costume jewelry throughout the second half of the 20th century. He was equally successful at cultivating a glittering client list, drawn largely from the ranks of the rich and famous.

Hagler specialized in faux pearl jewelry, using individually strung pearls to highlight their quality. This was in marked contrast to other makers of faux pearl jewelry who grouped them together to hide individual flaws and inconsistencies. His baroque pearls were hand-blown glass beads dipped in pearl resin up to 15 times to achieve maximum luminosity.

Opulent and complex, Stanley Hagler's jewelry combines contemporary design with antique components. He always used the finest materials, such as hand-blown glass, Swarovski crystals, and Russian-gold-plated filigree. Pieces were wired by hand, with stones and crystals prong-set into place rather than glued. His work has a strong architectural style and pieces look equally good whether they are viewed from the front or from the back. He also created some outstanding Christmas tree pins (*see pp.172–175*).

MULTI-PURPOSE DESIGN
One of the intriguing features of Stanley Hagler's jewelry is that it is often multi-purpose. The clasp of a necklace can be transformed into a hair ornament or a pin, necklaces can become double bracelets, and certain earrings can be given an alternative look, simply by adding or removing various components.

During the course of his career, Hagler won 11 Swarovski awards for "Great Designs in jewelry." He always designed jewelry he thought was "just plain pretty," although his earlier pieces were less complex than later ones.

Above: Flower pin with red and green Murano glass leaves and petals and a yellow glass cabochon center. *1960s* 4 in (10 cm) wide **$290–350 CRIS**

UPTOWN STYLE

Hagler produced jewelry for a range of middle and upmarket retail outlets, most notably Saks Fifth Avenue, Lord & Taylor, and Bergdorf Goodman. He started off selling through a prestigious West Coast fashion group called Joseph Magnin.

JEWELS FIT FOR A DUCHESS

Famed for her legendary jewelry collection, the stylish Wallis Simpson, Duchess of Windsor (*right*), enjoyed wearing both faux and genuine pieces. So when one of Stanley Hagler's friends remarked that he would never succeed as a jewelry designer, Hagler rose to the challenge and declared he would create something "fit for a queen." In fact, his first piece was designed for the woman whose husband famously gave up the British throne for her: the Duchess of Windsor. Stanley Hagler sent her the result, a bracelet, and she became the first in a long and illustrious line of clients.

Gold-plated bangle with polychrome molded glass and glass bead floral motifs, and clear crystal rhinestones. The original version of this bangle was made with seed pearls in the 1950s for Wallis Simpson. *1970s 7½ in (19 cm) circ* **$800–960 CRIS**

Hagler also gave much thought to how, when, and where a woman wears jewelry: earrings had to hang perfectly, while a necklace should lie in a particular way so as to be flattering. Although his jewelry was often large in scale, he varied the size according to current fashions. The name tags were also smaller or larger, depending on the size of the piece.

As well as his own jewelry, Hagler produced various designs for other companies, including jeweled swimming flippers, wigs, and jewelry that matched a prestigious range of luggage.

ABOUT IDENTIFICATION

Three designers were associated with the company: Stanley Hagler from the 1950s, Mark Mercy from 1979, and Ian St. Gielar from 1989. The marks from the 1950s had "Stanley Hagler" printed straight across an oval disc. On moving to Florida, Hagler added "N.Y.C." to read "Stanley Hagler N.Y.C." on the curve of the oval. Jewelry bearing the tag "Stanley Hagler NYC," with no period, has been designed by Ian St. Gielar since Hagler's death in 1996.

Vase of flowers pin in gilt metal with blue, green, red, and pink glass petals and beads. *1980s. 2¾ in (7 cm) long* **$190–240 CRIS**

Faux pearls were first dipped in opalescent dyed coating before being incorporated into a design, as in this stylized floral pin. It has pink champagne and lime green colored faux pearls and mother-of-pearl petals, hand-wired to a filigree gold-plated backing. *1980s 3 in (7.5 cm) wide* **$240–310 CRIS**

COLORED PEARLS

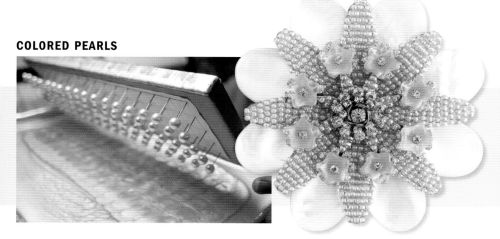

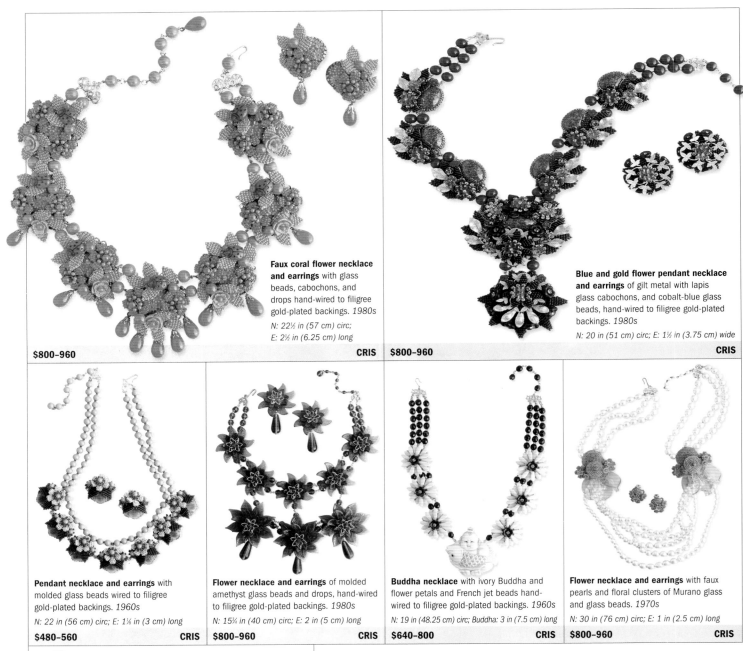

Faux coral flower necklace and earrings with glass beads, cabochons, and drops hand-wired to filigree gold-plated backings. *1980s*
N: 22½ in (57 cm) circ; E: 2½ in (6.25 cm) long

$800–960   **CRIS**

Blue and gold flower pendant necklace and earrings of gilt metal with lapis glass cabochons, and cobalt-blue glass beads, hand-wired to filigree gold-plated backings. *1980s*
N: 20 in (51 cm) circ; E: 1½ in (3.75 cm) wide

$800–960   **CRIS**

Pendant necklace and earrings with molded glass beads wired to filigree gold-plated backings. *1960s*
N: 22 in (56 cm) circ; E: 1⅛ in (3 cm) long

$480–560   **CRIS**

Flower necklace and earrings of molded amethyst glass beads and drops, hand-wired to filigree gold-plated backings. *1980s*
N: 15¾ in (40 cm) circ; E: 2 in (5 cm) long

$800–960   **CRIS**

Buddha necklace with ivory Buddha and flower petals and French jet beads hand-wired to filigree gold-plated backings. *1960s*
N: 19 in (48.25 cm) circ; Buddha: 3 in (7.5 cm) long

$640–800   **CRIS**

Flower necklace and earrings with faux pearls and floral clusters of Murano glass and glass beads. *1970s*
N: 30 in (76 cm); E: 1 in (2.5 cm) long

$800–960   **CRIS**

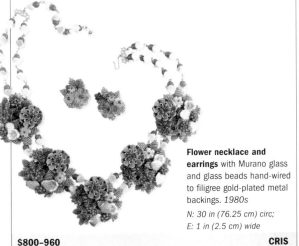

Flower necklace and earrings with Murano glass and glass beads hand-wired to filigree gold-plated metal backings. *1980s*
N: 30 in (76.25 cm) circ; E: 1 in (2.5 cm) wide

$800–960   **CRIS**

FAUX SEED PEARLS

Many of Stanley Hagler's imaginative pieces feature tiny faux seed pearls of Japanese origin. Made of glass, and produced in numerous colors, they are mostly hand-wired into floral and foliate motifs. The intricacy of these compositions is typical of Hagler's craftsmanship and counterbalances the boldness of his designs.

Necklace and earrings with floral rosettes of hand-wired, coral-colored faux seed pearls, crystal rhinestones, and faux coral cabochons. *1980s*
N: 17¾ in (45 cm) circ; E: 1 in (2.5 cm) wide **$560–640 CRIS**

Faux pearl necklace with an ornament of faux pearls and rose montées. *1970s*
15¾ in (40 cm) circ

$320–400 **CRIS**

Floral pin and earrings of faux and seed pearls and clear crystal rhinestones hand-wired to filigree gold-plated backings. *1990s*
P: 3 in (7.5 cm) wide; E: 1½ in (3.75 cm) long

$160–290 **PC**

Floral pin and earrings with petals and leaves of pressed glass and glass beads on filigree gold-plated backings. *1980s*
P: 3¾ in (9.5 cm) long; E: 1⅜ in (3.5 cm) wide

$160–240 **CRIS**

Although Hagler's designs were large in scale, he varied the size according to changing fashions.

Bib-of-bees necklace with hand-wired topaz crystal octagons and amber glass beads. *1960s*
N: 14½ in (36.75 cm) circ; Bib: 5 in (12.75 cm) drop

$720–800 **CRIS**

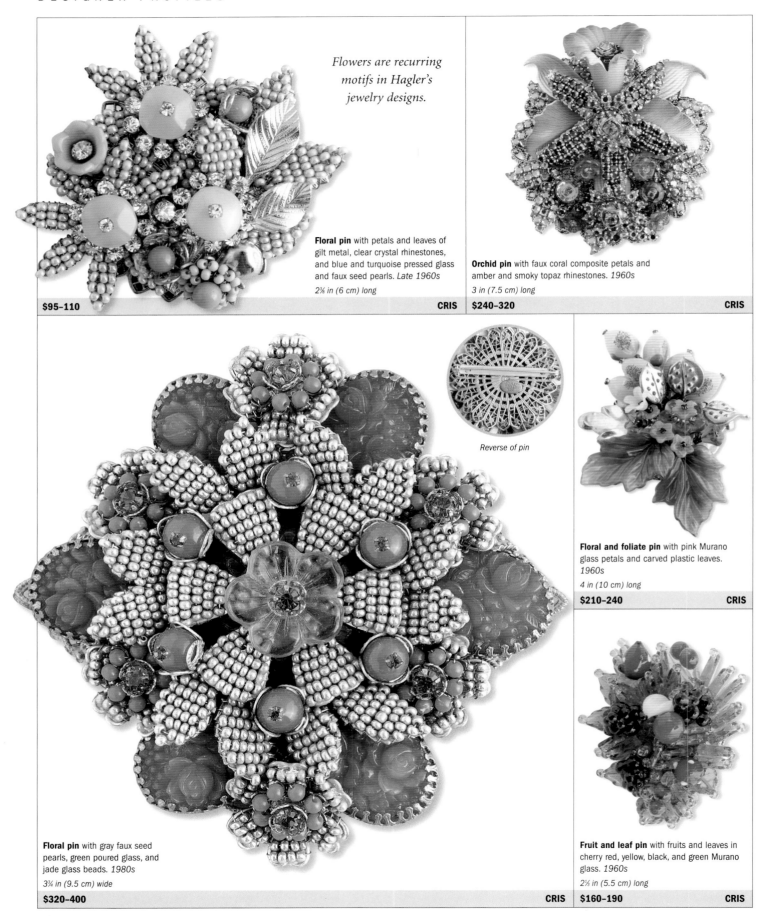

Flowers are recurring motifs in Hagler's jewelry designs.

Floral pin with petals and leaves of gilt metal, clear crystal rhinestones, and blue and turquoise pressed glass and faux seed pearls. *Late 1960s*

2⅜ in (6 cm) long

$95–110   CRIS

Orchid pin with faux coral composite petals and amber and smoky topaz rhinestones. *1960s*

3 in (7.5 cm) long

$240–320   CRIS

Reverse of pin

Floral and foliate pin with pink Murano glass petals and carved plastic leaves. *1960s*

4 in (10 cm) long

$210–240   CRIS

Floral pin with gray faux seed pearls, green poured glass, and jade glass beads. *1980s*

3¾ in (9.5 cm) wide

$320–400   CRIS

Fruit and leaf pin with fruits and leaves in cherry red, yellow, black, and green Murano glass. *1960s*

2⅛ in (5.5 cm) long

$160–190   CRIS

Floral pin with orange pressed glass and glass beads, coral faux seed pearls, and clear crystal rhinestones. *1980s*

3 in (7.5 cm) wide

$160–240 **CRIS**

Cameo floral pin with butter faux seed pearls and jonquil rhinestones around a carved ivory cameo. *1960s*

3 in (7.5 cm) long

$200–240 **CRIS**

Stylized camellia pin with pearlized metal blue petals, pressed red glass, red faux seed pearls, and clear crystal rhinestones. *1960s*

3¼ in (8.25 cm) wide

$320–400 **PC**

Panda and leaf pin with amethyst pressed glass, green and amethyst faux seed pearls, rhinestones, and ivory pandas. *1980s*

2½ in (6.5 cm) long

$320–400 **CRIS**

Flower and leaf pin with yellow and green pressed glass and yellow, red, and green faux seed pearls. *1980s*

5 in (12.75 cm) long

$400–480 **CRIS**

Turquoise pressed glass flower with powder blue faux seed pearls and a blue glass cabochon. *1970s*

3 in (7.5 cm) wide

$190–240 **CRIS**

Butterfly pin with white and peach pressed glass, yellow and peach glass beads, and seed pearls. *1980s*

3¾ in (9.5 cm) wide

$320–400

CRIS

Good, Better, Best

Age and rarity are significant, but the different prices these Hagler pins command are ultimately determined by their visual impact.

$120–160

This 1980s **floral pin** is a classic Hagler composition incorporating white, pink, and red pressed glass petals, green seed pearls, Venetian glass drops, and filigree gilt metal. *4¼ in (10.75 cm) long* **CRIS**

$240–320

This 1960s **vase of flowers pin** is in gold-tone metal with carved shell leaves, mother-of-pearl petals, and clear crystal rhinestones. Its rarity commands a high price. *3½ in (9 cm) long* **CRIS**

$320–400

This 1980s **head and flowers pin** features a central carved ivory oriental head encircled by rose quartz and green faux seed pearl leaves, rose quartz and violet pressed glass petals, and jade green rhinestones. It fetches the highest price because the inclusion of the head makes the composition more dramatic than that of the vase of flowers pin. *2½ in (6.25 cm) wide* **CRIS**

Trifari

Trifari has long been one of the United States' preeminent costume jewelry makers. Covering diverse styles and a full spectrum of price points, its pieces invariably display imaginative design and quality craftsmanship.

ITALIAN ORIGINS

Like many American costume jewelers, Trifari was founded on the skills of a newcomer to the country. Gustavo Trifari was born in Naples, Italy in 1883 and, prior to his arrival in New York in 1904, had trained as a goldsmith under his grandfather, Luigi. After initially working for an uncle, with whom he formed Trifari and Trifari in about 1910, Gustavo branched out on his own to make high-quality pieces under the name Trifari. The arrival of sales manager Leo Krussman in 1917, and the formation of Trifari and Krussman a year later, brought embryonic commercial success—further enhanced when salesman Carl Fishel came on board in 1923.

Two years later the three founded Trifari, Krussman and Fishel (T. K. F.), and the rest is history. Some seven decades on, T. K. F.—still best known as Trifari—remains one of the United States' largest and most prestigious designers and manufacturers of costume jewelry.

FOUNDATIONS OF SUCCESS

An essential part of Trifari's enduring success has been the powerful mix of glamorous clientele and prestigious publicity. From the 1930s onward, Trifari's creation of exclusive designs for Broadway musicals, such as *Roberta*, and for numerous stars of stage and screen, highlighted the desirability of its jewelry. This status was further enhanced by its commissions in the 1950s from First Lady Mamie Eisenhower. More recently, Madonna wore Trifari in the Hollywood blockbuster *Evita*.

Above: Patriotic American eagle pin of sterling silver with red enameling, white clear rhinestones, and blue Lucite belly. *1940s. 1¾ in (4.5 cm) long* **$200–300 ROX**

Rare and fabulous plant motif pin of sterling silver with green and brown enameling and a profusion of pavé-set clear crystal rhinestones. *1940s 7 in (18 cm) long* **$1,900–2,100 SUM**

Modern and sophisticated is how this late-1950s advertisement promotes a Trifari "Comet" necklace and earrings in gold Trifanium with clear crystal rhinestones.

Of course, such commissions would never have been forthcoming if the jewelry hadn't been of sufficient quality. In terms of materials and techniques, chief designer Alfred Philippe set the tone from early on with his use of fine, skillfully hand-set Austrian rhinestones in extremely convincing imitations of expensive precious jewelry (*see below*). Subsequently, when 1940s wartime restrictions prohibited the use of white metals for retail, Trifari produced fabulous pieces in heavy sterling silver, often with a luxurious vermeil (gold-plated) finish. Other attractive and convincing materials have included the plastic Lucite, which closely resembles rock crystal and was used in Trifari's 1940s Jelly Bellies (*see below and p.127*). Post-war examples range from pressed or molded glass, high-quality, milky colored pastes in imitation of moonstones and chalcedony, superb faux pearls, and Trifanium, a non-tarnishing, gold-finish alloy named after the company.

DIVERSITY OF STYLES

Above all, however, it is the way in which such materials have been used that has guaranteed Trifari's reputation. The range of its pieces—always astutely launched in sympathy with the prevailing sentiment of the time—has been incredibly diverse and encompasses most styles fashionable since the 1920s. All are collectible, but among the most coveted are the Jelly Belly figural pins and Crown pins (especially those designed by Alfred Philippe during the 1940s), and the patriotic jewelry, including American flag and eagle pins, hailing the American armed forces of World War II. Faux pearls and paste gemstones from the 1950s have recently enjoyed a revival, as have combinations of pearls and brushed gold. However, due to their eminent wearability, it is the pieces incorporating floral and foliate imagery that have proved the most consistently popular.

A fur clip, in two-tone yellow and rose gold-plated silver and set with faux rubies and diamonds. *1940s 3½ in (9 cm) long* **$720–800 CRIS**

COMMISSIONS

In addition to producing retail costume jewelry, Trifari also created pieces for private and commercial clients, including Broadway theaters and Hollywood film studios. Undoubtedly the most prestigious, however, were those designed in the 1950s for Mamie Eisenhower.

FIRST LADY

This necklace and earrings – part of a demi-parure of faux pearls, emeralds, and diamonds made to an original design by Alfred Philippe for First Lady Mamie Eisenhower. Trifari made other pieces for Mrs. Eisenhower, notably for the 1953 and 1957 Presidential Inaugural Balls. *1950s N: 15 in (38 cm) circ; E: 1⅛ in (3 cm) wide* **$640–800 CRIS**

EVITA

These "Jewels of India" pin and earrings are identical to those worn by Madonna when she starred in the movie *Evita*. Of brushed gold finish with green and red cabochons and clear rhinestones, they were inspired by the Mughal jewels popularized by Cartier in the 1920s. *1950s. P: 2⅜ in (6 cm) wide; E: 1 in (2.5 cm) wide* **$385–450 CRIS**

ALFRED PHILIPPE—CHIEF DESIGNER

Much of Trifari's success can be attributed to Frenchman Alfred Philippe, who joined the company as its chief designer in 1930, and didn't retire until 1968. Significant contributions included his use of high-quality Swarovski crystals, which gave rise to the company's epithet: the Diamanté Kings. Having previously designed pieces sold via the prestigious jewelers Cartier and Van Cleef and Arpels, Philippe also introduced sophisticated techniques such as the invisible setting usually confined to high-end precious jewelry. However, his most enduring legacy resides in his imaginative and commercially successful designs. Notable among many are the much-sought-after 1940s Crown pins (*see p.129*) and Lucite Jelly Bellies (*see p.127*).

Poinsettia pin designed by Alfred Philippe with faux rubies and diamonds configured in imitation of the invisible setting technique developed by Van Cleef and Arpels. *1950s 2¾ in (7 cm) wide* **$960–1,100 CRIS**

Jelly Belly seal pin designed by Alfred Philippe, of vermeil sterling silver with clear Lucite belly, clear and ruby rhinestones (for the eyes), and a large prong-set sapphire rhinestone ball. *1940s. 2⅜ in (6 cm) high* **$640–800 CRIS**

Necklaces, bracelets, and earrings

Numerous style influences are evident in Trifari necklaces, bracelets, and earrings, including neoclassical, Art Deco, romantic-historical, and oriental, to name but a few. With imagery ranging from floral to geometric to abstract, collectors have much to choose from.

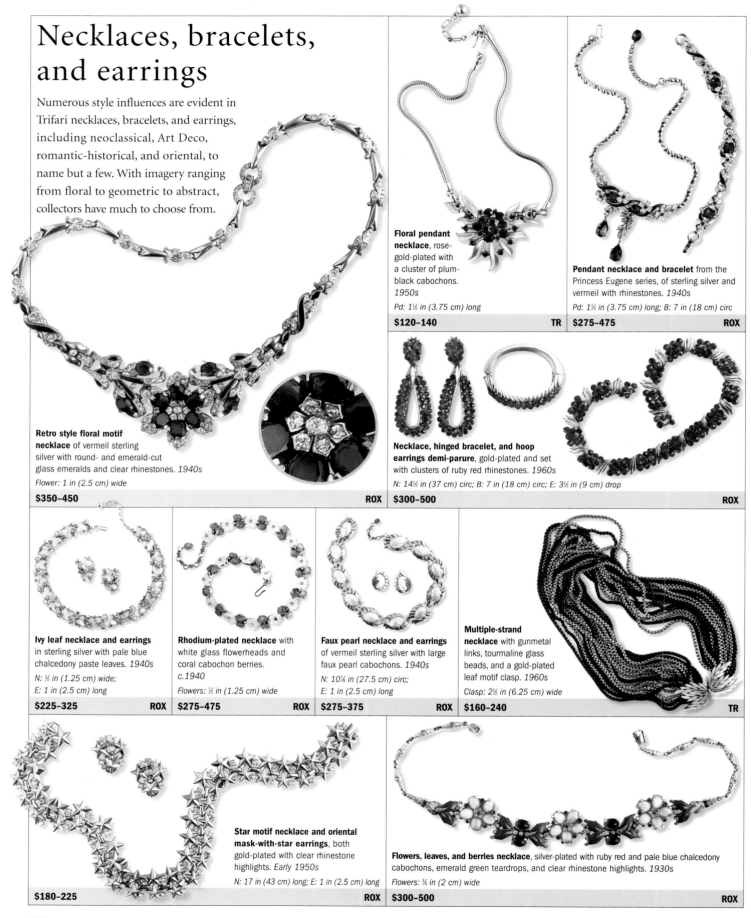

Floral pendant necklace, rose-gold-plated with a cluster of plum-black cabochons. *1950s*
Pd: 1½ in (3.75 cm) long
$120–140 · TR

Pendant necklace and bracelet from the Princess Eugene series, of sterling silver and vermeil with rhinestones. *1940s*
Pd: 1½ in (3.75 cm) long; B: 7 in (18 cm) circ
$275–475 · ROX

Retro style floral motif necklace of vermeil sterling silver with round- and emerald-cut glass emeralds and clear rhinestones. *1940s*
Flower: 1 in (2.5 cm) wide
$350–450 · ROX

Necklace, hinged bracelet, and hoop earrings demi-parure, gold-plated and set with clusters of ruby red rhinestones. *1960s*
N: 14½ in (37 cm) circ; B: 7 in (18 cm) circ; E: 3½ in (9 cm) drop
$300–500 · ROX

Ivy leaf necklace and earrings in sterling silver with pale blue chalcedony paste leaves. *1940s*
N: ½ in (1.25 cm) wide; E: 1 in (2.5 cm) long
$225–325 · ROX

Rhodium-plated necklace with white glass flowerheads and coral cabochon berries. *c.1940*
Flowers: ½ in (1.25 cm) wide
$275–475 · ROX

Faux pearl necklace and earrings of vermeil sterling silver with large faux pearl cabochons. *1940s*
N: 10⅞ in (27.5 cm) circ; E: 1 in (2.5 cm) long
$275–375 · ROX

Multiple-strand necklace with gunmetal links, tourmaline glass beads, and a gold-plated leaf motif clasp. *1960s*
Clasp: 2½ in (6.25 cm) wide
$160–240 · TR

Star motif necklace and oriental mask-with-star earrings, both gold-plated with clear rhinestone highlights. *Early 1950s*
N: 17 in (43 cm) long; E: 1 in (2.5 cm) long
$180–225 · ROX

Flowers, leaves, and berries necklace, silver-plated with ruby red and pale blue chalcedony cabochons, emerald green teardrops, and clear rhinestone highlights. *1930s*
Flowers: ¾ in (2 cm) wide
$300–500 · ROX

Good, Better, Best

With or without earrings or a pin, early Trifari necklaces from the 1930s and 40s generally command higher prices than those made in the 1950s and 60s, with a few exceptions.

$150–160

These mid-1950s **glass and rose gold necklace and earrings** set has carved, pale yellow glass flowerheads set in rose-gold-finish base metal. Their appeal lies in the simplicity of detail.
*N: 15 in (38 cm) circ;
E: 1½ in (3.75 cm) long* **CRIS**

$720–800

This 1940s **retro style twin-pendant necklace and bow pin** is of vermeil sterling silver with rhinestones which, together with greater intricacies of craftsmanship, command a substantially higher price.
*Pd: 3½ in (9 cm) long;
P: 2¼ in (5.75 cm) wide* **CRIS**

$1,000–1,100

This rare 1950s **floral garland necklace and earrings** with faux "baby's tooth" pearls and clear and black rhinestones on gold-plated castings, are brilliantly conceived and executed in both form and detail.
N: 15 in (38 cm) circ; E: 1⅛ in (3 cm) wide **CRIS**

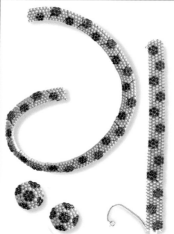

Necklace, bracelet, and earrings of vermeil sterling silver with turquoise cabochons and ruby red and blue rhinestones. *1940s*
N & B: ¾ in (2 cm) wide; E: 1 in (2.5 cm) wide

$300–500	ROX

Alfred Philippe necklace and earrings in vermeil sterling silver with carved coral glass leaves and clear rhinestone highlights. *1940s*
N: 16 in (40.5 cm) circ; E: 1½ in (3.75 cm) wide

$240–320	RG

Floral bracelet with clear navette-cut rhinestone flowerheads with faux pearl centers. *c.1950*
6 in (15 cm) circ

$225–375		LB

Jewels-of-India necklace and earrings of brushed gold alloy with navette-cut, square-cut, and round rhinestones. *1950s*
N: ¾ in (2 cm) wide; E: 1 in (2.5 cm) long

$275–375	ROX

Floral, foliate, and fruit pins

Trifari's flower, leaf, and fruit pins are a collecting field in their own right. Generally of more intricate design and craftsmanship, examples made during the 1930s and 40s almost invariably command higher prices than the simpler, albeit equally stylish pieces made thereafter.

Early, large, and rare sunflower pin, rhodium-plated with pavé-set clear and citrine rhinestones. *1930s*

3½ in (9 cm) wide

$640–800 CRIS

Early floral pin with trailing leaves, rhodium-plated with large blue baguettes and clear rhinestones. *1930s*

3⅛ in (8 cm) long

$275–375 ROX

Maltese Cross pin, gold-plated with blue cabochons, textured blue enamel, and clear rhinestones. *1950s*

2½ in (6.25 cm) wide

$110–130 CRIS

Large flower pin with yellow, green, and orange enamel and clear rhinestones. *1930s*

4 in (10 cm) long

$450–650 ROX

Bouquet-of-flowers pin of vermeil sterling silver with red and clear rhinestones. *1930s*

3⅛ in (8 cm) long

$350–380 TR

Lily pin of vermeil sterling silver with semi-translucent white Lucite leaves and clear rhinestones. *Late 1930s*

4 in (10 cm) long

$1,800–2,200 ROX

Bouquet-of flowers-pin, rhodium-plated with sapphire blue pastes and clear rhinestones. *1930s*

3¾ in (9.5 cm) long

$200–275 ROX

Basket-of-flowers pin, gold-plated with amethyst blue, jonquil, and rose pink rhinestones. *Mid-1950s*

1¾ in (4.5 cm) long

$55–65 CRIS

Very rare flower pin, gold-plated with white enameling and amber-red and pavé-set clear rhinestones. *1930s*

3 in (7.5 cm) long

$450–650 ROX

Large rare bouquet-of-flowers pin, gold-plated with aquamarine pastes, amber, red, and clear rhinestones, and green enameling. 1930s

4¾ in (12 cm) long

$1,500–2,000 ROX

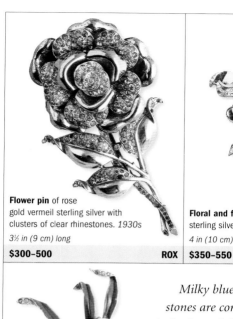

Flower pin of rose gold vermeil sterling silver with clusters of clear rhinestones. *1930s*
3½ in (9 cm) long

| $300–500 | ROX |

Floral and foliate bouquet pin of vermeil sterling silver with rhinestones. *1930s*
4 in (10 cm) long

| $350–550 | ROX |

Floral pin and earrings by Alfred Philippe, rhodium-plated with rose pink, caliber-cut pastes and pavé-set clear rhinestones. *1940s*
Flowerheads: 1⅜ in (3.5 cm) wide

| $600–1,000 | ROX |

Milky blue glass stones are convincing imitations of the mineral chalcedony.

Bouquet-of-flowers pin, gold-plated with green enameling, milky blue glass stones, and clear rhinestones. *1930s*
3½ in (9 cm) long

| $600–650 | TR |

Floral pin, rhodium-plated with sapphire navette and amethyst blue rhinestones. *1940s*
3½ in (9 cm) long

| $175–225 | ROX |

Floral and foliate pin, matte-finish gold-plated with graduated white faux pearls. *1950s*
3 in (7.5 cm) long

| $110–130 | CRIS |

Flower pin, rhodium-plated with small clear baguette and round rhinestones. *1930s*
4 in (10 cm) long

| $200–300 | ROX |

Good, Better, Best

All these pieces are very stylish and highly collectible. However, their different prices are determined by factors such as weight, contrasts of color, intricacy of workmanship, and the degree of naturalism.

$55–60

This late 1950s, silver-colored alloy **tulip pin** is eminently wearable and its petals and leaves are fluently styled. The absence of contrasting-colored materials gives it a nicely understated elegance. *3¼ in (8.25 cm) long* **CRIS**

$120–135

This mid-1950s, gold-plated **maple leaf pin** is set with bright red oval and teardrop coral cabochons. Boldly designed, it is, both visually and in weight, a more substantial piece than the tulip pin. *3 in (7.5 cm) long* **CRIS**

$720–880

This 1940s **hyacinth pin** is cold-enameled and studded with pavé-set clear rhinestones. It is highly naturalistic, exquisitely detailed, old, and rare—a compelling combination that makes this by far the most desirable piece of the three. *4½ in (11 cm) long* **CRIS**

Foliate pin and earrings of vermeil sterling silver with rectangular emerald green and round clear rhinestones. *1940s*

P: 3½ in (9 cm) long; E: 1 in (2.5 cm) long

$300–400   ROX

Grapes-and-leaves pin of sterling silver with vermeil highlights and pavé-set clear rhinestones. *1930s*

3 in (7.5 cm) long

$200–300   ROX

Pin and earrings with emerald green, ruby red, and sapphire blue rhinestones set around clear rhinestone flowerheads. *1930s*

P: 2½ in (6.5 cm) wide; E: 1 in (2.5 cm) wide

$300–400   ROX

Marine plant pin and earrings, gold-plated with fuchsia pink and faux moonstone cabochons and faux pearls. *1950s*

P: 3½ in (9 cm) long; E: 1 in (2.5 cm) long

$225–255   CRIS

Flower pin of green, purple, yellow, and pink enamel with clear rhinestone highlights. *1930s*

2¾ in (7 cm) long

$200–300   ROX

Foliate pin of sterling silver with "fruit salad" stones and clear and purple rhinestones. *1940s*

3½ in (9 cm) long

$225–250   TR

Alfred Philippe flower pin and earrings in sterling silver with invisible-set caliber-cut petals and green and clear rhinestones. *1940s*

P: 5 in (12.5 cm) long; E: 1⅛ in (3 cm) long

$550–850   ROX

Gold-plated leaf pin with pinkish red, blue, emerald green, and clear rhinestones. *1950s*

2¾ in (7 cm) long

$110–145   RG

Retro flower pin of pierced silver alloy with pear, navette, and round clear rhinestones. *1950s*

1½ in (4 cm) wide

$50–80   ABAA

Russian gold plating

Russian gold-plated leaf pin with chanel- and pavé-set clear rhinestones. *1950s*

7⅞ in (20 cm) long

$75–95   LB

Pea pod pin of matte-finish white metal with turquoise cabochons for the peas. Naturalistic in form with stylized color combinations; such pins are increasingly sought-after. *1930s*

2½ in (6.25 cm) long

$175–275   ROX

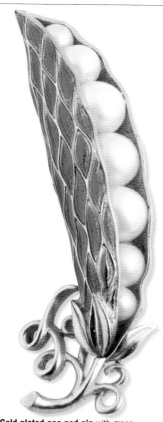

Fruit pin with two pairs of matching earrings (one pair pendant), gold-plated with clusters of fuchsia pastes. *1960s*

P: 2⅜ in (6 cm) long; E (left): 1 in (2.5 cm) long; E (above): 2⅜ in (6 cm) long

$85–125   **ROX**

Bunch of grapes pin with deep purple glass beads and gold-plated leaves. *1930s*

1½ in (3.75 cm) long

$200–275   **ROX**

Gold-plated pea pod pin with green cold enamel and faux pearls for the peas inside the pod. *1950s*

2¾ in (7 cm) long

$190–225   **CRIS**

Fruit motif pendant earrings in pierced, basket-weave patterned gold-plated base metal. *Mid-1950s*

1½ in (4 cm) long

$55–70   **CRIS**

Fruit pin and earrings of sterling silver, the fruits with ruby red rhinestones and clear rhinestone highlights, the leaves with pavé-set clear rhinestones. *1940s*

P: 1½ in (4 cm) long; E: ¾ in (2 cm) long

$560–880   **ROX**

MINI FRUITS

Trifari produced numerous miniature pins during the late 1950s and 1960s. They could be worn either individually, or scattered in groups of two, three, or more. Small fruits, as below, are particularly popular, but other ranges—notably their heraldic motifs—are equally collectible.

Miniature fruit pins with the apple, pineapple, and bunch of grapes in matte-finish silver alloy; the strawberry in a gold-tone equivalent. *Late 1950s*

¾–1 in (2–2.5 cm) long   **$25–30 each**   **CRIS**

Gold-plated fruit pin, sliced to reveal clusters of emerald green rhinestones. *1950s*

2⅜ in (6 cm) long

$95–110   **CRIS**

Leaves-and-berries pin and earrings, the stalks and leaves of matte-finish gold alloy with graduated white faux pearls. *1950s*

P: 4 in (10 cm) long;
E: 1½ in (3.75 cm) long

$225–255   **CRIS**

Gold-plated and pierced sponge earrings (with their original Trifari tag—not shown). *1960s*

⅞ in (2.25 cm) wide

$25–40   **TR**

Matte-finish gold alloy leaves-and-berries pin with elongated faux pearls. *1950s*

4 in (10 cm) long

$105–120   **CRIS**

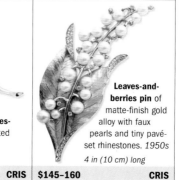

Leaves-and-berries pin of matte-finish gold alloy with faux pearls and tiny pavé-set rhinestones. *1950s*

4 in (10 cm) long

$145–160   **CRIS**

Creature pins

Trifari produced numerous, eminently collectible animal, bird, and insect pins. Better-quality components and greater intricacies of design make its earlier 1930s and 40s pins the most desirable.

Angel fish pin, silver-plated with blue Lucite belly and clear and ruby red rhinestones (for the eyes). *1950s*

2⅜ in (6 cm) long

$250–350   ROX

Shoal-of-fish pin of gold-plated casting with small ruby red cabochons for the eyes. *Late 1950s*

2½ in (6.5 cm) long

$120–135   ROX

Large hinged dragon's head watch ring set with clear rhinestones and green cabochon eyes. *1960s*

2½ in (6.5 cm) wide

$175–250   ROX

Jelly Belly crab pin of vermeil sterling silver with grey Lucite belly and clear rhinestone highlights. *1940s*

3 in (7.5 cm) wide

$900–1,000   TR

Châtelaine pin, gold-plated with faux pearls, enamel, and red cabochons. *1950s*

Coral: 1⅛ in (3 cm) long

$120–130   CRIS

Seahorse pin of matte-finish gold-plated casting with turquoise cabochons "belly" and ruby red glass cabochon eyes. *1950s*

4½ in (11.5 cm) long

$50–65   CRIS

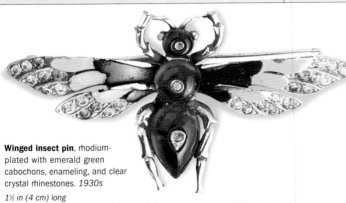

Winged insect pin, rhodium-plated with emerald green cabochons, enameling, and clear crystal rhinestones. *1930s*

1½ in (4 cm) long

$150–250   ROX

Fly pin, gold-plated with prong-set Lucite "belly," blue and aquamarine cabochons, ruby red baguettes, and clear rhinestones. *1940s*

1¾ in (4.5 cm) long

$175–250   ROX

Jelly Belly fly pin of vermeil sterling silver with grey Lucite belly and clear rhinestones. *1940s*

3 in (7.5 cm) long

$900–1,100   TR

Butterfly pin designed by Alfred Philippe of sterling silver with clear rhinestones and prong-set blue and red cabochons. *1940s*

2½ in (6.25 cm) long

$225–255   CRIS

Rare insect pin, gold-plated with blue navette paste body, and large and small red and emerald green cabochons. *1930s*

3 in (7.5 cm) long

$700–1,000   ROX

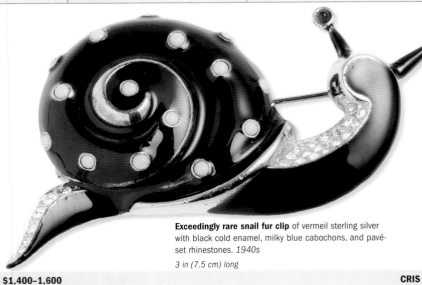

Exceedingly rare snail fur clip of vermeil sterling silver with black cold enamel, milky blue cabochons, and pavé-set rhinestones. *1940s*

3 in (7.5 cm) long

$1,400–1,600   CRIS

Bee pin with imperial purple enameling over a gold-plated casting. *1950s*

1⅜ in (3.5 cm) wide

$50–65   **CRIS**

Jelly Belly beetle pin of vermeil sterling silver with gray Lucite "belly" and clear rhinestone highlights. *1940s*

2 in (5 cm) long

$900–1,000   **TR**

Coiled snake pin and earrings, gold-plated with inset faux ruby and emerald cabochons. *1950s*

P: 2½ in (6.25 cm) long; E: 1 in (2.5 cm) wide

$190–240   **RG**

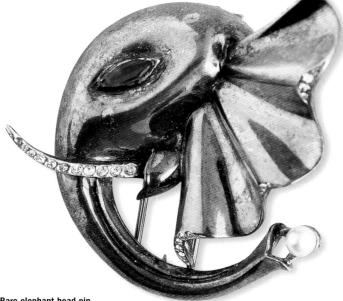

Rare elephant head pin, gold-plated with clear rhinestones, a faux pearl, and ruby red navettes (for the eyes). *1930s*

2 in (5 cm) long

$300–400   **ROX**

Set of duck and baby duck scatter pins, gold-plated with ruby red, emerald green, aquamarine, and sapphire blue cabochons and clear rhinestones. *1930s*

Largest: 1½ in (3.75 cm) long; Smallest: 1 in (2.5 cm) long

$300–400   **ROX**

Perching birds pin, silver-plated with red and turquoise enameling and clear rhinestones. *1930s*

2¼ in (5.75 cm) long

$300–500   **ROX**

JELLY BELLY PINS

Trifari's famous Jelly Belly pins have dramatically risen in price over the last five years. The Lucite Jelly Bellies made in the 1940s (*see below*) are generally considered the most desirable. Price differences between them primarily depend on the rarity of the motif—poodles, for example, being more scarce than roosters.

Jelly Belly rooster pin, gold-plated with Lucite belly and red rhinestones. *1940s*
2½ in (6.5 cm) long   **$640–900**   **CRIS**

Alfred Philippe bird-of-paradise pin of vermeil sterling silver with red rhinestone "belly," and teardrop and round rhinestones. *1940s*

3½ in (9 cm) long

$320–400   **RG**

Gray Jelly Belly chick pin, gold-plated with pavé-set clear rhinestone head and coral cabochon eyes. *1930s*

2 in (5 cm) long

$1,100–1,300   **TR**

American eagle pin of vermeil sterling silver with red, white, and blue enameling. *1940s*

2 in (5 cm) long

$190–215   **TR**

Jelly Belly poodle pin, gold-plated with Lucite belly and red rhinestones. *1940s*
2 in (5 cm) long   **$800–960**   **CRIS**

Miscellaneous pins

For many collectors the great appeal of Trifari pins lies in their sheer diversity. Bows, hearts, shells, and flags are the perennial favorites, but human-figural, architectural, pictorial, and abstract designs are also much sought-after, and the most prestigious of all are its classic crown pins.

The deep, lustrous shine of thick vermeil sterling silver is a recurring feature of Trifari pins made during the 1940s.

Bow pin of gold vermeil over sterling silver, with ruby red baguette and pavé-set clear rhinestones. *1940s*

3½ in (9 cm) wide

$600–900   LYNH

Heart pin of blue glass encased in vermeil sterling silver, with a rhodium-plated arrow and winged insect. *1940s*

2¾ in (7 cm) long

$200–300   ROX

Shell and seaweed pin of gold-plated casting with green and coral enameling and faux pearls. *1950s*

2½ in (6.5 cm) long

$190–225   CRIS

Heart pin and earrings of emerald green glass encased in scrolled vermeil silver with blue glass teardrops and clear rhinestones. *1940s*

P: 2½ in (6.25 cm) long; E: 1¼ in (3 cm) long

$290–320   CRIS

Rare swan and bridge pin with blue and dark ruby red enameling and clear rhinestones on a sterling silver casting. *1940s*

2¾ in (7 cm) wide

$700–1,000   ROX

Bow and fruit pin of vermeil sterling silver with large emerald green and small clear rhinestones. *1940s*

2⅜ in (6 cm) long

$160–210   RG

Lightweight gold plating

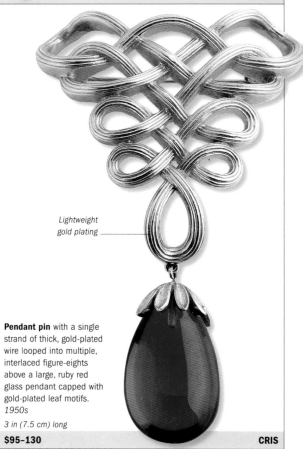

Pendant pin with a single strand of thick, gold-plated wire looped into multiple, interlaced figure-eights above a large, ruby red glass pendant capped with gold-plated leaf motifs. *1950s*

3 in (7.5 cm) long

Vermeil sterling silver pin with bands of rope molding alternated with blue enameling, and with clear rhinestones. *1940s*

1½ in (3.75 cm) long

$160–190   CRIS

Stars and Stripes flag pin with gold-plated staff, blue and red enamel, and clear rhinestone flag. *1940s*

2⅜ in (6 cm) long

$200–300   ROX

$95–130   CRIS

Early and relatively rare duette pin of vermeil sterling silver with large emerald pastes, small red and emerald baguettes, and small clear rhinestones. *1930s*
3⅜ in (8.5 cm) long

$300–500 ROX

Toadstool pin of textured gold alloy with blue cabochons, clear rhinestones, and faux angel skin coral eggs. *1950s*
1½ in (4 cm) long

$70–105 CRIS

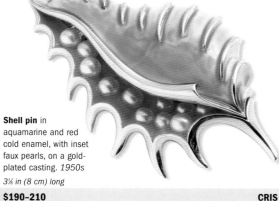

Shell pin in aquamarine and red cold enamel, with inset faux pearls, on a gold-plated casting. *1950s*
3⅛ in (8 cm) long

$190–210 CRIS

Sailor pin in white metal with clear rhinestones and flesh-tone enameled head and pale blue enameled globe. *1940s*
2¼ in (5.75 cm) long

$320–380 ROX

Balloon pin with heart-motif ballast, of satin finish gold-tone alloy. *1950s*
2¼ in (5.75 cm) long

$50–65 CRIS

Rare Chinese lantern pin with red, black, and white enameling and clear rhinestones, on a gold-plated casting. *1930s*
2¾ in (7 cm) long

$600–800 ROX

Faux fabric bow-tie pin by Diane Love, who designed for Trifari from 1971 to 1974. *1970s*
3 in (7 cm) wide

$65–75 TR

Figure-eight bow pin with small turquoise and ruby red cabochons on a gold-plated, rope-molded casting. *1950s*
3 in (7.5 cm) wide

$255–305 CRIS

CROWN PINS

From the late 1930s to the 1950s, Trifari astutely produced a series of crown pins to coincide with a string of hugely popular romantic-historical movies that fired public interest in the lifestyle and trappings of European royalty. The inclusion of the crown silhouette in Trifari's trademark from around 1937 is testament to the commercial success of an enduring line that encompassed a wide range of fanciful designs, including the "Coronation Gems" launched in 1953. However, the most sought-after pins are those designed by Alfred Philippe in the 1940s. Incorporating large cabochons on heavy vermeil sterling silver encrusted with rhinestones, they are opulent masterpieces of design. These 1940s vermeil silver examples should not be confused with Trifari's 1980s reissues in lighter-weight base metals, which command significantly lower prices.

Large crown pin designed by Alfred Philippe, of vermeil sterling silver with prong-set sapphire blue and ruby red cabochons, emerald green baguettes, and emerald green, ruby red, and clear rhinestones. *1940s. 1¾ in (4.5 cm) long* **$190–240 CRIS**

Fleur-de-lys finial crown pin of sterling silver set with round-cut clear crystal rhinestones. The design is of medieval inspiration and comprises stylized foliate and floral forms topped with a heraldic fleur-de-lys finial. *1940s. 2½ in (6.25 cm)* **$150–170 TR**

Crown pin of vermeil sterling silver with emerald green, ruby red, and clear rhinestones, and a ring of faux pearls. *1940s*
2⅛ in (5.5 cm) long **$275–300 TR**

1944 Coro company first uses "Vendome" mark on some of its high-end jewelry

1953 Full Vendome line is introduced as the successor to the Corocraft line, and Vendome begins to operate as a subsidiary company

1957 Together with Coro, Vendome is purchased by the Richton International Corporation of New York

1960s onward Helen Marion is appointed as Chief Designer and rejuvenates flagging sales

1979 Production ceases

Bangle and earrings of highly polished silver-plated metal castings with prong-set aquamarine and sapphire blue crystal rhinestones, and powder blue prong-set crystal cabochons. *Late 1950s* B: 8 in (20 cm) circ; E: 1½ in (4 cm) wide **$320–480 CRIS**

Vendome

Originally Coro's top-of-the-range line, and later a semi-autonomous company, Vendome combined fine-quality materials and excellent craftsmanship with elegant and often highly innovative designs.

HAUTE JEWELRY

Named after the Place de Vendôme, the center of the Parisian *haute* jewelry trade, Vendome first appeared in 1944 as a mark on charm bracelets and faux pearl jewelry produced by the Coro company (*see pp.68–71*). Conceived as a replacement brand for Coro's top-end Corocraft range, and aimed at a wealthy American clientele aspiring to post-war Parisian chic, the full Vendome line was eventually introduced in 1953—at which point Vendome was also established as a Coro company in its own right.

Vendome jewelry is characterized by the use of high-quality materials: silver- and gold-plated or gold-tone metals; crystal faceted beads and

rhinestones of Austrian and Czechoslovakian origin; clear and colored Lucite; lustrous faux pearls; and delicate enameling. Prior to the 1960s, motifs and imagery were fairly traditional—mostly floral, but sometimes geometric. Thereafter, following the appointment of Helen Marion as Chief Designer and until the company ceased trading in the late 1970s, more radical designs were introduced. Notable among these were some sumptuous reinterpretations of ethnic jewelry and a series of fine art collage pins (*see opposite*). Regardless of style, however, all Vendome pieces are now avidly sought-after by costume jewelry collectors.

Above: Floral motif earrings of gold-tone metal casting with clear and *aurora borealis* rhinestones and red faux stone centers. *1950s. 2 in (5 cm) wide* **$25–30 MILLB**

Vendome advertisement from *Harper's Bazaar*, November 1958, promoting a "Royal Empire" line parure, comprising an adjustable collar necklace, bracelet, pin, and pendant earrings.

Bouquet-of-flowers pin and earrings with rhinestone petals, emerald navette centers, and emerald and jade pendants. *1950s*
P: 3¼ in (8.25 cm) long

$180–225   **CRIS**

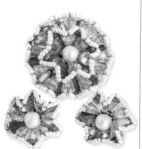

Floral motif pin and earrings with crystal rhinestones and faux pearls wired to filigree backs. *Mid-1950s*
P: 2 in (5 cm) wide; E: 1 in (2.5 cm) wide

$130–160   **CRIS**

Floral motif pin and earrings with blue and white Lucite petals, green Lucite leaves, and clear crystal rhinestone centers. *Mid-1950s*
P: 2 in (5 cm) wide; E: 1 in (2.5 cm) long

$190–210   **CRIS**

AFTER GEORGES BRAQUE

Among many stylistic innovations conceived by Vendome designer Helen Marion was a series of six collage-like pins inspired by the work of Cubist artist Georges Braque (1882–1963). Single pins surface from time to time, but complete sets are exceedingly rare and worth more than twice the sum of six individual pins.

"Georges Braque" pin of gold-plated metal with enameling, crystal rhinestones, a faux pearl, and a glass cabochon. *1960s*
2¼ in (5.75 cm) long **$320–400 CRIS**

Four-strand necklace of polychrome, clear, and *aurora borealis* crystal beads. *c.1960*
17 in (43 cm) long

$85–95   **ABIJ**

Link and hoop necklace of brushed gold-tone metal; half of the hoops with pale amethyst crystal rhinestone centers. *1970s*
18 in (45.75 cm) circ

$50–65   **ABIJ**

Extendable necklace with pin and earrings of gold-plated metal and polychrome crystal baguettes. *1965*
N: 16 in (40.5 cm) circ; P & E: 2 in (5 cm) long

$240–310   **WAIN**

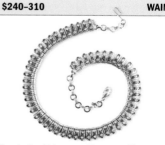

Brushed gold-tone necklace set with magenta, white, and blue crystal rhinestones. *1960s*
16 in (40.5 cm) circ

$75–85   **ABIJ**

Watch with casing and bracelet of antiqued silver-tone chain mail discs. *c.1970*
7 in (17.75 cm) circ.

$100–120   **MILLB**

1942 Albert Weiss sets up his own jewelry company in New York City

1943 onward Pieces are marked either "Weiss" in script or block letters, "Albert Weiss," or "AW Co." with the "W" shaped like a crown

1950s The company thrives and some of the work is contracted out to Hollycraft

1960s Albert Weiss retires and his son Michael takes over the business

1971 The company closes

Weiss

Admired by its contemporaries for its exquisite rhinestone work, Weiss has long been undervalued by collectors. Recent upward price trends indicate that this is now changing.

FROM A SMALL FISH IN A BIG POND

Albert Weiss honed his jewelry-making skills at the massive Coro company (*see pp.68–71*) during the 1930s, and left in 1942 to set up his own decidedly smaller Weiss enterprise in New York City. By the late 1940s, Weiss had begun to thrive, to the point where in the 1950s and 60s some of its output had to be contracted out for manufacture by Hollycraft (*see p.167*) in order to keep up with consumer demand. The majority of Weiss's designs are floral, foliate, fruit, or figural, although it also produced some geometric pieces, notably a range of Art Deco style necklaces, bracelets, pins, and earrings. Across all subject matters and styles, the materials used and the standards of craftsmanship were exceptionally high. Gold and silver metal or alloys were usually employed and sometimes enameled or, especially in the 1960s, japanned. However, it is Weiss's Austrian crystal rhinestones that are most impressive.

QUALITY CRYSTALS

Whether citrine, aquamarine, sapphire, emerald, jade, ruby, or topaz, all Weiss rhinestones display exceptional purity of color—a quality most clearly evident in the prong-set stones it used in its series of butterfly, insect, and single flower pins (sometimes with matching earrings) made in the late 1940s and 50s, and in its Christmas tree pins of the 1950s and 60s (*see pp.172–175*). Weiss's reproductions of fine German smoky quartz crystals, known as "black diamonds," were also highly convincing, and its enthusiastic use of Swarovski *aurora borealis* rhinestones from the mid-1950s onward was often innovative (*see below*).

Above: Fleur-de-lys earrings of antique gold-tone metal casting with green round- and navette-cut crystal rhinestones. *1950s. 1 in (2.5 cm) long* **$25–30 MILLB**

Flower pin of gold-plated metal with prong-set navette-cut colored Austrian crystal rhinestone petals and leaves, and a faceted sapphire blue crystal center. *c.1950 3 in (7.5 cm) long* **$160–185 JJ**

AURORA BOREALIS

Weiss was quick to exploit the decorative potential of the *aurora borealis* rhinestones that Swarovski developed with Dior in the mid-1950s. Named after the shimmering atmospheric phenomenon also known as the Northern Lights, the iridescent fantasy finishes of these stones were created with a polychrome metallic coating. In this pin (*right*), Weiss has made ingenious use of the stones, inverting them to display the more densely colored undersides.

Fantasy colored pin of gold-tone metal casting set with inverted, polychromatic, 3-D *aurora borealis* crystal rhinestones. *Early 1970s. 1¾ in (4.5 cm) wide* **$105–110 ABIJ**

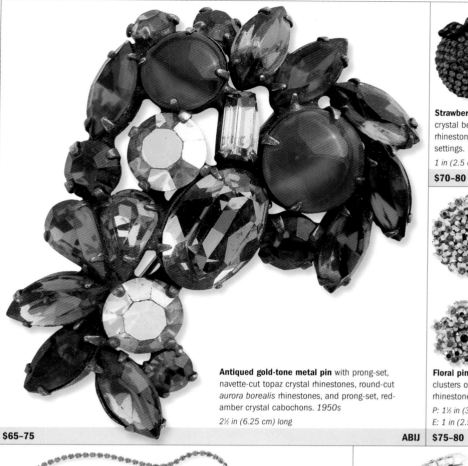

Antiqued gold-tone metal pin with prong-set, navette-cut topaz crystal rhinestones, round-cut *aurora borealis* rhinestones, and prong-set, red-amber crystal cabochons. *1950s*
2½ in (6.25 cm) long

$65–75 | | | **ABIJ**

Strawberry earrings with ruby crystal beads and emerald crystal rhinestones in japanned metal settings. *1940s*
1 in (2.5 cm) long

$70–80 | | **JJ**

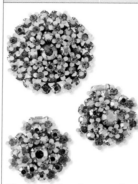

Floral pin and earrings set with clusters of yellow enameled and rhinestone flowerheads. *1950s*
P: 1½ in (3.75 cm) wide;
E: 1 in (2.5 cm) wide

$75–80 | | **JJ**

FIGURAL PINS

Of the figural pins produced by Weiss, the most coveted by collectors are its 1950s butterflies and insects. Glittering compositions of crystal rhinestones hand-wired with gilt metal, they are now commanding high prices. More affordable are some excellent novelty figurals, such as this jack-in-the-box pin, made in the 1940s.

Jack-in-the-box pin of gilt metal with enameling and rhinestones. *1940s*
2 in (5 cm) long **$95–105 JJ**

Necklace, bracelet, and earrings of solid and meshed gold-tone metal with pink and *aurora borealis* crystal rhinestones. *1960s*
N: 15 in (38 cm) circ; B: 7 in (17.75 cm) circ; E: 1 in (2.5 cm) long

$120–130 | | **JJ**

Silver-tone white metal necklace set with Austrian crystal rhinestones. *1940s*
17 in (43 cm) circ

$90–100 | | **JJ**

Flower pin with white enamel petals and green enamel leaves and stem. *c.1970*
3 in (7.5 cm) long

Cross pin of japanned base metal set with "black diamond" Austrian crystal beads. *1970s*
2½ in (6.25 cm) long

$45–50 | **MILLB**

Floral wreath pin and earrings in antiqued silver-tone metal with topaz, sapphire, and *aurora borealis* rhinestones. *1950s*
P: 3½ in (9 cm) wide; E: 1¾ in (4.5 cm) long

$65–75 | **ABIJ**

Floral motif pin and earrings with smoky quartz and *aurora borealis* crystal rhinestones in antiqued gold-tone metal settings. *1950s*
P: 2 in (5 cm) wide; E: 1¼ in (3.25 cm) long

$65–75 | **ABIJ**

$20–25 | **MILLB**

A–Z of designers and makers

A gallery of highly collectible costume jewelry

The costume jewelry designers and makers profiled over the following pages are drawn from both sides of the Atlantic. Some of them are relatively large companies that have produced a huge number of diverse pieces, while others are much smaller enterprises, specializing in handcrafted, limited-edition pieces. Some of the designers had already established a reputation by the start of the 20th century, while others are very much in the limelight now and have only recently risen to prominence. All of them, however, have their devotees, and collectively their work encompasses the extraordinary wealth of styles, materials, techniques, and prices available to contemporary costume jewelry collectors.

Accessocraft

Founded in the 1930s, Accessocraft produced tens of thousands of war relief pins in World War II, but then became known for its heavy, stylish jewelry and accessories. During the 1960s, its distinctive gothic designs and blended antique gold-tone or bronzed metals with unusual stones were particularly popular.

Many Accessocraft pieces have Renaissance, Victorian, or Art Nouveau touches.

Eagle and globe pin, the eagle casting of bright gold-tone metal; the globe of mottled red Lucite. *1940s*

2¾ in (7 cm) long

$45–50   **BB**

Bead necklace of pearlized brown plastic, clear Lucite with white inclusions, and clear rhinestone roundels. *c.1970*

16 in (40.5 cm) circ

$75–85   **ABIJ**

Alcozer

The Italian company Alcozer & J. was founded in Florence in 1994 by designer Giampiero Alcozer. The company specializes in antique-style costume jewelry and accessories. Every piece is handcrafted from hypoallergenic gold-tone metal set with seed pearls, rhinestones, and semi-precious stones.

Vase of flowers pin with semi-precious stones, cultured pearls, and clear and ruby rhinestones on a rose-gold-plated casting. *Late 1990s*

4¼ in (11 cm) long

$290–320   **CRIS**

Basket-of-flowers pin with semi-precious stones, cultured pearls, beads, and rhinestones on a rose-gold-plated casting. *Late 1990s*

3⅜ in (8.5 cm) wide

$240–285   **CRIS**

Angela Hale

London-based jewelry designer Angela Hale creates feminine, delicate jewelry with a glamorous retro look. Inspired by the Victorian and Art Deco periods, each piece is handcrafted from hypoallergenic bronze and set with faux pearls and sparkling Swarovski crystals in myriad rainbow colors.

Pendant earrings of antiqued gold-tone metal with faux pearls and large prong-set oval rhinestones. *1990s*

1⅛ in (3 cm) long

$50–65   **PC**

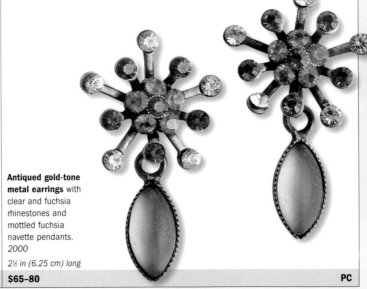

Antiqued gold-tone metal earrings with clear and fuchsia rhinestones and mottled fuchsia navette pendants. *2000*

2½ in (6.25 cm) long

$65–80   **PC**

Alice Caviness

Costume designer Alice Caviness began making jewelry just after World War II, and her company, based in Long Island, New York, continued production following her death in 1983. Pieces range from parures and demi-parures to earrings and single pins, including carved cameos, fruits, and animal figurals. All her pieces are characterized by the use of high-quality materials, notably crystal stones of unusual colors. Mostly marked "Alice Caviness," they are relatively scarce and increasingly sought-after by collectors.

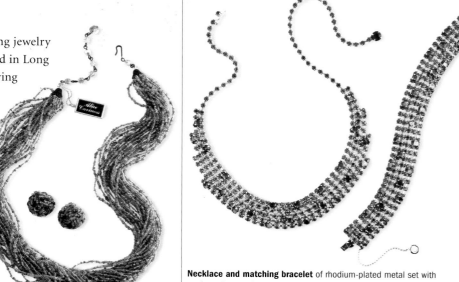

Interwoven multiple-strand necklace and matching earrings of polychrome beads and seed pearls. *1970s*
N: 25 in (63.5 cm) circ; E: 1 in (2.5 cm) wide

$125–150   ABIJ

Necklace and matching bracelet of rhodium-plated metal set with graduated rows of lavender, pink, and black rhinestones. *1960s*
N: 16½ in (42 cm) circ; B: 7 in (17.75 cm) circ

$400–425   ABIJ

Japanned metal necklace and matching bracelet with olivine and ruby glass cabochons and prong-set rhinestones. *1960s*
N: 16 in (40.5 cm) circ;
B: 7½ in (19 cm) circ

$350–375   ABIJ

Umbrella and turtle pin of white metal with prong-set ruby rhinestones, French jet teardrops, and a pink glass cabochon. *c.1980*
2¾ in (7 cm) long

$70–80   JJ

Umbrella and poodle pin of gilt base metal with prong-set pale and dark amber rhinestones and French jet teardrops. *c.1980*
2¾ in (7 cm) long

$80–90   JJ

Raspberry and raspberry leaf pin of textured gold-tone metal with pavé-set faux ruby cabochons for the berries. *1960s*
2¾ in (7 cm) long

$75–90   ABIJ

Andrew Logan

A contemporary British artist and sculptor of international repute, Andrew Logan creates vibrant jewelry from new and used glass. Each piece of jewelry is a miniature piece of sculpture, individually handmade from multicolored mirrored glass and semi-precious stones set in a light and durable resin. Favorite motifs include hearts, fauna, flora, planets, and gods.

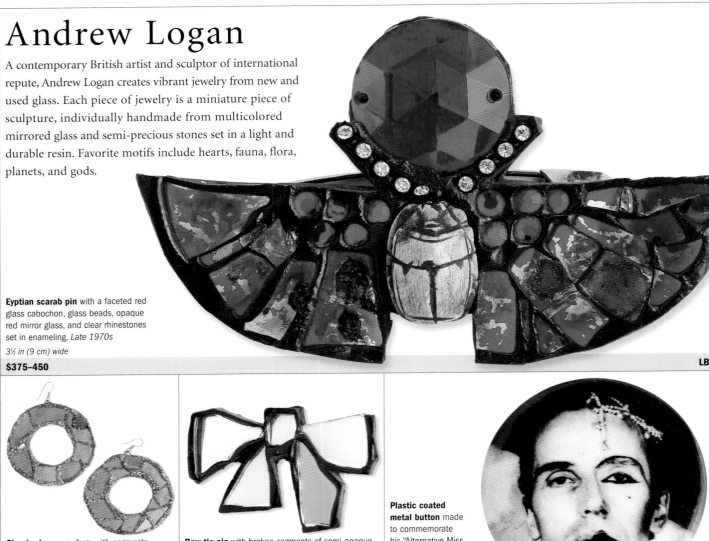

Eyptian scarab pin with a faceted red glass cabochon, glass beads, opaque red mirror glass, and clear rhinestones set in enameling. *Late 1970s*

3½ in (9 cm) wide

$375–450　　LB

Circular hoop earrings with segments of orange glass set in gold glittered metal castings. *Late 1990s*

2¾ in (7 cm) wide

$210–240　LB

Bow-tie pin with broken segments of semi-opaque, clear mirror glass set in a black resin casting. *Late 1970s*

2½ in (6.25 cm) wide

$145–180　LB

Plastic coated metal button made to commemorate his "Alternative Miss World Contest". *Late 1970s*

2¼ in (5.75 cm) wide

$NPA　LB

Argy-Rousseau

From 1921 to 1931, the glassworks Les Pâtes-de-verre d'Argy-Rousseau produced finely crafted glassware made from *pâte-de-verre* (poured glass), which was popular in the Art Nouveau and Art Deco periods. As well as highly collectible vases and bowls, Gabriel Argy-Rousseau created glowing pendants and pins depicting stylized fruit and flowers, butterflies, and figures drawn from mythology.

Art Nouveau belt buckle of stamped brass with bead molding edges and three blue stone cameos carved with crab motifs. *c.1905*

4¾ in (12 cm) wide

$320–400　　RITZ

Art

From the 1940s to the late 1960s, Art (also known as ModeArt) produced costume jewelry in a diverse range of styles, including replicas or reinterpretations of Renaissance, Victorian, and Art Deco pieces. While flower, fruit, and leaf motifs are most prevalent, figural imagery—especially animal subjects—was also employed. Characteristic materials and techniques include fine filigree metalwork, enameling, carved or molded polychrome plastics, and rhinestones—the latter often uniquely colored and pavé-set in eye-catching clusters. Usually marked and displaying middle to high-end standards of craftsmanship, Art jewelry is increasingly sought-after and prices have been rising accordingly.

Bouquet of flowers pin and earrings with pink, yellow, amber, and green Lucite petals, and clear rhinestone highlights, on gilt castings. *Mid-1950s*
P: 2 in (5 cm) long; E: ¾ in (2 cm) wide

$95–120   **CRIS**

Necklace, bracelet, and earrings demi-parure with antique gilt metal leaf motifs, ruby glass cabochons, and *aurora borealis* rhinestones. *Mid-1950s*
N: 15¼ in (39 cm) circ; B: 7 in (17 cm) circ; E: 1⅛ in (3 cm) long

$200–240   **CRIS**

Fruit pin and earrings with blue, green, and *aurora borealis* rhinestones on gunmetal castings. *Mid-1950s*
P: 1¾ in (4.5 cm) long; E: 1⅛ in (3 cm) long

$150–175   **CRIS**

Pear fruit pin of yellow and green enamel over a gold-plated casting. *Late 1950s*
1⅜ in (3.5 cm) long

$65–70   **CRIS**

Flower pin and earrings of silver and gilt metal; the surface of the leaves has an engraved "Florentine" finish. *1960s*
P: 2 in (5 cm) wide; E: 1 in (2.5 cm) wide

$45–55   **JJ**

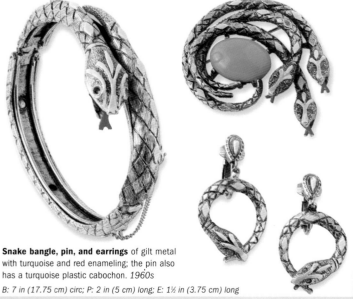

Snake bangle, pin, and earrings of gilt metal with turquoise and red enameling; the pin also has a turquoise plastic cabochon. *1960s*
B: 7 in (17.75 cm) circ; P: 2 in (5 cm) long; E: 1½ in (3.75 cm) long

$65–95   **JJ**

Atwood & Sawyer

Founded in England in 1956 by Horace Atwood (Sawyer was a silent partner), Atwood & Sawyer produced copies of 18th- and 19th-century precious jewelry, many pieces for the *Dallas* and *Dynasty* TV series, and glittering diamanté compositions for the Miss World competitions. In recent years, however, it is their exquisite Christmas jewelry *(see pp.172–175)* that has really proved popular with collectors.

Snowman pin with gold-plating, green and blue enameling, and ruby and pavé-set clear rhinestones. *Late 1990s*

1⅜ in (3.5 cm) long

$55–65 (plus $30 if with original box)   **CRIS**

Auguste Bonaz

Innovative French designer Auguste Bonaz worked from the Bonaz Studios in France during the 1920s and 30s. Much of his jewelry is made from Bakelite or Galalith and has the simple lines, strong geometric shapes, and bold contrasting colors typical of the Art Deco period. Bonaz's pieces are among the rarest and most valuable of all Bakelite jewelry.

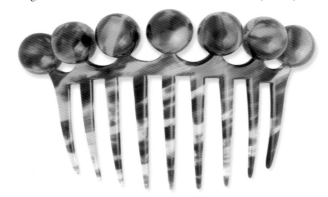

Crown tiara of faux tortoiseshell Galalith, a plastic similar to Bakelite and made from formaldehyde and a derivative of sour milk. *1900*

5½ in (14 cm) wide

$240–400   **LB**

Avon

The American company Avon was founded in 1886 as the California Perfume Company. In the late 1920s it introduced the Avon line of jewelry and subsequently changed its name to Avon Products, Inc. Avon has been very successful at introducing reasonably priced, good-quality jewelry to American homemakers. The jewelry is not particularly valuable, but is of interest to those who collect Avon memorabilia.

Paisley motif earrings of gold-tone metal casting with three shades of pink enameling. *1980s*

1½ in (3.75 cm) long

$15–20   **MILLB**

Apple pendant necklace of antiqued gold-tone metal with semi-opaque clear plastic pendant. *1970s*

N: 27 in (68.5 cm) circ;
Pd: 1½ in (3.75 cm) wide

$25–30   **MILLB**

As well as earrings in suitably festive colors, Avon also produced a number of Christmas tree pins.

Christmas earrings with faux pearls, ruby rhinestones, and green enameling on goldwashed metal castings. *1980s*

1½ in (3.75 cm) long

$25–30   **MILLB**

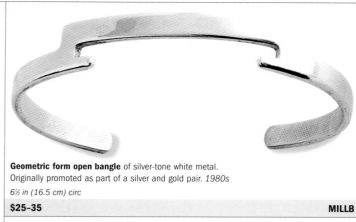

Geometric form open bangle of silver-tone white metal. Originally promoted as part of a silver and gold pair. *1980s*

6½ in (16.5 cm) circ

$25–35   **MILLB**

Knotted rope earrings made from molded faux white ivory plastic. *Late 1970s*

1⅛ in (3 cm) long

$15–20   **MILLB**

New Millennium clock pin of polished silver-tone metal casting with sapphire rhinestone star centers and a paper-under-glass clock face. *2000*

1¾ in (4.5 cm) long

$15–20   **MILLB**

Perfume basket pin (with hinged lid) of goldwashed metal casting with clear rhinestone highlights. *c.1980*

1½ in (3.75 cm) long

$25–35   **MILLB**

Perfume owl pin (with hinged head) of goldwashed metal casting with emerald green rhinestone eyes. *c.1980*

2 in (5 cm) long

$30–40   **MILLB**

Christmas present earrings of goldwashed metal casting with clear rhinestone highlights. *1990s*

½ in (1.25 cm) long

$20–25   **MILLB**

Goldwashed metal chain necklace and antiqued goldwashed pendant with faux white and pink pearls and a pink plastic cabochon. *Late 1970s*

N: 24 in (60 cm) circ;
Pd: 2 in (5 cm) long

$25–35   **MILLB**

B.S.K.

Little is known about B.S.K. other than that it was based in New York and was in business from about 1950 to the early 1970s. The letters stand for the first initials of the three owners' names, Benny Steinberg, Slovitt, and Kaslo. Some B.S.K. jewelry is interesting in design, but much of it is of average quality. It was produced initially as the demand for affordable jewelry boomed in the early 1950s. The line was reasonably priced and was sold through department stores such as Woolworths.

Bust of an Asian lady pin in gold-tone metal casting with faux pearl drop earrings. *1970s*
2 in (5 cm) long

$30–40   **JJ**

Asian man pin of gold-tone metal casting with faux jade sacks. *1970s*
1¼ in (3 cm) high

$30–40   **JJ**

Balenciaga

The famous Spanish couturier Cristóbal Balenciaga founded his *haute couture* line in 1919 and opened the House of Balenciaga in Paris in 1937. The simple lines of his costume jewelry were designed to complement the classical elegance of his clothes, and were often inspired by indigenous Spanish forms and motifs.

Couture choker with four interwoven strands of faceted black glass beads, and a gilt metal clasp with turquoise glass cabochons and clear rhinestones. *c.1960*
N: 14¾ in (38 cm) circ; Clasp: 1½ in (3.75 cm) wide

$2,400–2,600   **SUM**

Barry Parman

Originally a theater set designer, London-based Barry Parman turned his creative talents to jewelry design for just a few years prior to his death in the late 1980s. The distinctive and superbly modeled pieces he originally designed for leading costume jewelry dealers such as Linda Bee are rare, and are now hot collectibles.

1920s "flapper" pin in shades of gray and black plastic with enameled makeup and clear rhinestone highlights. *c.1975*
3½ in (9 cm) long

$160–240   **LB**

Beaujewels

Beaujewels was run by Bowman & Foster from the late 1940s to the early 1970s. Flowers and leaves are recurring motifs, often portrayed in rich colors and unexpected color combinations. Although reasonably priced, the jewelry incorporated fruit salad stones that were popular in the more expensive jewelry of the day.

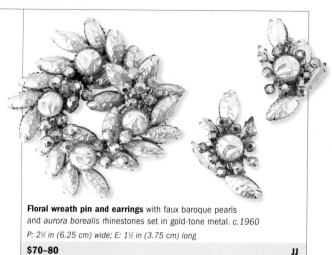

Floral wreath pin and earrings with faux baroque pearls and *aurora borealis* rhinestones set in gold-tone metal. *c.1960*
P: 2½ in (6.25 cm) wide; E: 1½ in (3.75 cm) long

$70–80 JJ

Twin leaf pin of bold naturalistic design in brushed matte sterling silver and signed "Beau Sterling." *1950s*
2 in (5 cm) long

$45–55 BBG

Floral pin and earrings with pink *aurora borealis* and fuchsia pink rhinestones set in gold-tone metal. *1940s*
P: 2 in (5 cm) long;
E: 1⅛ in (3 cm) long

$70–80 JJ

Bettina von Walhof

Contemporary designer Bettina von Walhof, based in California, is known for her imaginative jewelry. Her whimsical figural pins feature motifs such as lobsters, parrots, and whales, as well as flowers. Each piece is unique, handcrafted from vintage glass beads, poured glass leaves and flowers, and sparkling Swarovski crystals.

Flowers, animals, and birds are recurring motifs in Bettina von Walhof's jewelry designs, all crafted with minute attention to detail and a sense of fun.

Floral pin with hand-wired yellow, green, and clear poured glass leaves and flowers, and jonquil crystal rhinestones set above a carved red and black medallion. *c.1980*
3⅜ in (8.5 cm) long

$720–880 SUM

Billy Boy

An American company with workshops and a small team of assistants in Paris, Billy Boy has produced jewelry in diverse and interesting styles. These include a range of strongly colored resin pieces inspired by Schiaparelli's work, and a number of "barbaric" tribal designs. Other examples recall the geometric forms of ancient amulets, necklaces, and belts executed in rough-textured metals with square and pyramid-form glass beads.

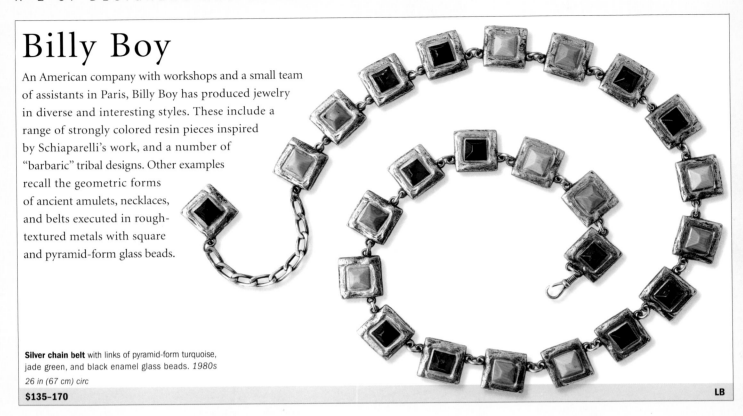

Silver chain belt with links of pyramid-form turquoise, jade green, and black enamel glass beads. *1980s*
26 in (67 cm) circ

$135–170 LB

Blackinton

Founded in 1862, in North Attleboro, Massachusetts, R. Blackinton & Co. produced silver and gold jewelry, and accessories such as compacts and cigarette cases. Although not well known, the company produced many fine pieces at the end of the 19th century, often influenced by Art Nouveau designs.

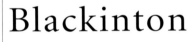

Goldwashed sterling silver bangle with graduated bead molding and turquoise glass cabochons. *c.1895*
3 in (7.5 cm) wide

$240–260 CGPC

Scrolling leaf motif bangle of goldwashed sterling silver with amethyst glass cabochons. *c.1895*
3 in (7.5 cm) wide

$340–360 CGPC

Bogoff

Throughout the 1950s and 60s, the Bogoff Spear Novelty Company, based in Chicago, made elegant and interesting costume jewelry that imitated high-cost designer jewelry. Crafted from good-quality materials, the pieces usually had rhodium backings and hand-set stones.

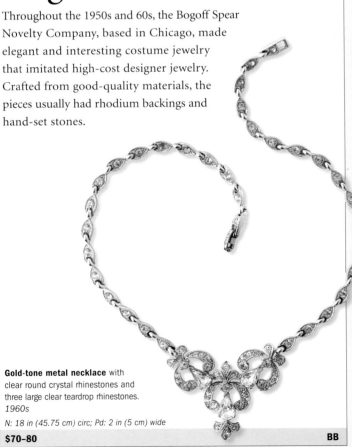

Gold-tone metal necklace with clear round crystal rhinestones and three large clear teardrop rhinestones. *1960s*
N: 18 in (45.75 cm) circ; Pd: 2 in (5 cm) wide

$70–80 BB

Butler & Wilson

After selling antique jewelry from London market stalls, Nicky Butler and Simon Wilson opened a shop in the early 1970s and started marketing their own jewelry based on reproductions of period styles. By the late 1980s, they were selling their jewelry all around the world. Butler and Wilson's 1980s pieces are glitzy and diamanté-studded, harking back to the Art Deco period. Their lizard and spider pins became classics, and their early 1970s designs in particular are now highly collectible.

Dancing couple pin with prong-set clear paste and black and clear rhinestones.
1980s

4¾ in (12 cm) long

$65–80   **PC**

Glittering clusters of pavé-set rhinestones feature in many Butler & Wilson designs from the 1980s and 90s.

Oriental dragon pin with blue and green metallic enameling, pavé-set clear crystal rhinestones, and ruby red cabochon eyes set in a gold-plated casting.
Mid-1990s

4¼ in (11 cm) long

$150–190   **CRIS**

Three-strand faux pearl necklace, champagne-colored with gilt metal clasp.
1980s

16½ in (42 cm) circ

$50–65   **PC**

Plaid butterfly pin with red, blue, and green enamel on a gold-plated casting.
Late 1980s

2½ in (6.25 cm) wide

$55–65   **CRIS**

Charm bracelet of antiqued gold-tone metal with pendant crowns, fleur-de-lys motifs, and faux pearl drops. *1980s*

7 in (18 cm) circ

$65–80   **PC**

Austrian Fruits

Made in Austria almost exclusively for export to the United States, these exquisite glass fruit pins have become highly collectible. All marked "Austria," the pins come in a wide variety of fruits, as well as a wonderful range of rich and glowing colors.

OLD WORLD APPEAL IN A TIME OF CHANGE
Austrian fruit pins were created during the 1940s and 50s and represent the more traditional side of costume jewelry during the postwar period. The pins were made at different factories in Austria, but some earrings are marked "Germany." None of the fruit is marked with the name of a designer or manufacturer.

The pins are mostly single, although some have matching earrings. Strawberries, cherries, pears, and bunches of grapes are the most common motifs. Reminiscent of delicate Christmas tree decorations, the fruit pins are made of molded or carved glass, usually transparent or translucent, but sometimes opaque or frosted. The vibrant colors range from rich scarlets and purples to gold, amber, and even pure white. The glowing appearance of the fruit is enhanced by the fact that the glass is backed with gold or silver foil, making it both richer in color and more light-reflective.

The leaves and stems of the fruit are made from silver, gilt, or japanned metal. The navette-cut leaves are often enameled or have crystal highlights, adding to the lasting appeal of these desirable pieces.

Strawberries pin of red glass with stamped silver alloy leaves and stalks. *1950s 2½ in (6.5 cm) long* **$135–160 CRIS**

Strawberries pin and earrings of red glass with green glass and gilt leaves, and gilt metal stalks. *1940s. P: 2¾ in (7 cm) long; E: 1¼ in (3.25 cm) long* **$80–120 ROX**

Pears pin of blue and yellow glass with japanned metal stalks, and a crystal rhinestone. *1950s. 2¾ in (7 cm) long* **$70–80 BY**

Bunches-of-grapes pin of clear and yellow glass, metal stalks, and a crystal rhinestone. *1950s. 2¼ in (5.75 cm) long* **$60–70 BY**

Cherries pin with black and green glass, japanned metal, and a crystal rhinestone. *1950s. 2 in (5 cm) long* **$60–70 BY**

Pear pin of opaque green glass, enameled leaves, gilt metal stalks, and crystal rhinestones. *1950s. 2¼ in (5.75 cm) long* **$60–70 BY**

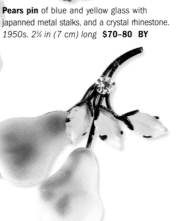

Pears pin of clear and yellow glass, japanned metal stalks, and a crystal rhinestone. *1950s. 2½ in (6.5 cm) long* **$70–80 BY**

Cherries pin of red and yellow glass, japanned metal, and a red crystal rhinestone. *1950s. 2¼ in (5.75 cm) long* **$110–130 CRIS**

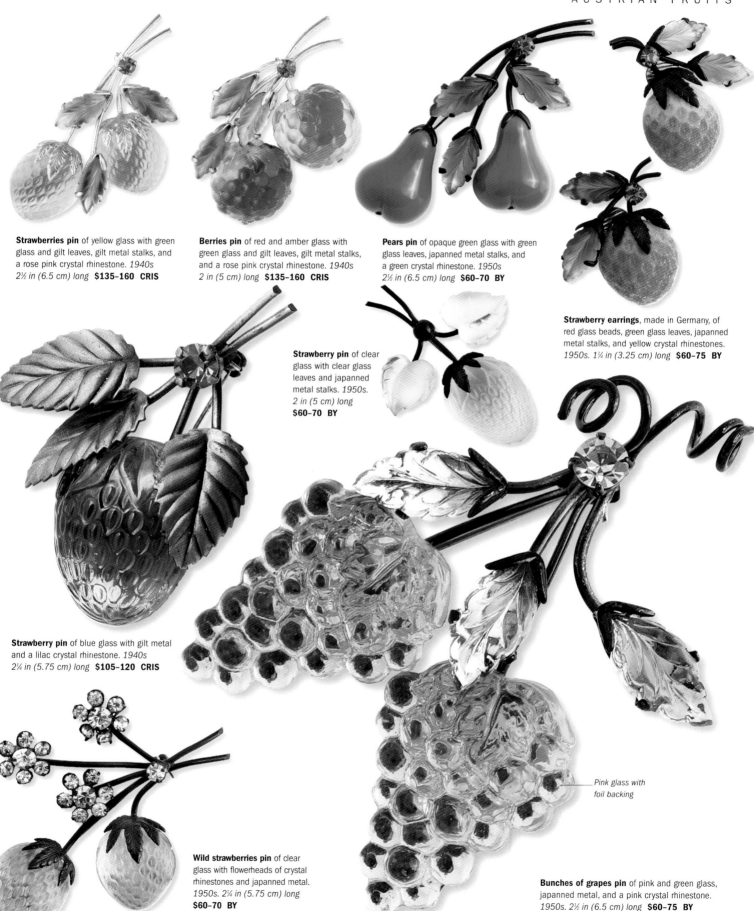

Strawberries pin of yellow glass with green glass and gilt leaves, gilt metal stalks, and a rose pink crystal rhinestone. *1940s 2½ in (6.5 cm) long* **$135–160 CRIS**

Berries pin of red and amber glass with green glass and gilt leaves, gilt metal stalks, and a rose pink crystal rhinestone. *1940s 2 in (5 cm) long* **$135–160 CRIS**

Pears pin of opaque green glass with green glass leaves, japanned metal stalks, and a green crystal rhinestone. *1950s 2½ in (6.5 cm) long* **$60–70 BY**

Strawberry earrings, made in Germany, of red glass beads, green glass leaves, japanned metal stalks, and yellow crystal rhinestones. *1950s. 1¼ in (3.25 cm) long* **$60–75 BY**

Strawberry pin of clear glass with clear glass leaves and japanned metal stalks. *1950s. 2 in (5 cm) long* **$60–70 BY**

Strawberry pin of blue glass with gilt metal and a lilac crystal rhinestone. *1940s 2¼ in (5.75 cm) long* **$105–120 CRIS**

Pink glass with foil backing

Wild strawberries pin of clear glass with flowerheads of crystal rhinestones and japanned metal. *1950s. 2¼ in (5.75 cm) long* **$60–70 BY**

Bunches of grapes pin of pink and green glass, japanned metal, and a pink crystal rhinestone. *1950s. 2½ in (6.5 cm) long* **$60–75 BY**

Carolee

The American company Carolee was founded in 1972 and is still in business today, creating classic, high-quality jewelry. Most of the pieces are made of sterling silver, sometimes gold-plated with faux or cultured pearls and rhinestones. A popular 1980s line called the "Duchess of Windsor" is considered highly collectible.

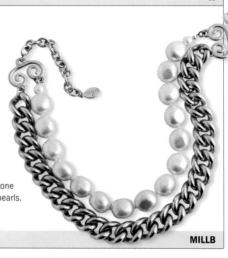

Crystal bracelet with round-cut clear crystal rhinestones set in white metal castings. *c.1980*

7 in (17.75 cm) circ

$165–170   JJ

Pearls, both faux and cultured, play a key role in Carolee's jewelry collections.

Star pin in gold-plated base metal with embossed studs. *1950s*

3 in (7.75 cm) wide

$75–100   MILLB

Chain necklace of antiqued gold-tone metal and a single strand of faux pearls. *c.1990*

16 in (40.5 cm) circ

$25–35   MILLB

Castlecliff

Founded in New York by Clifford Furst in 1945, Castlecliff created bold but intricate jewelry made from good-quality materials. Its designs show an imaginative use of stones, and styles range from Art Deco to Gothic and Native American. Large signed pieces that have stood the test of time are the most sought-after.

Floral motif earrings set with bands and rings of ruby red crystal rhinestones. *Late 1950s.*

1 in (2.5 cm) wide

$100–150   LB

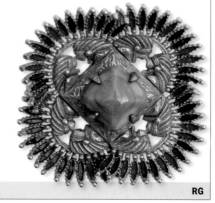

Native American-style pin of gold-plated metal with green enameling and a faux green agate stone. *1960s*

2¾ in (7 cm) wide

$65–80   RG

Pendant necklace and earrings with gold-plated Mesoamerican heads and motifs, and polychrome semi-precious stone beads and drops. *Late 1940s*

Pd: 4¾ in (12 cm) drop; E: 2 in (5 cm) long

$300–375   RITZ

Ciner

The Ciner Manufacturing Company was founded in 1892 by Emanuel Ciner to produce fine jewelry. Since 1931, the company has manufactured classic, upmarket costume jewelry. Ciner pieces look like fine jewelry, but are set with rhinestones rather than jewels. Swarovski crystals are often used, hand-set in gold-tone metalwork. Early pieces are often unmarked, but most pieces after 1945 were marked "Ciner."

Ciner jewelry uses small, delicate stones, in a glittering array of rainbow colors.

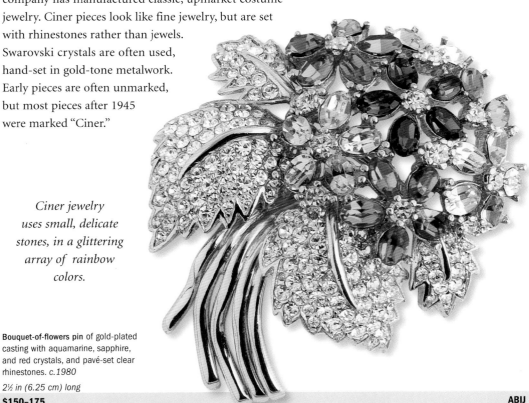

Flower pin of gold-plated casting with green and pavé-set clear Swarovski crystal rhinestones. *Mid-1960s*

2¾ in (7 cm) long

$130–140   **WAIN**

White metal earrings with navette-cut clear crystal rhinestones and Japanese luminescent faux pearl drops. *1970s*

2½ in (6.25 cm) long

$160–170   **JJ**

Bouquet-of-flowers pin of gold-plated casting with aquamarine, sapphire, and red crystals, and pavé-set clear rhinestones. *c.1980*

2½ in (6.25 cm) long

$150–175   **ABIJ**

Cow and dog pin of gold-plated castings set with small turquoise glass cabochons and larger ruby glass cabochons. *1950s*

1⅛ in (3 cm) long

$225–255 for the pair   **CRIS**

Starburst motif bracelet of vermeil and rose vermeil sterling silver set with clear and jonquil crystal rhinestones: *1940s*

7 in (18 cm) circ

$320–330   **CBU**

Woven gold-plated metal bracelet with interwoven bands of clear crystal rhinestones. *1980s*

8 in (20.25 cm) circ

$120–130   **JJ**

Floral motif bracelet of gold-plated castings set with turquoise, aquamarine, ruby, emerald, and black crystal cabochons. *1950s*

7½ in (19 cm) circ

$300–350   **CRIS**

Cristobal

Founded in London in 1986, Cristobal is an internationally renowned retailer of 20th-century costume jewelry. In addition, in the late 1990s, owners Steven Miners and Yai Thammachote launched their own limited-edition designs, currently divided into four series: the "Butterfly Collection," the "Secret Garden Collection," the "London Collection" (comprising necklaces and earrings), and the "X-mas Collection" (including some Christmas Tree pins shown on pp.172–175). Increasingly sought after by collectors around the world, these distinctive pieces use only the highest-quality Austrian crystals (mostly dating from the 1940s and 50s) hand-set in gorgeous, eye-catching color combinations.

Bouquet of flowers pin from the "Secret Garden Collection" of polychrome French poured glass and clear rhinestones set in a brass wire frame. *Late 1990s*

3½ in (9 cm) long

$480–560   **CRIS**

Bib necklace and pendant earrings from the "London Collection" with citrine, topaz, and *aurora borealis* rhinestones in gunmetal settings. *Late 1990s*

N: 18 in (45.5 cm) circ; Bib: 3 in (7.5 cm) drop; E: 3 in (7.5 cm) drop

$160–240   **CRIS**

Apple pin from the "Secret Garden Collection," with 1950s ruby, fuchsia, aquamarine, amethyst, and emerald rhinestones. *Late 1990s*

3¾ in (9.5 cm) long

$145–190   **CRIS**

Rhinestone necklace of 1950s amber and topaz rhinestones in a ruthenium-plated casting. *Late 1990s*

15⅜ in (39 cm) circ

$160–240   **CRIS**

Butterfly pin from the "Butterfly Collection," ruthenium-plated with navette-cut blue and clear rhinestones. *Late 1990s*

3¾ in (9.5 cm) long

$135–160   **CRIS**

Butterfly pin from the "Butterfly Collection," ruthenium-plated with sapphire, lime green, and *aurora borealis* rhinestones. *Late 1990s*

3 in (7.5 cm) long

$80–110   **CRIS**

Sunflower pin from the "Secret Garden Collection," ruthenium-plated and set with Swarovski jet, emerald, peridot, and rainbow rhinestones. *Late 1990s*

4¾ in (12 cm) long

$80–110   **CRIS**

Czech Jewelry

From the 1890s to the late 1930s, the jewelry-makers of Gablonz, Czechoslovakia produced a distinctive and romantic style of costume jewelry. Glass stones in rich purples and delicate pastels were set into filigree backings. Pins were usually set with multicolored pastes. Necklaces and bracelets are rarer, and the more complex the piece, the more collectible it is. Czech jewelry is usually unsigned, but is sometimes marked "Czech" or "Czechoslovakia."

Floral pin and earrings with crystal rhinestones prong-set in a gilt metal casting. *c.1930*

P: 1 in (2.5 cm) long; E: ¾ in (2 cm) long

$90–130   **MILLB**

Multiple-pendant necklace of gilt metal with sapphire blue rhinestones and a large, dark amethyst cabochon. *Early 1900s*

N: 21 in (57 cm) circ; Pd: 4½ in (11.5 cm) long

$125–150   **JJ**

Pale pink necklace with a chain of silvered metal and pink beads, and a pendant with a glass cabochon and rhinestones. *1920s*

N: 20 in (51 cm) circ; Pd: 3 in (7.5 cm) long

$85–125   **MILLB**

Stylized floral motif pin with ruby, jade, amethyst, and sapphire crystal rhinestones of various cuts set in a filigree gilt metal backing. *1940s*

2⅛ in (6.25 cm) wide

$35–65   **LB**

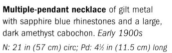

Rectangular pin with a filigree gilt metal backing set with numerous crystal rhinestones of various cuts and gemstone colors. *Early 1900s*

2½ in (6.25 cm) wide

$75–95   **JJ**

Long glass bead necklaces were popular with the "flappers" of the 1920s.

Scrolled cartouche triple-pendant pin of gilt metal with large prong-set Burmese-ruby colored oval cabochons. *1930s*

3½ in (9 cm) wide

$200–220   **JJ**

Heart-shaped pin with filigree blackened steel backing and dark and light sapphire blue crystal rhinestones. *1930s*

2½ in (6.25 cm) wide

$35–65   **LB**

Four-pendant necklace of gilt metal with round-, oval-, and square-cut red glass beads and stones. *c.1930*

N: 16½ in (42 cm) circ

$240–320   **ECLEC**

DRGM

Although also applied to numerous other items ranging from clocks and corkscrews to cameras and toys, jewelry stamped with the German patent mark DRGM— *Deutsches Reichs Gebrauchsmuster*—is a collecting field in its own right. Used from about 1891 until the early 1950s by various, and often now anonymous, German jewelry makers, the DRGM mark is commonly associated with pieces incorporating clear crystal rhinestones set in zinc alloys, which are often rhodium-plated. The majority of pieces are of geometric Art Deco design, although earlier Art Nouveau forms can also be found.

Most German DRGM jewelry displays the streamlined geometric forms of the Art Deco movement and the Machine Age.

Rhodium-plated chain and bib necklace
set with clear crystal rhinestones and a
central cluster of rhinestones configured
in a floral motif. *c.1930*
N: 14½ in (37 cm) circ;
Bib: 1¾ in (4.5 cm) wide

$400–465   **LB**

"Woven" alloy link bracelet with
highly polished rhodium-plated clasp.
c.1930
7½ in (19 cm) circ

$280–400   **LB**

Art Deco bracelet with safety chain in rhodium-plated
alloy set with clear crystal rhinestones. *1920s*
7 in (18 cm) circ

$95–160   **MARA**

Art Deco geometric-form bracelet in rhodium-plated alloy
set with clear crystal rhinestones. *1920s*
7 in (18 cm) circ

$95–160   **MARA**

Danecraft

In 1939, Danecraft was founded by Victor Primavera in Providence, Rhode Island. The company is now known as the Felch-Wehr Company, but it continues to manufacture silver and vermeil jewelry, which it markets under the name of Danecraft to the better department stores. Danecraft specializes in quality sterling silver. Reminiscent of Scandinavian jewelry design, its pieces have a handcrafted look.

Sterling silver bracelet with die-stamped seashell motifs and bands of pink enameling. *1950s*

7¾ in (20 cm) circ

$35–45   **BBG**

Umbrella pin of white metal with selected gilding, iridescent blue enameling, and emerald green rhinestones. *1980s*

1¾ in (4.5 cm) long

$45–50   **JJ**

Sterling silver bracelet with vermeil sterling silver links and medallions, the latter with large faceted purple pastes. *1940s*

7 in (17.75 cm) circ

$120–130   **JJ**

David-Andersen

Goldsmith David Andersen founded his company in Christiana (now called Oslo), Norway, in 1876, and it is still trading today. The company produces beautifully designed silver jewelry decorated with fine enamelwork and has commissioned work from many talented designers. Marks on the jewelry include "David-Andersen" and "D-A."

Seahorse pin of vermeil sterling silver casting with blue and turquoise enameling. *1940s*

2 in (5 cm) high

$170–180   **MAC**

De Nicola

Founded by Jerry De Nicola in 1957, De Nicola produced beautifully crafted, fine-quality costume jewelry during the late 1950s and early 60s. It then became part of the Capri Jewelry Company, before ceasing operations altogether in 1973. Signed De Nicola pieces are now rare and are therefore highly collectible.

Floral pin with six gilt metal flowers with faux turquoise cabochon centers encircled by tiny clear rhinestone highlights. *1950s*

2 in (5 cm) wide

$100–110   **MG**

DeRosa

Founded by Ralph DeRosa in New York in about 1935, DeRosa was one of the first manufacturers of good-quality costume jewelry to use local craftsmanship. Its pieces are striking in design, featuring richly colored stones with unusual cuts, and high-quality enamelwork. The floral pieces are especially good, particularly those in the retro style of Hollywood precious jeweler Paul Flato. Unfortunately, many DeRosa pieces are not marked. The signed pieces, however, are very collectible and command high prices.

Vermeil sterling silver pin with prong-set cranberry glass cabochons encircling clear crystal rhinestones and a dark blue glass cabochon center. *1940s*

2¼ in (5.75 cm) wide

$140–160　　　　MG

Bowl of flowers pin with vermeil sterling silver bowl and leaves, and red enameled roses. *1940s*

2 in (5 cm) long

$340–360　　　　ROX

Vermeil sterling silver bracelet with three black enameled roundels set with clear crystal rhinestones. *1940s*

7 in (17.75 cm) circ

$240–290　　　　RG

DeRosa's crystals display exceptional depth and purity of color.

Floral fur clip of vermeil sterling silver with ruby red crystals, rose montées, and clear crystal rhinestones. *1940s*

3 in (7.5 cm) long

$320–400　　　　RG

Gold-plated bangle and earrings with black enameling and pavé-set clear crystal rhinestones. *1950s*

B: 8 in (20.25 cm) circ; E: 1 in (2.5 cm) long

$120–130　　　　MG

Sterling silver pin with two faux sapphire cabochons, and clear and jonquil crystal rhinestones. *1940s*

2 in (5 cm) wide

$130–175　　　　RG

Dinny Hall

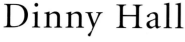

One of Great Britain's leading jewelry designers, Dinny Hall opened her first boutique in London in 1992. Her elegant, modern designs feature colorful stones in pared-down settings that reflect simple, natural forms, such as leaves and starfish. Each piece is handcrafted using fine materials and following traditional techniques.

Dinny Hall's impressive list of celebrity clients includes Madonna, Uma Thurman, Kristin Scott-Thomas, and Liz Hurley.

Gold-plated silver earrings in the form of elongated, stylized leaf motifs. *2001*

1⅜ in (3.5 cm) long

$130–160   **PC**

Large circular hoop earrings in silver (also produced in gold-plated silver). *2001*

1⅜ in (3.5 cm) long

$95–110   **PC**

Mauve icicle earrings with handcrafted, antiqued silver in Classical scrolling forms with three icicle-form pendants of mauvish-blue resin. *2002*

2½ in (6.5 cm) long

$95–130   **PC**

Pendant earrings with gold fishhooks and pendant caps with semi-translucent white resin drops. *Late 1990s*

1½ in (4 cm) long

$80–95   **PC**

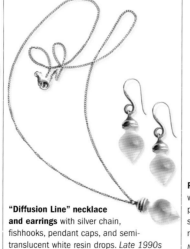

"Diffusion Line" necklace and earrings with silver chain, fishhooks, pendant caps, and semi-translucent white resin drops. *Late 1990s*

N: 18 in (46 cm) circ; E: 1½ in (4 cm) long

$145–160   **PC**

Pendant necklace with silver chain and pendant cap with semi-translucent blue resin drop. *1992*

N: 18 in (46 cm) circ; Pd: 1⅛ in (3 cm) long

$130–145   **PC**

"Diffusion Line" necklace and earrings with gold chain, fish hooks, and scrolling hoops with baroque pearl drops. *Mid-1990s*

N: 15¾ in (40 cm) circ; E: 1⅛ in (3 cm) long

$145–175   **PC**

Eisenberg

American clothing company Eisenberg Original was founded in 1914 and, in 1930, began accessorizing its dresses with its own pins. These pins soon proved so popular that they were sold separately—and are still produced to this day. Incorporating fine materials such as Swarovski rhinestones, Eisenberg pieces are large and display a boldness and clarity of design. The early 1940s figurals are now particularly sought-after. Pieces from 1930 to 1945 are marked "Eisenberg Original," and thereafter, marked "Eisenberg Ice."

Eisenberg Original Russian dancer pin in vermeil sterling silver with red enamel and prong-set Swarovski crystal rhinestones. *Early 1940s*

3½ in (9 cm) long

$1,300–1,400   **CRIS**

Eisenberg Original stylized floral pin of rhodium-plated metal with sapphire, turquoise, and clear Swarovski crystal rhinestones. *Early 1940s*

3 in (7.5 cm) wide

$250–300   **ABIJ**

Eisenberg Original pin of sterling silver set with clear Swarovski crystal rhinestones and champagne and gray faux pearls. *1930s*

3 in (7.5 cm) long

$750–850   **TR**

Eisenberg Original bow-tie pin of rhodium-plated metal set with unfoiled Swarovski clear crystal rhinestones. *Early 1940s*

3½ in (9 cm) wide

$250–300   **ABIJ**

Eisenberg Original flower pin of gilt metal with emerald poured glass, an Austrian crystal cabochon, and four ruby crystal rhinestones *c.1940*

4 in (10 cm) wide

$1,000–1,200   **SUM**

Eisenberg Original pin of rhodium-plated metal with Swarovski crystal rhinestones, a round faux pearl, and nine faux pearl drops. *Late 1930s*

3 in (7.5 cm) long

$175–225   **ABIJ**

Eisenberg Original fur clip with tiered scrolls of sterling silver and prong- and bezel-set Swarovski crystal rhinestones. *Early 1940s*

2¼ in (5.75 cm) long

$250–300   **ABIJ**

Eisenberg Original fur clip of rhodium-plated metal with prong- and bezel-set Swarovski emerald and clear crystal rhinestones. *1940s*

3 in (7.5 cm) long

$320–400   **ABIJ**

Fischel and Nessler

Founded in New York in the late 19th century, Fischel and Nessler produced costume jewelry until it ceased trading in 1937. It is best known for its Art Deco style necklaces and earrings made in the late 1920s and 30s. Marked with a fish motif with an "L" at its nose, these elegant and highly desirable pieces are almost invariably made in silver and set with high-quality Austrian crystal rhinestones, beads, or cabochons.

Sterling silver necklace with carved tubular and round emerald molded glass beads, and a carved pendant of jade green glass. *1930s*

Pd: 2½ in (6.5 cm) wide

$240–320   RG

Necklace and pendant earrings of sterling silver with round- and baguette-cut clear crystal rhinestones, and prong-set cranberry glass beads. *1920s*

N: 18 in (45.75 cm) circ; E: 2¾ in (7 cm) long

$560–720   RG

Florenza

Daniel Kosoff set up Florenza in the late 1940s in New York, where it continued in business until 1981. Along with costume jewelry, Florenza also made enameled and jeweled boxes and picture frames, often for other companies. Many pieces reflect Renaissance and Victorian styles, and typical components include antiqued gold-tone metal, enameling, carved cameos, and frosted and *aurora borealis* rhinestones. Most pieces are marked "Florenza."

Intricate filigree work features strongly in Florenza jewelry, and is often combined with colored rhinestones.

Shield-shaped pin of scrolled gold-tone metal with green enameling, clear and emerald rhinestones, a ring of faux pearls, and a faux pearl drop, with gold-tone metal chains. *Late 1970s*

3½ in (9 cm) long

$80–90   JJ

Gold-tone metal bracelet with floral motif clusters of faux pearls and rhinestones, and a central white-on-pink carved cameo. *c.1970*

6½ in (16.5 cm) circ

$120–130   JJ

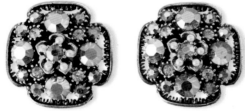

Clover motif earrings of antiqued gold-tone metal with jade green beads, faux pearls, and round-cut *aurora borealis* rhinestones. *1960s*

1 in (2.5 cm) wide

$40–50   JJ

Floral bow pin of antiqued silver-tone metal set with rows of small turquoise glass cabochons. *1950s*

2½ in (6.5 cm) long

$50–60   ABIJ

Bakelite

Fashionable in the 1920s and 30s, Bakelite jewelry was seemingly "old hat" by the end of World War II. The successful sale of Andy Warhol's Bakelite jewelry collection in 1988 at Sotheby's in New York proved otherwise.

A THOUSAND USES

Preceded by 19th-century celluloid and Galalith, and supplanted by mid-20th-century innovations such as Lucite, Bakelite was neither the first nor the last "plastic" to be used in costume jewelry. Its popularity, however, can be gauged by the fact that it is frequently employed as a catch-all term for early plastic jewelry. For example, the open bangle opposite would often be labeled Bakelite, but is actually made from a more translucent Lucite.

Patented in 1907 by Dr. Leo Baekeland, Bakelite was used initially as an electrical insulator but, tagged "the material of 1,000 uses," it was soon utilized for numerous useful and decorative wares—notably radio and clock casings, and kitchenalia. Enthusiastically adopted by the costume jewelry industry from the 1920s to the 1940s, it was exploited for its attractive coloring and the fact that it could be carved on a lathe into diverse shapes. Geometric Art Deco forms dominated the late 1920s and early 30s, while figural subjects later became more prevalent. Typical colors, often embellished with rhinestones or chromed steel, include black, white, and shades of red, brown, and yellow, two or more of which were often combined in the same piece.

Egyptian-style motif pin in iridescent pink, red, and taupe with a small, central mauve cabochon. *Early 1930s. 3 in (8 cm) long* **$80–110 ABAA**

Red Bakelite bead

Art Deco belt buckle of mirror-image stylized leaves in black and amber-red. *1930s 3½ in (9 cm) wide* **$65–80 ABAA**

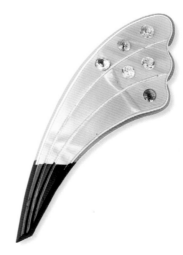

Stylized feather pin with gold edging, incised linear decoration, and clear rhinestones. *1930s. 2¾ in (7 cm) long* **$80–110 ABAA**

Carved Egyptian Revival pendant necklace with red beads and black tassel. *Late 1920s Pd: 6⅝ in (17 cm) long* **$350–400 RBRG**

Brown scrolling pin of geometric form encrusted with clear rhinestones. *c.1930 2⅜ in (6 cm) long* **$30–50 ABAA**

Egyptian Revival camel pin typical of the animal figurals popular in the 1920s and 30s. *c.1930. 1½ in (4 cm) high* **$40–55 ABAA**

Brown swinging monkey pin with baby monkey on the branch above. *1930s 2¾ in (7 cm) long* **$40–55 ABAA**

Art Deco stylized twin-leaf pin in blue with gray linear incisions. *1930s 2¾ in (7 cm) long* **$40–55 ABAA**

Extremely rare head pin of "apple juice" color with multicolor headdress. *c.1940. 2¾ in (7 cm) long* **$2,000–3,000 ROX**

Victorian-style red hand pin with lace cuff of brass and brass wire. *c.1930 2 in (5 cm) long* **$40–55 ABAA**

Dice cufflinks of "apple juice" and white Bakelite. *1940s. ¾ in (2 cm) wide* **$40–55 PC**

Green and gold lapel pin or hat pin, with tiny brass beads and rhinestones. *1930s. 5¼ in (13.5 cm) long* **$50–65 ABAA**

Art Deco flower pin with black stem and translucent white petals with incised linear decoration. *1930s 4 in (10 cm) long* **$40–55 ABAA**

Black and ivory snake bangle with clear rhinestones and tiny inset brass beads. *1930s. 9 in (23 cm) circ* **$40–55 ABAA**

Rare open bangle of translucent "apple juice" color with shoal-of-fish decoration. *1940s 2½ in (6.5 cm) wide* **$1,000–2,000 ROX**

Art Deco geometric pin of chromed steel with red Bakelite insert and clear rhinestone highlights. *1930s. 2½ in (6.5 cm) long* **$50–65 ABAA**

Black hoop-pendant clip earrings encrusted with clear rhinestones and tiny faux pearls. *c.1930. 2¾ in (7 cm) long* **$30–50 ABAA**

Black Scottie dog figural pin with a red collar and tongue. *Early 1930s 2 in (5 cm) wide* **$40–55 ABAA**

Brown Art Deco loop and buckle pin with clear rhinestones. *c.1930 2 in (5 cm) wide* **$30–50 ABAA**

Dark green cufflinks with gilt links, by Birkby's of Liversedge, England. *1920s Face: ¾ in (2 cm) long* **$30–50 MHC**

Brown stylized shoe-shaped pin encrusted with clear rhinestones. *1920s. 2⅜ in (6 cm) long* **$30–50 ABAA**

Black stylized scrolling leaf pin with a row of clear rhinestones. *1920s 1½ in (4 cm) long* **$30–50 ABAA**

"Five and six" large dice cufflinks of black and white Bakelite set in giltmetal. *Early 950s Face: ¾ in (2 cm) wide* **$80–130 CVS**

Stretching black cat pin with mauve collar and ruby red glass eyes. *Early 1930s 1½ in (4 cm) long* **$40–55 ABAA**

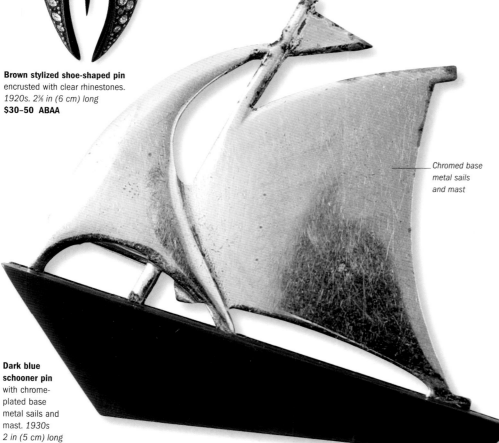

Chromed base metal sails and mast

Dark blue schooner pin with chrome-plated base metal sails and mast. *1930s 2 in (5 cm) long* **$50–65 ABAA**

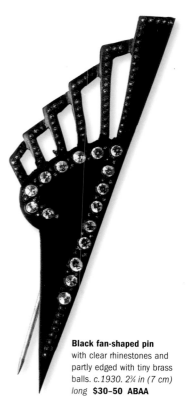

Black fan-shaped pin with clear rhinestones and partly edged with tiny brass balls. *c.1930. 2¾ in (7 cm) long* **$30–50 ABAA**

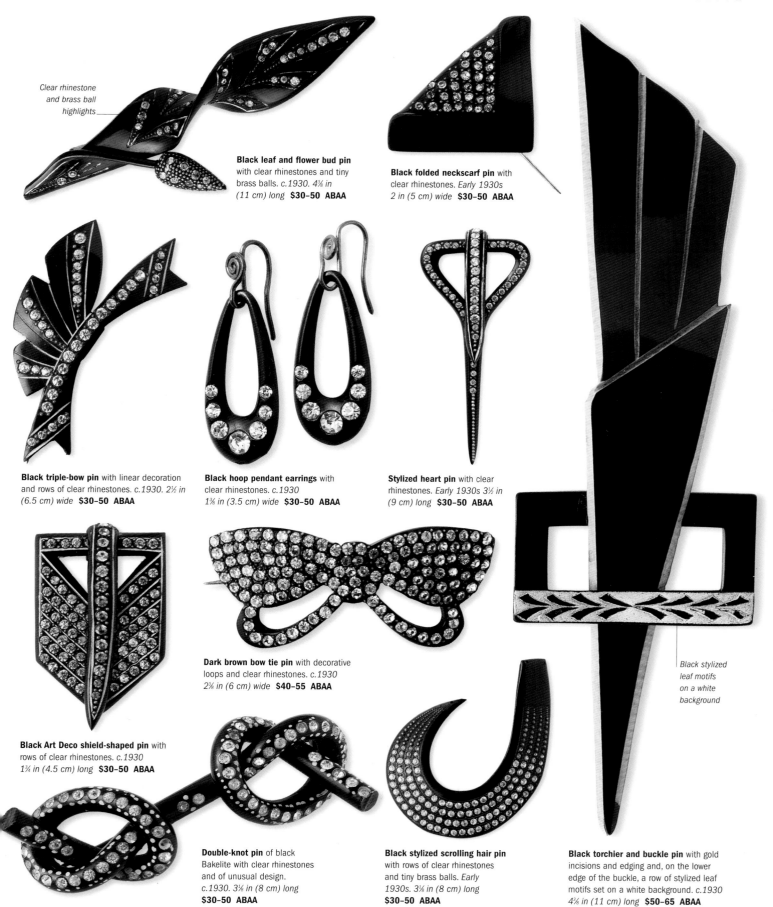

Clear rhinestone and brass ball highlights

Black leaf and flower bud pin with clear rhinestones and tiny brass balls. *c.1930. 4⅜ in (11 cm) long* **$30–50 ABAA**

Black folded neckscarf pin with clear rhinestones. *Early 1930s 2 in (5 cm) wide* **$30–50 ABAA**

Black triple-bow pin with linear decoration and rows of clear rhinestones. *c.1930. 2½ in (6.5 cm) wide* **$30–50 ABAA**

Black hoop pendant earrings with clear rhinestones. *c.1930 1⅜ in (3.5 cm) wide* **$30–50 ABAA**

Stylized heart pin with clear rhinestones. *Early 1930s 3½ in (9 cm) long* **$30–50 ABAA**

Black Art Deco shield-shaped pin with rows of clear rhinestones. *c.1930 1¾ in (4.5 cm) long* **$30–50 ABAA**

Dark brown bow tie pin with decorative loops and clear rhinestones. *c.1930 2⅜ in (6 cm) wide* **$40–55 ABAA**

Black stylized leaf motifs on a white background

Double-knot pin of black Bakelite with clear rhinestones and of unusual design. *c.1930. 3⅛ in (8 cm) long* **$30–50 ABAA**

Black stylized scrolling hair pin with rows of clear rhinestones and tiny brass balls. *Early 1930s. 3⅛ in (8 cm) long* **$30–50 ABAA**

Black torchier and buckle pin with gold incisions and edging and, on the lower edge of the buckle, a row of stylized leaf motifs set on a white background. *c.1930 4⅜ in (11 cm) long* **$50–65 ABAA**

Fred A. Block

Based in Chicago, Fred A. Block, Inc. made costume jewelry from the 1930s to the 1950s, initially to promote and accessorize its *prêt-à-porter* clothing lines. Many of its rare, collectible, and increasingly expensive pieces—especially its whimsical figural pins—are made in high-quality vermeil sterling silver with colorful enameling and large rhinestones or beads.

Strong contrasts of color— like the golden luster of vermeil against turquoise in this pin—are an eye-catching feature of many Fred A. Block designs.

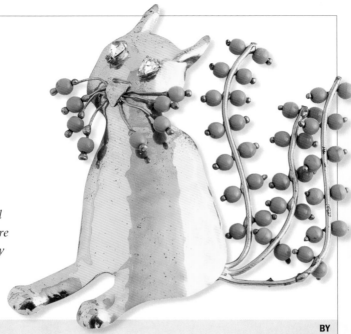

Cat pin of vermeil sterling silver with turquoise glass beads and clear crystal rhinestone eyes. *1940s*

4 in (10 cm) long

$300–400   **BY**

Geoff Roberts

Contemporary British jewelry designer Geoff Roberts is based in northern Scotland. His quirky and distinctive pieces are bold in form, vibrant in color, and spiked with humor. Roberts incorporates printed acrylics and mixed media in his work, much of which is made of flamboyant multicolored foils laminated over acrylic sheeting.

"Fishwife" pin and earrings composed of polychrome metallic foils laminated over acrylic sheeting. *Late 1990s*

P: 5½ in (14 cm) wide; E: 2½ in (7 cm) wide

$65–95   **PC**

Stylized floral motif earrings of metallic foils laminated over acrylic sheeting. *Late 1990s*

2½ in (6.5 cm) long

$30–40   **PC**

"Broken Heart" pin and earrings in red and gold metallic foils laminated over acrylic sheeting. *Late 1990s*

P: 3¼ in (8.25 cm) long; E: 2 in (5 cm) long

$65–80   **PC**

Fish earrings of polychrome metallic foils laminated over acrylic sheeting. *Late 1990s*

3¼ in (8.25 cm) long

$30–50   **PC**

Giorgio Armani

Celebrated Italian fashion designer Giorgio Armani established his own label in 1974. His jewelry complements the simple lines, understated elegance, and neutral colors of his fashion designs. Large rings, chokers, and bracelets are bold and vibrant, using an eclectic mix of silver, gemstones, and wood, often with global cultural references.

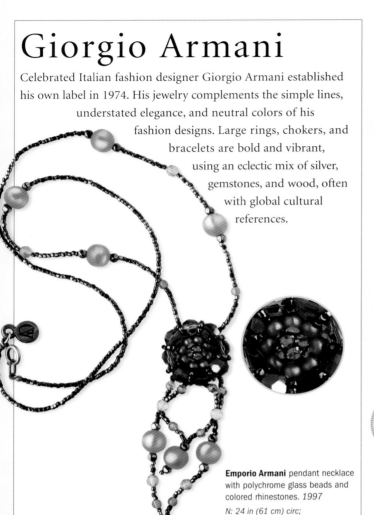

Emporio Armani pendant necklace with polychrome glass beads and colored rhinestones. *1997*

N: 24 in (61 cm) circ;
Pd: 6 in (15.25 cm) long

$30–50   PC

Givenchy

The House of Givenchy, which opened in Paris in 1952, was influential throughout the 1950s and 60s, its simple, elegant style best epitomized by Audrey Hepburn. Givenchy's jewelry features classic designs on a large scale, with much use of gold plating, Lucite, and other plastics.

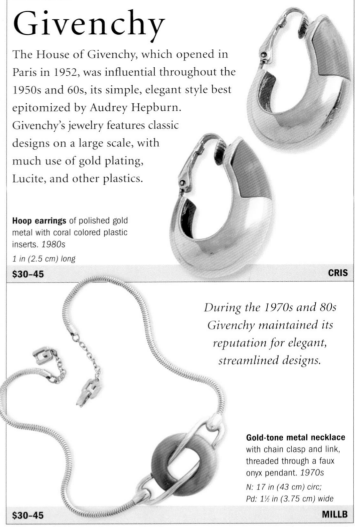

Hoop earrings of polished gold metal with coral colored plastic inserts. *1980s*

1 in (2.5 cm) long

$30–45   CRIS

During the 1970s and 80s Givenchy maintained its reputation for elegant, streamlined designs.

Gold-tone metal necklace with chain clasp and link, threaded through a faux onyx pendant. *1970s*

N: 17 in (43 cm) circ;
Pd: 1½ in (3.75 cm) wide

$30–45   MILLB

Gorham & Co.

Founded in 1813, the Gorham Manufacturing Company was the largest 19th-century silversmith in the United States. The chief designer William Codman produced a "martelé" (hand-hammered) line of silverware, which combined the free-flowing lines of Art Nouveau with the craftsmanship of the Arts and Crafts movement.

Native American motif belt buckle of sterling silver with selected gold plating and a marbled turquoise cabochon. *c.1900*

2 in (5 cm) long

$500–550   CGPC

Twin fish pin of goldwashed sterling silver with green enameling and a central amethyst glass cabochon. *c.1900*

2¼ in (5.75 cm) wide

$800–900   CGPC

Rare, irregularly shaped pin of 14-carat gold with a miniature enameled romantic bacchanalian portrait. *1906*

1 in (2.5 cm) wide

$1,200–1,300   CGPC

Har

Other than the fact that it was made in New York in the 1950s, the history of Har jewelry is shrouded in mystery. If anything, this has only enhanced the desirability of a limited but exceptionally distinctive range of exotic, fantastical designs. Har's signature subjects are genies, oriental men, and, especially, sinuous snakes and dragons. The latter, of green-enameled gold-tone metal encrusted with fantasy stones, are the most sought-after of all.

Hinged dragon bangle of gold-tone metal with green enameling and *aurora borealis* rhinestones. *1950s*

7 in (18 cm) circ

$720–800   **CRIS**

Oriental head pendant bracelet with silver-tone chain and faux ivory head with glass cabochons and *aurora borealis* rhinestones. *1950s*

B: 7 in (18 cm) circ; Pd: 1⅛ in (3 cm) long

$160–190   **CRIS**

Dragon pin and earrings of gold-tone metal with green enameling and ruby, turquoise, and *aurora borealis* rhinestones. *1950s*

P: 2¾ in (7 cm) wide; E: 1⅛ in (3 cm) wide

$1,000–1,200   **SUM**

Swirling wheat-sheafs pin of brushed gold-tone base metal. Its simple decoration is uncharacteristic of most Har pieces. *1950s*

2¼ in (5.75 cm) wide

$30–40   **MILLB**

Exotic pendant necklace with silver-tone metal chain, fantasy colored stones, and *aurora borealis* rhinestones. *1950s*

Pd: 4 in (10 cm) wide

$440–480   **SUM**

Fortune-teller male genie pin of gilt base metal with round-cut clear and star-cut sapphire blue rhinestones. *1950s*

2½ in (6.25 cm) long

$880–1,040   **SUM**

Rare cobra necklace, pin, bracelet, and earrings parure of gold-tone base metal with green enameling and fantasy colored glass stones, including navette-cut *aurora borealis* rhinestones. *1950s*

N: 15 in (38 cm) circ; P: 2¾ in (7 cm) wide; B: 7 in (18 cm) circ; E: 1⅛ in (3 cm) long

$3,200–4,000   **SUM**

Henry Schreiner

New York jeweler Henry Schreiner opened his own company in 1951, after designing some early pieces for Christian Dior in the late 1940s and early 50s (*see pp.60–65*). Schreiner's exuberant costume jewelry, worn by stars such as Marilyn Monroe, is characterized by its unconventional combinations of colors and paste stones, inverted-set rhinestones, and its use of high-quality diamanté and crystal. Full parures by Schreiner are rare and therefore highly collectible.

Necklace and earrings of gilt metal with aquamarine, jonquil, and *aurora borealis* crystal rhinestones. *1950s*

N: 17½ in (44.5 cm) circ; E: ½ in (3 cm) long

$1,100–1,300

CRIS

Necklace and pendant earrings of silver gilt metal with clear crystal rhinestones and prong-set, pear-cut, ruby red glass drops. *1950s*

N: 15 in (38 cm) circ; E: 2 in (5 cm) long

$720–800

CRIS

Bush pin of gilt wire backing with prong-set ruby, emerald, and clear crystal rhinestones, square-cut aquamarine pastes, and carved pear-cut emerald glass drops. *1950s*

4⅜ in (11 cm) wide

$1,900–2,100

SUM

Necklace and earrings of gilt metal with prong-set rhinestones and drops of colored glass. *1950s*

N: 2 in (5 cm) wide; E: 1½ in (4 cm) long

$1,200–1,400

SUM

Prong-set faux moonstone pin with a cluster of inverted amber-colored rhinestones. *1950s*

2¾ in (7 cm) wide

$145–160

CRIS

Jonquil keystone crystal pin with a prong-set matrix-cut jonquil glass cabochon. *1950s*

3 in (7.5 cm) wide

$560–640

CRIS

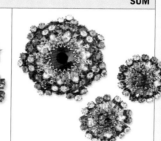

Floral motif pin and earrings of gunmetal plating with crystal rhinestones and cabochons. *1950s*

P: 2½ in (6.25 cm) wide; E: 1½ in (3.75 cm) wide

$320–400

CRIS

Hermès

Thierry Hermès founded his saddlery
company in 1837 and gradually introduced
the production of boots, jewelry, items for
the home, scarves, and bags. Today, Hermès
is mainly famous for its silk scarves,
ties, and exclusive bags and luggage.
Everything produced by Hermès is characterized
by stylish designs, quality materials, and high
standards of craftsmanship.

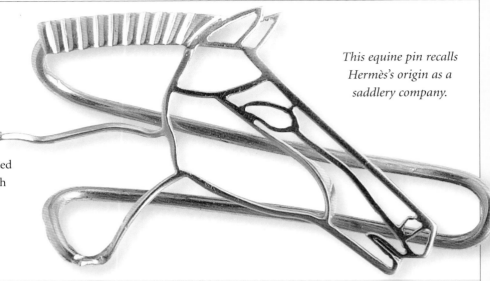

*This equine pin recalls
Hermès's origin as a
saddlery company.*

Silhouette horse-head tie pin of hand-looped,
soldered, and indented gold wire. *c.1980*
1¾ in (4.5 cm) wide

$120–190   **LB**

Hervé van der Straeten

Also known for his furniture designs, Paris-based Hervé van der
Straeten began making limited-edition costume jewelry in the
1990s. Rare and increasingly collectible,
many of his bold compositions are
hand-finished in gold-plated brass,
and set with pearls or
semi-precious stones.

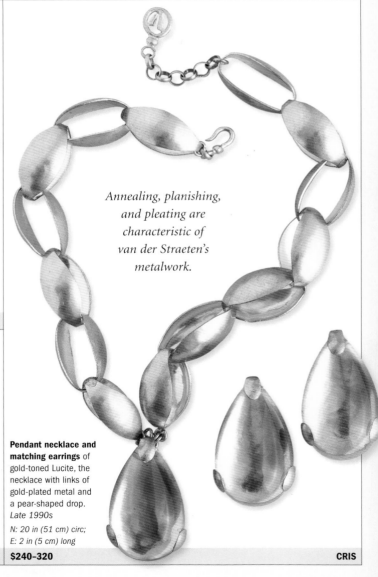

*Annealing, planishing,
and pleating are
characteristic of
van der Straeten's
metalwork.*

**Stylized flower pin with
matching earrings** of hand-
beaten gold-plated metal with prong-
set faux pearl centers. *Late 1990s*
P: 2¾ in (7 cm) wide;
E: 1¾ in (4.5 cm) long

$160–240   **CRIS**

Bow pin with matching earrings of
hand-beaten and looped gold-plated metal.
Late 1990s
P: 4 in (10 cm) long; E: 1¾ in (4.5 cm) long

$160–240   **CRIS**

Link necklace of gold-plated metal
alternated with ovals of gold-toned Lucite.
Late 1990s
19 in (48 cm) circ

$240–320   **CRIS**

**Pendant necklace and
matching earrings** of
gold-toned Lucite, the
necklace with links of
gold-plated metal and
a pear-shaped drop.
Late 1990s
N: 20 in (51 cm) circ;
E: 2 in (5 cm) long

$240–320   **CRIS**

Hollycraft

Hollycraft was founded in 1938 as the Hollywood Jewelry Manufacturing Company, but adopted the "Hollycraft" trademark in 1948 and continued in business until the mid-1970s. It is best known for its 1950s costume jewelry and Christmas tree pins. Intricate and Victorian in style, its pieces have antiqued gold-tone settings with rhinestones, beads, and enameling adding a characteristic dazzle of rainbow colors. Hollycraft jewelry is highly collectible because, unusually, it is always signed.

Butterfly pin of gilt and silver-gilt metal with black and white enamel. *c.1970*

2¼ in (5.75 cm) wide

$45–55   JJ

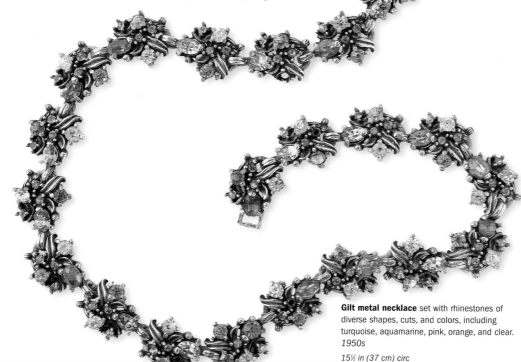

Gilt metal necklace set with rhinestones of diverse shapes, cuts, and colors, including turquoise, aquamarine, pink, orange, and clear. *1950s*

15½ in (37 cm) circ

$140–160   MG

Floral motif necklace with gilt metal chain and castings, the latter set with pink and clear crystal rhinestones. *1960s*

15 in (38 cm) circ

$280–320   JJ

Floral and foliate pin with faux coral, dark amethyst, and blue *aurora borealis* navettes and channel-set clear rhinestones. *1950s*

3 in (7.5 cm) long

$90–100   MG

Gilt metal bracelet and earrings with prong-set blue *aurora borealis* rhinestones, and diverse polychrome and *aurora borealis* foil-backed glass cabochons. *1950s*

B: 8 in (20.25 cm) circ; E: 1½ in (3.75 cm) long

$240–260   MG

Howard & Co.

Established in Providence, Rhode Island, in 1878, Howard & Co. changed its name to the Howard Sterling Company in 1891. It ceased trading in about 1902. The plated and sterling silver jewelry it produced for a quarter of a century—notably buckles, brooches, buttons, and cuffs—is now very collectible. Its mark includes an ornamental lower-case "h" and a four-leaf clover.

Belt buckle of sterling silver with applied sterling silver floral imagery. *c.1887*

3¼ in (8.25 cm) long

$170–180　　　　　　　　　　　　　　　　**CGPC**

Circular buckle of goldwashed textured sterling silver with ruby and amethyst glass stones and blister pearl center. *c.1901*

1½ in (3.75 cm) wide

$340–360　　　　　　　　　　　　　　　　**CGPC**

Ian St. Gielar

Florida-based jewelry designer Ian St. Gielar was the chief designer for Stanley Hagler until Hagler's death in 1996 (*see pp.112–117*). St. Gielar then set up on his own, designing both under his own name and as Stanley Hagler NYC.

Superbly crafted, St. Gielar's pieces have delicate filigree backings, embellished with fine materials such as Murano glass, mother-of-pearl, glass pearls, Limoges porcelain, and antique ivory. All pieces are in limited editions and are signed on a tag.

Tasseled scarf of mauve, cranberry, red, and pale green glass beads. *Late 1990s*

44 in (112 cm) long

$480–560　　　　　　　　　　　　　　　　**CRIS**

Bib necklace with pale blue and clear glass drops cascading from a "woven" collar of clear crystal rhinestones. *Late 1990s*

12½ in (32 cm) circ

$320–400　　　　　　　　　　　　　　　　**CRIS**

Flower pin with iridescent shell petals and an amber-red glass center encircled by topaz crystal rhinestones. *Late 1990s*

3½ in (9 cm) wide

$240–300　　　　　　　　　　　　　　　　**CRIS**

Iradj Moini

Although originally trained as an architect, Iranian-born Iradj Moini's career really took off after he began designing catwalk jewelry for Oscar de la Renta in the late 1980s. A string of prestigious clients and retail outlets (*see below*) have confirmed his reputation as one of the most imaginative of contemporary designers. His handmade pieces are invariably large, exquisitely detailed, and three-dimensional. Other characteristics include diverse figural and floral imagery, and unusual combinations of materials such as brass, bone, wood, and brightly colored European crystal and oriental gemstones.

Frog pin with 1950s jade green baroque pastes, clear rhinestones, and ruby red glass cabochon eyes set in a brass wire frame. *Early 1990s*

3¾ in (9.5 cm) wide

$640–800 CRIS

HIGH PROFILE

In addition to being the *couture* jeweler for Oscar de la Renta, New York-based Iradj Moini has also produced pieces for Bill Blass, Carolina Herrera, and Arnold Scaasi. Not surprisingly, working for such influential fashion designers has led to numerous private commissions from fashion cognescenti on both sides of the Atlantic. Considerable demand has also resulted in his jewelry being retailed through Saks Fifth Avenue and other up-market boutiques in New York City and Beverly Hills. The actress Drew Barrymore, for example, purchased a Moini Austrian crystal, gold-plated bracelet from a Los Angeles boutique to wear to the 1999 Academy Awards.

Apple pin with ruby red and emerald green glass stones and clear rhinestones in a brass wire frame. *Early 1990s*

4⅜ in (11 cm) long

$640–800 CRIS

En tremblant flower pin with prong-set clear and emerald green rhinestones set in a brass wire frame. *Mid-1990s*

6¼ in (16 cm) long

$1,400–1,500 CRIS

En tremblant rose motif pin with prong-set, round-cut clear rhinestones on a ruthenium-plated frame. *Mid-1990s*

5⅛ in (13 cm) long

$1,400–1,500 CRIS

Flower pin with mother-of-pearl petals and clear rhinestones on a ruthenium-plated frame. *Late 1990s*

5½ in (14 cm) long

$960–1,120 CRIS

Bouquet-of-flowers pin and earrings with hand-blown French glass petals, carved jade leaves, and clear rhinestone highlights. *Early 1990s*

P: 4 in (10 cm) long; E: 1 in (2.5 cm) long

$1,000–1,200 CRIS

Jewelerama

Made primarily in the 1960s, Jewelerama jewelry is unique. An offshoot of the Edmund Scientific Co. of Barrington, New Jersey, its novelty pins—mostly figural and floral, but also subjects such as musical instruments—incorporate machine-polished, circular convex metal discs that produce shimmering refractions of light.

Jewelerama's "Refraction Jewels" have become an interesting and affordable collecting field.

Turbaned genie pin of antiqued gold-tone casting, and magic lamp with gold-tone refractive disc. *1960s*
2 in (5 cm) long

$25–30   **JJ**

Floral pin of antiqued white metal casting and a pewter-tone refractive disc center. *1960s*
2½ in (6.25 cm) long

$25–30   **JJ**

Banjo pin and earrings of antiqued gold-tone metal castings with gold-tone refractive disc centers. *1960s*
P: 2½ in (6.25 cm) long; E: ¾ in (2 cm) wide

$30–40   **JJ**

J.J.

The Jonette Jewelry Company, known as J.J., was founded in 1935 in East Providence, Rhode Island. Following its early success with ballerina and mother-of-pearl figural pins, J.J. became renowned for its Christmas tree pins and novelty pins, featuring animals, charms, and Art Deco motifs with rhinestone details.

Flower pin and earrings of gold-tone metal castings set with clear and sapphire blue rhinestones. *1950s*
P: 2½ in (6.25 cm) long; E: ¾ in (2 cm) wide

$50–60   **MILLB**

Pendant necklace with gold-tone chain and casting, white enameled quarters, and a central cabochon. *1970s*
N: 18 in (45.75 cm) circ; Pd: 2 in (5 cm) wide

$20–25   **MILLB**

Puppy and mirror pin in gold-tone base metal and semi-opaque mirror glass. *c.1990*

2 in (5 cm) wide

$35–45 ABIJ

Fish pendant of gold-tone casting with black rhinestone eye and red painted belly set with polychrome plastic cabochons. *1970s*

3 in (7.5 cm) long

$40–50 JJ

Cat and goldfish bowl pin of pewter-colored base metal casting and gray-tone glass. *c.1990*

2½ in (6.5 cm) wide

$35–45 ABIJ

Inside of pin

Safe pin of bronze and gold-tone base metal casting with hinged door revealing a bag of money. *c.1980*

1½ in (3.75 cm) wide

$25–30 JJ

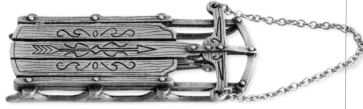

Sled pin of pewter-tone base metal casting inscribed with an arrow motif, and a gold-tone base metal chain. *1990s*

2¼ in (5.75 cm) long

$15–20 MILLB

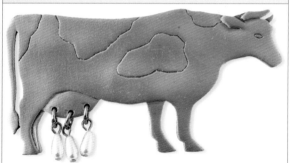

Cow pin of brown-tone metal casting with three faux pearl drop udders. *c.1980*

2½ in (6.5 cm) wide

$25–30 JJ

Contrasting textured and polished metal finishes feature in many J.J. designs.

Fruit pin of antiqued and part brown-enameled gilt metal casting with fruits of gold-red rhinestones. *1980s*

2 in (5 cm) long

$20–25 BB

Biblical figure and snake pin of antiqued gold-tone casting with ruby and *aurora borealis* rhinestone highlights. *1950s*

3½ in (9 cm) long

$70–80 JJ

Fish pendant of gold-tone metal casting with semi-translucent white plastic eye with black bead pupil. *1970s*

3 in (7.5 cm) wide

$40–50 JJ

Christmas Tree Pins

Originally a collecting phenomenon in the United States, Christmas tree pins are now internationally sought-after. Seasonal by design, these often exquisite pins have become a hot collecting field year-round.

KICK-STARTED IN CONFLICT

The convention of wearing a festive corsage at Christmastime dates back to the late 19th century. Composed of cloth, ribbon, and various trinkets, these fragile adornments rarely survived more than a few years. In the 1940s, however, more durable metal-frame Christmas jewelry began to appear. Typical pieces included wreaths, bows, Santas, snowmen, sleighs, reindeer, and, most notably, Christmas tree pins. The popularity of the latter really took off during Christmas 1950, when mothers and wives of American servicemen started wearing them and sending them to sons and husbands fighting overseas in the Korean

War. The fashion stuck, and ever since, jewelry manufacturers have annually introduced new, limited-edition and instantly collectible Christmas tree pin designs.

In keeping with the traditional colors of Christmas, most trees are of silver- or gold-tone metal and many feature red and green beads, stones, or enameling. Most pins exhibit exquisite standards of craftsmanship, and many of the costume jewelry designers featured in this book have produced Christmas tree pins. However, there are also numerous unsigned but desirable pieces. Prices start at under $50, but can exceed $500 for rare examples by prestigious names.

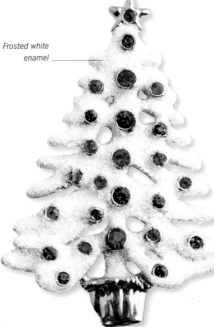

Frosted white enamel

Eisenberg Ice pin with frosted white enamel, gilt metal, and ruby and emerald rhinestones. *1980s. 2⅜ in (6 cm) long* **$50–65 CRIS**

Stanley Hagler Christmas tree pin with hand-wired red and green Murano glass beads and yellow Murano glass fruit drops. *c.1970. 2¾ in (7 cm) long* **$145–160 CRIS**

Stanley Hagler Christmas tree pin with hand-wired red and green Murano glass beads and gilt wire stars. *c.1970 2⅛ in (5.5 cm) long* **$145–160 CRIS**

Trifari pin with jade glass and ruby rhinestones. *1960s. 2 in (5 cm) long* **$80–120 ROX**

Mylu pin with carved stones and rhinestones. *1950s. 2¾ in (7 cm) long* **$170–190 ROX**

Trifari pin of brushed gold with faceted beads. *1950s 2 in (5 cm) long* **$105–110 CRIS**

Stanley Hagler Christmas tree pin with mother-of-pearl petals, red rose montée centers, and jade rhinestones. *1960s 3⅜ in (8.5 cm) long* **$240–270 CRIS**

Eisenberg Ice pin with polychrome rhinestones on pierced gilt metal casting. *1980s. 2 in (5 cm) long* **$30–40 CRIS**

Cristobal pin with 1950s Swarovski crystals and peridot and emerald glass. *1990s 3 in (7.5 cm) long* **$50–55 CRIS**

Hollycraft Christmas tree pin of textured gilt metal with polychrome rhinestones. *1950s 2 in (5 cm) long* **$70–80 CRIS**

Semi-matte Russian gold plating

Sphinx Christmas tree pin with green enamel and clear and ruby rhinestones. *1960s. 2¾ in (7 cm) long* **$55–65 CRIS**

Cadora cherubs Christmas tree pin of gilt metal with faux pearls. *1950s 2¾ in (7 cm) long* **$130–140 ROX**

Stanley Hagler pin with colored glass beads and *aurora borealis* angel. *1980s. 2⅜ in (6 cm) long* **$130–145 CRIS**

Art pin with green enameling and polychrome rhinestones. *1950s 2⅜ in (6 cm) long* **$65–70 CRIS**

Cristobal pin with prong-set red, emerald green, and clear crystal rhinestones. *1990s. 2¾ in (7 cm) long* **$40–50 CRIS**

Eisenberg Ice pin with clear, ruby, and emerald rhinestones (some prong-set), and ruby and emerald navettes. *1980s 2⅜ in (6 cm) long* **$70–80 CRIS**

Larry Vrba pin with prong-set dark blue teardrop cabochons, and ruby and clear rhinestones. *1990s. 4½ in (11.5 cm) long* **$190–210 CRIS**

Unsigned French potted pin of gilt metal with green enameling, and polychrome and clear rhinestones. *1980s. 2 in (5 cm) long* **$55–65 CRIS**

Sphinx pin of gilt metal with green enameled leaves and ruby red and clear rhinestones. *1960s 2 in (5 cm) long* **$50–55 CRIS**

Stanley Hagler pin with textured gilt basket, ruby baguette rhinestones, and emerald glass beads. *c.1970. 2¼ in (5.75 cm) long* **$130–160 CRIS**

Larry Vrba pin with large *aurora borealis* and round-cut clear rhinestones and square-cut Montana blue rhinestones. *1990s 4½ in (11.5 cm) long* **$130–190 CRIS**

Trifari partridge-in-a-pear-tree pin of gilt metal with green, red, and blue enameling. *1950s. 2 in (5 cm) long* **$130–140 ROX**

Eisenberg Ice pin, gold-plated with clear and ruby rhinestones and emerald navettes. *1980s. 2⅛ in (5.5 cm) long* **$40–50 CRIS**

Cristobal pin with pavé-set clear and emerald baguette rhinestones, and ruby glass cabochons. *1990s* 4¼ in (11 cm) long **$150–160 CRIS**

Clear crystal rhinestones

Art pin of textured gilt metal with clear, red, green, and blue beads and rhinestones. *1950s* 2⅜ in (6 cm) long **$65–80 CRIS**

Atwood & Sawyer pin with bow base, gold-plated with ruby and emerald rhinestones. *Late 1990s* 2 in (5 cm) long **$55–65 CRIS**

Unsigned Austrian pin with ruby, amethyst, emerald, and clear rhinestones and clear rhinestone candles. *1950s.* 3 in (7.5 cm) long **$70–80 CRIS**

Unsigned French pin with matte gold-tone metal basket, large ruby, emerald, and amber glass navettes, carved clear glass flowers, and clear, ruby, and aquamarine rhinestones. *1980s* 2¾ in (7 cm) long **$55–65 CRIS**

Matte gold-tone metal

175

Judy Lee

Judy Lee jewelry was sold at parties in people's homes from the 1950s to the 1970s. The 1950s pieces are mostly of floral design and are Victorian in style, using glittering rhinestones and faux pearls set on gold- or silver-tone filigree backings. Later pieces display other historical influences and use various stones set in antiqued metalwork.

Floral burst pin and matching earrings of gold-tone filigree backing with navette- and round-cut clear, topaz, ruby, and gray-green rhinestones. *c.1970*

P: 2¾ in (7 cm) wide; E: 1½ in (3.75 cm) long

$55–65   ABIJ

Antiqued gold-tone metal bracelet with metallic polychrome glass cabochons. *1970s*

7 in (17.75 cm) circ

$55–65   ABIJ

Bracelet and earrings of antiqued silver-tone metal set with ruby, sapphire, aquamarine, and *aurora borealis* rhinestones. *Late 1970s*

7 in (17.75 cm) circ

$75–85   ABIJ

Karl Lagerfeld

German fashion designer Karl Lagerfeld worked for various Paris designers before joining Chanel in 1983 and launching his own-name label. The costume jewelry he created in the 1980s was bold and distinctive. He took well-known motifs, such as coins, pearls, and Chanel's "CC" motif, and made them larger and more flashy. These pieces are now very collectible.

Stylized plant form earrings in goldwashed metal, each set with a faux pearl. *c.1990*

1 in (2.5 cm) long

$45–55   MILLB

"Louis XIV-style" bergère armchair earrings in goldwashed metal with clear crystal beads at the sides. *1980s*

1⅛ in (3 cm) long

$60–70   JJ

Kerr & Co.

Founded in New Jersey in 1855, and originally known as Kerr and Thierry, the firm of William B. Kerr & Co. started by making tableware and gold and silver jewelry. From 1892 to 1900, however, the company made Art Nouveau costume jewelry. It produced large quantities of hollow-backed jewelry stamped with imitation repoussé work. Most of the jewelry was heavily influenced by French Art Nouveau designs and was marked with a fleur-de-lys.

Extremely rare two-part cherub belt clasp of silver-plated metal which, when joined, shows the male and female cherubs dancing. *c.1900*

2¾ in (7 cm) wide

Belt clasp undone (above) and joined (right)

$650–750 CGPC

Art Nouveau floral motif pin of goldwash over sterling silver with three faux moonstone cabochons. *c.1900*

2½ in (6.25 cm) wide

$350–400 CGPC

Art Nouveau double peacock motif belt buckle of goldwash over sterling silver set with ruby glass cabochons. *c.1900*

3½ in (9 cm) wide

$450–550 CGPC

Goldwash over sterling silver necklace comprising floral swags intertwined with cherubs. *c.1900*

15 in (38 cm) circ

$700–800 CGPC

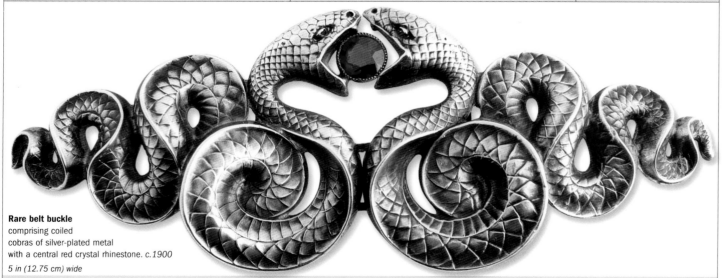

Rare belt buckle comprising coiled cobras of silver-plated metal with a central red crystal rhinestone. *c.1900*

5 in (12.75 cm) wide

$500–600 CGPC

Kramer

Kramer Jewelry Creations was founded in New York in 1943 and continued production until the late 1970s. Kramer's exuberant and artistic jewelry features high-quality sparkling Austrian rhinestones, both clear and colored. In the early 1950s, Kramer manufactured pieces for Christian Dior. Kramer's more extravagant styles, especially when in intact parures, are much sought-after.

Circular pin of antiqued, brushed gilt metal with a large faceted "watermelon" glass center. *1950s*
2¼ in (5.75 cm) wide

$65–70 ABIJ

Leaf motif pin and earrings of antiqued, brushed, and pierced gilt metal with crystal rhinestones. *1970s*
P: 3¼ in (8.25 cm) long;
E: 1½ in (3.75 cm) long

$55–65 ABIJ

Leopard pin with articulated tail of gilt metal with black enamel spots, emerald rhinestone eyes, and a saddle of pavé-set clear rhinestones. *1950s*
2 in (5 cm) long

$65–75 ABIJ

Bracelet and earrings with gilt metal clasp and links, and clear and textured white glass beads. *c.1960*
B: 7 in (17.75 cm) circ; E: 1½ in (3.75 cm) long

$45–55 MILLB

Stylized leaf motif earrings of gilt metal with black enameling and faux pearl cabochons. *1950s*
1⅛ in (3 cm) long

$20–25 MILLB

Geometric motifs and bright colors were extremely fashionable in the 1950s.

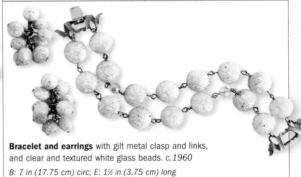

Button earrings of gold-tone metal with twisted rope moldings encircling highly polished centers. *1950s*
1⅛ in (3 cm) wide

$15–20 MILLB

Choker necklace of gold-tone metal links and castings, the latter with turquoise glass crosses. *1950s*
15½ in (39.5 cm) circ

$35–45 MILLB

La Pierre

The La Pierre Manufacturing Company was founded in 1885 in New York City, but relocated its factory to Newark in 1893. Until 1929, in addition to silverware it produced good-quality jewelry—notably bangles, belt buckles, and pins, also in silver but sometimes made with "novelty" materials such as celluloid.

Belt buckle with frame and applied scrolling leaves of sterling silver, and two romantic-historical celluloid miniatures. *c.1904*
4 in (10 cm) wide

$700–800　　　　　　　　　　　　　　　　　　　　CGPC

Art Nouveau sterling silver bangle with plant form motifs. *c.1902*
3 in (7.5 cm) circ

$150–170　　　　　　　　　CGPC

Lanvin

The House of Lanvin, established by Jeanne Lanvin in 1889, is the oldest of the Paris fashion houses and creates stylish, elegant jewelry to complement its collections. After a makeover in the late 1960s, Lanvin produced a series of carved Op Art plastic pendants on chains, which have become highly collectible.

Couture **belt** of black velvet with a stylized leaf motif buckle of black glass beads with clear rhinestone highlights around a large pear-cut clear paste stone. *c.1970*
34 in (87.5 cm) circ

$400–480　　　　　　　　SUM

Hinged bangle of gilt metal casting with classic key motif border against red enameling. *1970s*
8 in (21 cm) circ

$120–150　　　　　　　　　　　　　　LB

Space Age necklace with gilt metal wire hoop and a circular pendant of black plastic set with a large red plastic cabochon. *1960s*
Pd: 3 in (8 cm) wide

$190–240　　　　　　　　LB

Larry Vrba

From a lowly administrative role at Miriam Haskell (*see pp.98-107*) in 1969, Nebraska-born Larry Vrba enjoyed a remarkably rapid rise to prominence. On leaving Haskell after only nine months of employment, he worked briefly for Castlecliff and then William DeLillo before, just a year later, at age 22, returning as Haskell's chief designer. For seven years he designed over a thousand different lines for Haskell—traditional in style, but with a contemporary, often exotic twist. After two years with Les Bernard in the early 1980s, Vrba embarked on a highly imaginative solo career unfettered by corporate restraints. His pieces—large, ornate, and often outrageous—are particularly sought after in the theatrical and transvestite communities (*see box below*).

Larry Vrba's unique designs are visually arresting in their sheer size and profusion of color. Equally engaging in their imaginative compositions and finely worked detail, they never fail to make a powerful statement.

Basket-of-flowers pin with carved orange and yellow glass, and jade, coral, and yellow glass beads, on a gunmetal frame. *Late 1990s*
4½ in (11.5 cm) long

$200–240   **CRIS**

Large flower pin of gunmetal frame with abalone shell, faux pearls, glass beads, and clear crystal rhinestones. *Late 1990s*
8 in (20 cm) long

$290–320   **CRIS**

Vase-of-flowers pin with white mother-of-pearl flowers, carved jade leaves, coral bead berries, and poured glass vase. *Late 1990s*
4¾ in (12 cm) long

$240–320   **CRIS**

Knotted bow pin with rope-molding motif, oxidized gunmetal wire frame, set with fuchsia and rose pink pastes and rhinestones. *1990s*
5⅛ in (13 cm) wide

$255–290   **CRIS**

THEATRICAL GESTURES

It isn't at all surprising that Larry Vrba's bold conceptions have appeared in numerous stage productions. Theater designers have long appreciated that, rather like stage makeup, costume accessories have to be larger-than-life in order to "read" up in the mezzanine or down in the orchestra. For similar reasons, Vrba has also received numerous commissions from transvestites requesting ever more dramatic pieces to go with equally innovative and extravagant costumes—mostly for New York's annual charity drag balls. His big, colorful designs are fully in the spirit of dressing up outrageously, and they also serve the purpose of making larger bodies look more petite.

Heart-shaped vase-of-flowers pin of gold-plated base metal with mother-of-pearl, glass beads, and rose pink rhinestones. *Late 1990s*
4½ in (11.5 cm) long

$240–320   **CRIS**

Liberty

Arthur L. Liberty opened his first shop in London in 1875. From 1894 onward, he commissioned designs from talented jewelers, such as Archibald Knox, a leading figure of the Arts and Crafts Celtic Revival movement, and Jessie King. Liberty pieces are often made of hammered silver to create a handcrafted effect. The swirling, interlaced metal designs are decorated with peacock blue and green enameling and semi-precious stones.

The Celtic influence on Liberty pieces is unmistakable, as are the Arts and Crafts standards of workmanship.

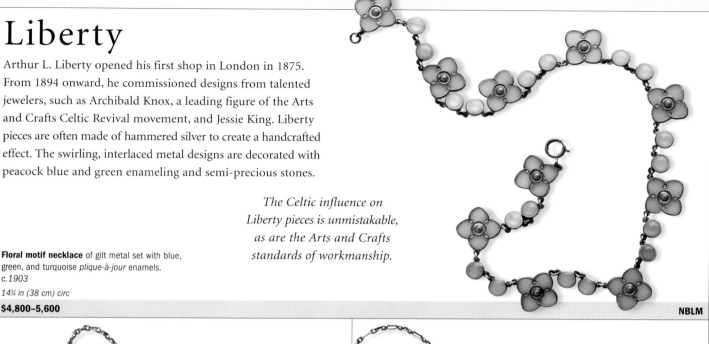

Floral motif necklace of gilt metal set with blue, green, and turquoise *plique-à-jour* enamels. *c.1903*

14¾ in (38 cm) circ

$4,800–5,600   **NBLM**

Necklace detail

Pendant necklace (unsigned) with gilt metal chain and floral motif castings with enameling and faux pearl cabochons. *c.1905*

16½ in (42 cm) circ

$1,300–1,400   **RG**

Necklace detail

Pendant necklace (unsigned) with silvered metal chain and clover motif castings, enameling, and faux pearl cabochons and drop. *c.1910*

16½ in (42 cm) circ

$1,600–1,900   **RG**

Marvella

Weinrich Bros. Co., founded in 1911, used the name "Marvella" as its trademark and only changed its name to Marvella, Inc. in 1965. The Weinrich brothers specialized in imitation jewelry and faux pearls. Necklaces are made of several strands of faceted crystal beads, and faux pearls are combined with rhinestones. The jewelry is marked with different trademarks, many of which include Marvell or Marvella in a longer name, such as "Marvellesque." The company was bought by Trifari in 1982.

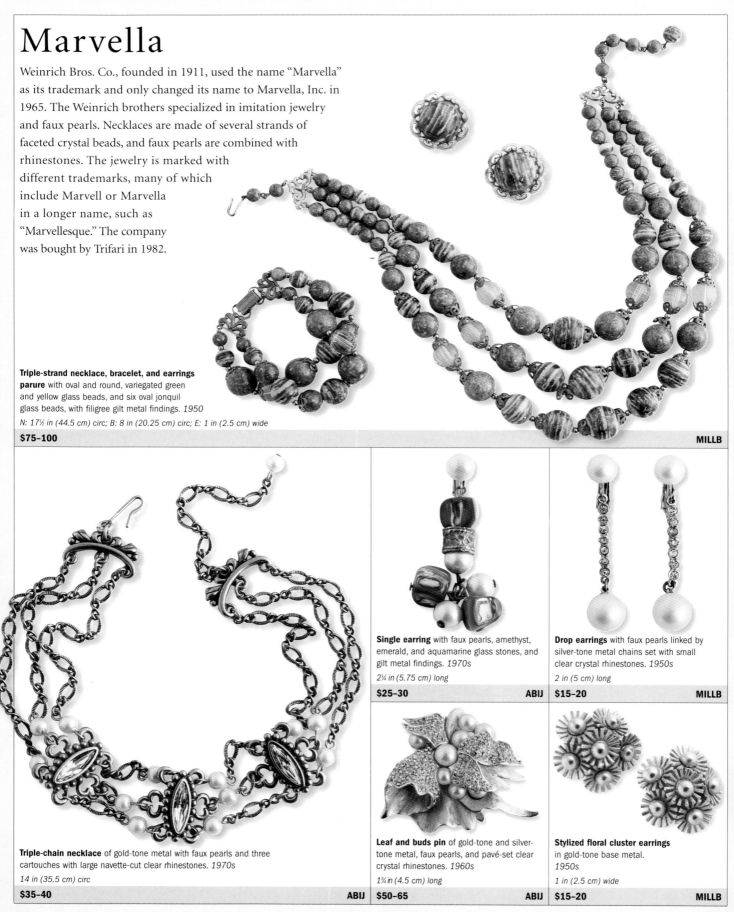

Triple-strand necklace, bracelet, and earrings parure with oval and round, variegated green and yellow glass beads, and six oval jonquil glass beads, with filigree gilt metal findings. *1950*

N: 17½ in (44.5 cm) circ; B: 8 in (20.25 cm) circ; E: 1 in (2.5 cm) wide

$75–100　　　　　　　　　　　　　　**MILLB**

Triple-chain necklace of gold-tone metal with faux pearls and three cartouches with large navette-cut clear rhinestones. *1970s*

14 in (35.5 cm) circ

$35–40　　　　**ABIJ**

Single earring with faux pearls, amethyst, emerald, and aquamarine glass stones, and gilt metal findings. *1970s*

2¼ in (5.75 cm) long

$25–30　　　　**ABIJ**

Drop earrings with faux pearls linked by silver-tone metal chains set with small clear crystal rhinestones. *1950s*

2 in (5 cm) long

$15–20　　　　**MILLB**

Leaf and buds pin of gold-tone and silver-tone metal, faux pearls, and pavé-set clear crystal rhinestones. *1960s*

1¾ in (4.5 cm) long

$50–65　　　　**ABIJ**

Stylized floral cluster earrings in gold-tone base metal.
1950s

1 in (2.5 cm) wide

$15–20　　　　**MILLB**

Monet

Founded by Jay and Michael Chernow in 1929, and known as Monocraft until 1937, Monet became one of the leading costume jewelers during the 1940s. Its simple, classic designs in silver and gold tones, sometimes accented with Austrian crystal highlighters, appealed to the working women of the postwar era. It also pioneered comfortable clip-on earrings, which became very popular. Monet produced jewelry for Yves Saint Laurent during the 1980s and, by constantly adapting to changing fashions, has remained successful right up until today.

Over the years, Monet has continually adapted its jewelry designs to reflect the social scene of the time.

Cross pin of gold-plated casting set with pear-shaped faux pearls and navette-, baguette-, and round-cut clear crystal rhinestones. *1980s*

2 in (5 cm) diam

$30–40   **ABIJ**

Gold-plated necklace with chain links and oval ornament, the latter with rope molding border and a glass cabochon. *1980s*

18 in (45.75 cm) circ

$45–55   **MILLB**

Flower pin with borders of gold-plated metal; the petal surfaces are strands of base metal with white enameling. *c.1970*

2 in (5 cm) long

$25–35   **MILLB**

Starfish pins of textured gold-plated metal with pavé-set clear crystal rhinestones. *1980s*

Large: 1 in (2.5 cm) wide; Small: ¾ in (2 cm) wide

$35–45   **ABIJ**

Snail pin of gilt metal with clear rhinestone eyes and a shell set with ruby and emerald glass cabochons. *c.1980*

2 in (5 cm) long

$30–35   **JJ**

Gold-plated necklace with stylized floral design pendant of scrolling, interlaced forms. *1970s*

N: 23 in (58.5 cm) circ; Pd: 2 in (5 cm) wide

$15–20   **MILLB**

Moschino

Italian fashion designer Franco Moschino launched his own label in 1983, after working as an illustrator for Gianni Versace. He started with jeans and casual wear, which were soon followed by shoes, lingerie, innovative evening wear, and jewelry. Provocative and iconoclastic, Moschino approached fashion and accessories with a touch of irony and a strong sense of humor. His jewelry is stamped with the mark "Moschino Bijoux."

Antiqued gold-tone metal earrings, the clips with central faux pearl cabochons encircled by a stamped "Moschino Bijoux" mark, and chained to peace symbol pendants. *1980s*

3 in (7.5 cm) long

$25–30   **MILLB**

Antiqued gold-tone metal earrings, the clips with faux pearl cabochons and the hoop pendants with latticework pattern. *1980s*

3¾ in (9.5 cm) long

$30–35   **MILLB**

FRANCO MOSCHINO

1950 Born near Milan, Italy

1971 After studying at the Fine Arts Academy in Milan, he began his career working as an illustrator for Giorgio Armani, with whom he continued working for 11 years

1983 The Moschino label is launched

1994 Franco Moschino dies and Rossella Jardini, who worked with the designer for many years, becomes Creative Director of Moschino

Murrle Bennet & Co.

From 1884 to 1914, this Anglo-German agency marketed inexpensive jewelry similar to Liberty's. Often designed by Theodor Fahrner (*see pp.72–73*) in Germany, the pieces were usually made of silver or low-carat gold, set with green and blue enamelwork, semi-precious stones, mother-of-pearl, or glass. Fahrner's work was abstract or semi-organic in form, often based on stylized plants or birds. Most pieces bear a mark, either "MB" or "MB & Co." Those attributed to a particular designer are the most valuable.

Arts and Crafts pendant of silver casting with a raised central lozenge of mottled blue and green enameling, with indented slivers of turquoise enameling. *c.1905*

1¾ in (4.5 cm) long

$480–560   **RBRG**

$375–450   **LYNTT**

Art Nouveau pin of goldwashed sterling silver with a central mottled green and brown semi-precious stone cabochon. *c.1905*

1¾ in (4.5 cm) wide

Arts and Crafts pendant necklace with Celtic Revival motifs. The chain and pendant are of silver set with blue enamel. *c.1905*

N: 16½ in (41.5 cm) circ;
Pd: 1¾ in (4.5 cm) long

$1,000–1,200   **RG**

Napier

Founded in 1875, Napier originally made silverware, but shifted emphasis to modern jewelry after World War I and stayed in business until 1999. Its early designs are highly collectible, as are its Egyptian-style pieces of the 1920s and 30s. During the 1950s and 60s, Napier produced a wide variety of chunky gilt metal charm bracelets, which became very popular. Coins, antique seals, and oriental motifs are much sought-after. Another favorite line is its simple gilt mesh and silver-toned jewelry.

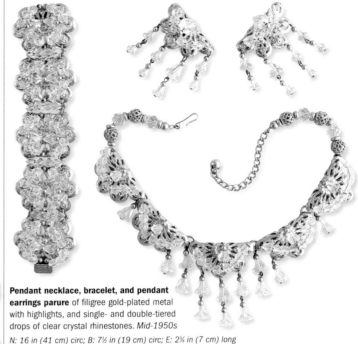

Pendant necklace, bracelet, and pendant earrings parure of filigree gold-plated metal with highlights, and single- and double-tiered drops of clear crystal rhinestones. *Mid-1950s*

N: 16 in (41 cm) circ; B: 7½ in (19 cm) circ; E: 2¾ in (7 cm) long

$160–200   **CRIS**

Grapes-and-leaves pin, the leaves of textured, matte-finish gilt metal; the bunch of grapes and wire spiral of polished gilt metal. *1950s*

5 in (12.75 cm) long

$105–120   **CRIS**

Elephant pin of gold-plated casting with a sapphire paste stone capped with filigree metal, and a faux ruby and pearls. *Mid-1950s*

1½ in (3.75 cm) high

$80–90   **CRIS**

Turtle pin of engraved gilt metal casting with a large jade green glass cabochon with rope molding border. *1980s*

2 in (5 cm) long

$40–45   **JJ**

Gold-plated charm bracelet of various motifs, with faux emerald, turquoise, ruby, amethyst, and pearl stones and beads. *Mid-1950s*

B: 7 in (18 cm) circ; Longest charm: 2 in (5 cm) long

$160–200   **CRIS**

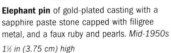

Unusual bracelet with "carved" twin fruit pendants and chain of silver-tone metal. *Late 1950s*

B: 8 in (20.25 cm) circ; Fruits: 1½ in (3.75 cm) long

$120–150   **CRIS**

Ethnic-style necklace, bracelet, and earrings parure with gold findings and diverse polychrome beads and stones of various cuts. *1960s*

N: 60 in (152.5 cm) circ; B: 7 in (17.75 cm) circ; E: 1½ in (3.75 cm) long

$130–150   **ABIJ**

Coro Duettes

The first major American manufacturer of costume jewelry to make double clips, Coro soon became famous for its animal and floral "Duettes." Much sought-after, they have now become a collecting field in their own right.

FAMED FOR THEIR VERSATILITY

Clips were a mainstay of 1920s jewelry, worn on furs or dresses to highlight an attractive feature, such as a lapel or plunging neckline. In 1927, the French fine jeweler Louis Cartier patented the double clip, an ingenious mechanism (*see below right*) that allowed two identical or similar clips to be fastened together and worn as one pin, or detached and worn separately— for example, on both sides of a neckline, or on a lapel and a hat or scarf. The versatility of the double clip made it a huge success.

Quick to follow suit, Coro created its own version of the double clip, the Coro Duette, in 1931. The initial designs were often Art Deco in style and decorated with pavé-set clear rhinestones. Coro's greatest success, however, came with the creation of its figural Duettes, featuring flowers, birds and other animals, and characters such as cherubs. Mostly made of vermeil sterling silver, these were decorated with colorful enameling and crystal rhinestones. Each Duette had a name and was sometimes sold with matching earrings.

Coro Duettes were popular throughout the 1940s, but were waning in popularity by the early 50s, although they were still being marketed in smaller, lighter versions. They are now avidly collected, particularly the unusual and complex pieces such as the "Quivering Camellias" Duette, featuring delicate trembler flowers mounted on springs.

Yellow metal parrots with green, blue, and pink enameling and pavé-set clear crystal rhinestones. *1940s 2½ in (6.25 cm) long* **$150–200 ABIJ**

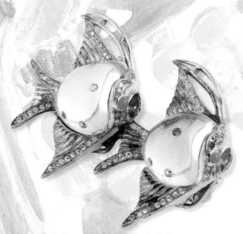

Vermeil sterling silver fish with Lucite bellies, pink and sapphire cabochons, and clear crystal rhinestones. *1940s 1¾ in (4.5 cm) long* **$600–675 CRIS**

Sterling silver owls with blue enamel and aquamarine and pavé-set clear crystal rhinestones. *1940s 1½ in (3.75 cm) long* **$240–270 CRIS**

DOUBLE CLIP MECHANISM

Duettes were sold on a metal frame fitted with a brooch pin. When clipped onto the frame, the two individual pieces looked like a single pin. The mechanism varied in styling for each design, but the way in which the pieces locked together remained much the same.

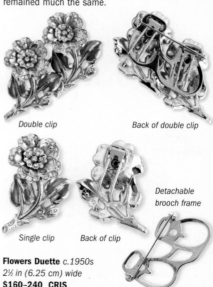

Double clip   *Back of double clip*

Single clip   *Back of clip*

Detachable brooch frame

Flowers Duette *c.1950s 2½ in (6.25 cm) wide* **$160–240 CRIS**

Silver leaves in rhodium-plated metal with clear crystal rhinestones. *c.1940. 2½ in (6.25 cm) wide* **$160–240 CRIS**

Vermeil sterling silver cherubs with ruby and emerald crystal rhinestones and faux pearls. *1940s. 1⅜ in (3.5 cm) high* **$320–400 CRIS**

Hearth and mantel motifs of white metal with clear crystal rhinestones and ruby glass "fires." *c.1940 3 in (7.5 cm) long* **$150–200 MILLB**

Clear crystal rhinestones

Énameling over vermeil

Bouquets of flowers in enameled silver with glass beads and crystal rhinestones. *1930s. 2¾ in (7 cm) long* **$250–300 ROX**

Dutch couple pin in vermeil sterling silver with ruby, aquamarine, and clear crystal rhinestones. *1940s. 2 in (5 cm) long* **$575–640 CRIS**

Horse-heads of vermeil sterling silver with ruby and aquamarine crystal navettes. *1940s 2¼ in (5.75 cm) long* **$225–290 CRIS**

Owls on branches of vermeil sterling silver with topaz and clear crystal rhinestones. *1940s. 1½ in (3.75 cm) long* **$230–260 JJ**

"Brave and squaw" in vermeil sterling silver with red and green enamel and ruby and clear crystal rhinestones. *1940s. 1¾ in (4.5 cm) long* **$1,000–1,100 CRIS**

Nettie Rosenstein

From the 1930s to the 1960s, fashion designer Nettie Rosenstein designed costume jewelry in addition to clothes. She is best known for her colorful rhinestone pins and earrings, and her unusual silver and enamel pieces of the 1930s Art Deco period. Favorite imagery includes animals, butterflies, flowers, and heraldic motifs.

Crab fur clip of vermeil sterling silver with green, brown, yellow, and red enameling. *1940s*

1¾ in (4.5 cm) wide

| $160–190 | RG |

Minstrel pin of vermeil sterling silver with turquoise glass cabochons and clear crystal rhinestones. *1940s*

2¾ in (7 cm) long

| $240–260 | ROX |

Butterfly fur clip of vermeil sterling silver with dark and pale green, pink, and red enameling, and faux seed pearls. *1940s*

3½ in (9 cm) wide

| $400–560 | RG |

Crowned heart motif bangle of vermeil and antiqued vermeil sterling silver with glass cabochons encircling a large red paste cabochon. *Late 1930s*

Motif: 2¾ in (7 cm) long

| $425–475 | MG |

Panetta

After working for Trifari and Pennino, Italian-born Benedetto Panetta set up his own company in New York City in 1945. Working with platinum-colored metal, he crafted replicas of fine jewelry, from enameled and floral pins to Art Deco-style rhinestone pieces, all of which are now highly collectible.

Snake bangle with two matching rings of gilt metal with black enamel and black and clear crystal rhinestones. *1960s*

B: 2¾ in (7 cm) wide; R: 2¾ in (7 cm) circ

| $280–320 | MG |

Platinum-colored metal ring set with bands and navette-shaped cups of pale amethyst crystal rhinestones. *1960s*

¾ in (2 cm) wide

| $75–85 | BBG |

Small floral motif pin of gold-tone metal set with turquoise colored glass beads. *1970s*

1⅛ in (3 cm) wide

| $25–35 | BB |

Floral motif pin of antiqued gilt metal, the center and petals with pavé-set clear crystal rhinestones. *1950s*

1¾ in (4.5 cm) long

| $220–230 | BBG |

Pennino Bros.

The New York-based Pennino Bros., founded by Frank and Oreste Pennino, produced fine-quality costume jewelry from around 1926 to 1961. Mostly made by skilled Italian *émigrés*, such as Adrian Scannavino and Beneditto Panetta, its pieces are characterized by intricate workmanship, the use of best-quality Austrian rhinestones, and vermeil sterling silver. Favorite—and highly collectible—forms and features include flowers, bows, scrolls, drapery effects, and abstract designs.

Flower pin and earrings
of vermeil sterling silver with crystal rhinestones. *c.1940*
P: 2¾ in (7 cm) long;
E: 1⅜ in (3.5 cm) long

$400–560   **SUM**

Bouquet-of-flowers pin and earrings of rose gold vermeil sterling silver with rose pink and clear crystal rhinestones. *Mid-1940s*
P: 2¾ in (7 cm) long; E: ¾ in (2 cm) wide

$640–720   **CRIS**

Bow pin of vermeil sterling silver with aquamarine and rose pink crystal rhinestones. *Mid-1940s*
3¾ in (9.5 cm) long

$320–370   **CRIS**

High-quality Austrian rhinestones are a fine feature of Pennino jewelry.

Bow-and-flowers pin
of vermeil sterling silver with aquamarine and small rose pink crystal rhinestones. *Mid-1940s*
2⅜ in (6 cm) long

$320–400   **CRIS**

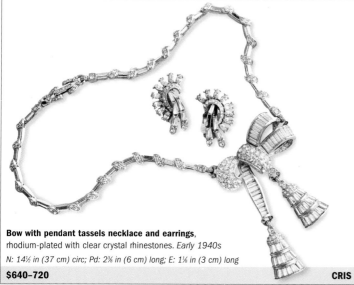

Bow with pendant tassels necklace and earrings,
rhodium-plated with clear crystal rhinestones. *Early 1940s*
N: 14½ in (37 cm) circ; Pd: 2⅜ in (6 cm) long; E: 1⅛ in (3 cm) long

$640–720   **CRIS**

Stylized flower pin with trailing tendrils of vermeil sterling silver and aquamarine and clear crystal rhinestones. *Mid-1940s*
2¾ in (7 cm) long

$320–400   **CRIS**

Stylized flower pin with trailing tendrils of vermeil sterling silver and rose pink and clear crystal rhinestones. *Mid-1940s*
2¾ in (7 cm) long

$320–400   **CRIS**

Pop Art Jewelry

Pop Art was a vibrant expression of the youth movement of the 1960s and early 70s, which created art to reflect popular culture. Pop Art costume jewelry reflects influences ranging from the Space Age to "flower power," and includes pastiches of traditional or classic forms. Bold, often highly colorful designs in plastics and metals, these pieces are rarely signed.

Large papier mâché hoop earrings painted to look like traditional stone, bone, or leather American Indian earrings. Unsigned. *1960s*

3¾ in (9.5 cm) long

$45–55   **MILLB**

Large straw boater pendant earrings in candy-stripe plastic and gold-tone base metal. Unsigned. *Early 1970s*

3½ in (9 cm) long

$20–25   **MILLB**

"Flower power" earrings with semi-translucent petals and opaque, deep purple centers. Unsigned. *Late 1960s*

1½ in (3.75 cm) wide

$20–25   **MILLB**

Gold-tone metal link belt with candy-colored plastic and a long disc pendant. *Early 1970s*

40 in (101.5 cm) long incl. pd

$20–25   **MILLB**

Plastic necklace comprising elastic-strung crimson, tangerine, banana, and white plastic beads. *Early 1970s*

19⅝ in (50 cm) circ

$20–25   **MILLB**

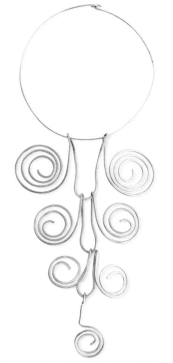

Large pendant choker made from gold-tone wire, the spiral pendants a pastiche of ancient Roman forms. *Early 1970s*

N: 17 in (43 cm) circ; Pd: 8 in (20.5 cm) long

$75–100   **MILLB**

Open bangle of gold-tone metal set with citrine rhinestones and smoky quartz. *Early 1970s*

7½ in (19 cm) circ

$45–55   **MILLB**

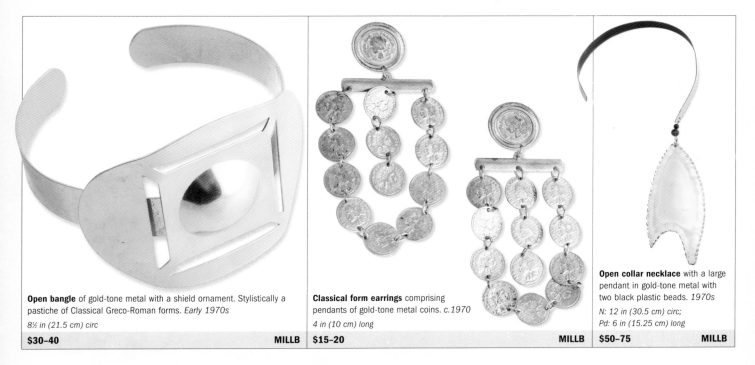

Open bangle of gold-tone metal with a shield ornament. Stylistically a pastiche of Classical Greco-Roman forms. *Early 1970s*

8½ in (21.5 cm) circ

$30–40   **MILLB**

Classical form earrings comprising pendants of gold-tone metal coins. *c.1970*

4 in (10 cm) long

$15–20   **MILLB**

Open collar necklace with a large pendant in gold-tone metal with two black plastic beads. *1970s*

N: 12 in (30.5 cm) circ; Pd: 6 in (15.25 cm) long

$50–75   **MILLB**

Rebajes

Jeweler and sculptor Francisco Rebajes was born in Spain in 1906. In 1934 he opened a studio shop in New York City, selling jewelry and *objets d'art*. He ran his business until 1967, then returned to Spain, where he made jewelry until his death in 1990. Rebajes was a star of the Modernist jewelry movement. His bold, dramatic pieces, with their characteristic soft finish, were carefully handcrafted and drew their inspiration from sources as diverse as ethnic masks and Surrealism.

A master of copper jewelry, Rebajes created distinctive pieces with a soft patina.

Stylized "African head" copper pin with copper wire necklace and earrings. *Late 1940s*

3 in (8 cm) long

$320–385   **CRIS**

Cast copper hoop earrings in the form of flying wings or flames. *c.1950*

1⅛ in (3 cm) long

$25–30   **BB**

Copper chain pendant necklace with three scrolled feather or leaf motifs. *1950s*

N: 19 in (48 cm) long; Pd: 2¼ in (5.75 cm) wide

$100–150   **MILLB**

Regency

Little is known about the history of Regency costume jewelry, other than that it was made from the 1950s to 70s by the Polowitz family–owned Regina Novelty Company, based in New York City. Such scant provenance has, however, in no way detracted from its desirability to collectors. Regency's signature piece is the butterfly, which was made in various colorways and slightly differing forms. Like the mostly floral and foliate motif pieces also made under the Regency brand, much of their attraction resides in the consistently high quality of the rhinestones employed. Usually prong-set in sumptuous complementary or contrasting colors, they are invariably a feast for the eye.

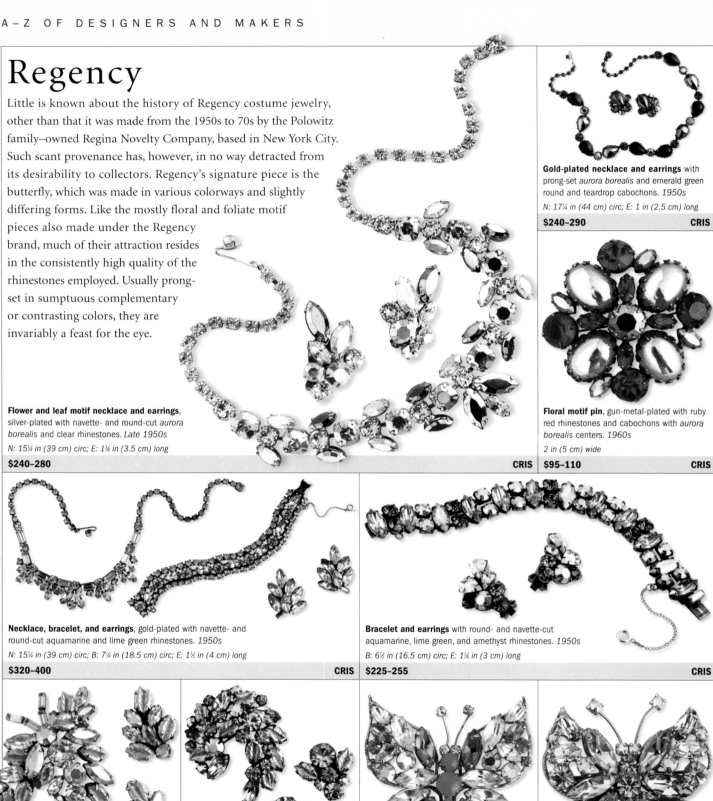

Gold-plated necklace and earrings with prong-set *aurora borealis* and emerald green round and teardrop cabochons. *1950s*
N: 17¼ in (44 cm) circ; E: 1 in (2.5 cm) long

$240–290   CRIS

Floral motif pin, gun-metal-plated with ruby red rhinestones and cabochons with *aurora borealis* centers. *1960s*
2 in (5 cm) wide

$95–110   CRIS

Flower and leaf motif necklace and earrings, silver-plated with navette- and round-cut *aurora borealis* and clear rhinestones. *Late 1950s*
N: 15¼ in (39 cm) circ; E: 1⅜ in (3.5 cm) long

$240–280   CRIS

Necklace, bracelet, and earrings, gold-plated with navette- and round-cut aquamarine and lime green rhinestones. *1950s*
N: 15¼ in (39 cm) circ; B: 7¼ in (18.5 cm) circ; E: 1½ in (4 cm) long

$320–400   CRIS

Bracelet and earrings with round- and navette-cut aquamarine, lime green, and amethyst rhinestones. *1950s*
B: 6½ in (16.5 cm) circ; E: 1⅛ in (3 cm) long

$225–255   CRIS

Leaf motif pin and earrings, gold-plated with round- and navette-cut *aurora borealis* and lime green rhinestones. *Mid-1950s*
P: 2⅛ in (5.5 cm) long; E: 1⅛ in (3 cm) long

$160–200   CRIS

Scrolling leaf pin and earrings, gold-plated with round- and navette-cut, prong-set aquamarine and amethyst rhinestones. *1950s*
P: 2 in (5 cm) long; E: 1 in (2.5 cm) long

$120–135   CRIS

Butterfly pin, gold-plated with prong-set, navette and round orange-red glass cabochons and jonquil, *aurora borealis*, and amber rhinestones. *Mid 1950s*
2⅛ in (5.5 cm) wide

$135–145   CRIS

Butterfly pin, gold-plated with prong-set round- and navette-cut *aurora borealis*, aquamarine, and jade rhinestones. *Mid-1950s*
1¾ in (4.5 cm) wide

$135–145   CRIS

Réja

Founded by Sol Finkelstein in 1939, Déja Costume Jewelry, Inc. of New York changed its name to the Réja Jewelry Co. in 1941. Up until production ceased in 1952, it created many pieces of exceptional design and craftsmanship. Although best known for its dramatic figural pins (including human, animal, fish, bird, and insect designs), Reja also made exquisite floral pieces. Most were produced in vermeil sterling silver, the thickness and warm tones of which impart a feeling of quality and substance. Other characteristic materials include enamel, faux pearls, rhinestones, and large, colored glass stones of American origin.

Flower pin of vermeil sterling silver with green, pink, and white enameling, aquamarine pastes, and clear rhinestones. *c.1939*

3⅜ in (8.5 cm) long

| $400–640 | ROX |

Stylized jellyfish pin of sterling silver with faux pearls, small faux sapphires, and clear rhinestones. *1940s*

3½ in (9 cm) long

| $240–320 | RG |

Bacchanalian mask design of vermeil sterling silver with rose-gold-plated grapes and green enameled leaves. *Mid-1940s*

P: 3 in (7.5 cm) long; E: 1⅜ in (3.5 cm) long

| $960–1,100 | CRIS |

Blackamoor head pin and earrings of vermeil and black-enameled sterling silver with clear rhinestones. *1940s*

P: 2⅜ in (6 cm) long; E: 1⅛ in (3 cm) long

| $600–900 | ROX |

Stork pin of vermeil sterling silver with clear rhinestones and a large faux aquamarine. *1940s*

2¾ in (7 cm) long

| $130–175 | RG |

Leaping stag pin of vermeil sterling silver with clear rhinestones and a large faux aquamarine. *1940s*

3 in (7.5 cm) wide

| $190–225 | RG |

Turtle pin of vermeil sterling silver with clear and pavé-set green rhinestones. *1940s*

2 in (5 cm) wide

| $190–240 | RG |

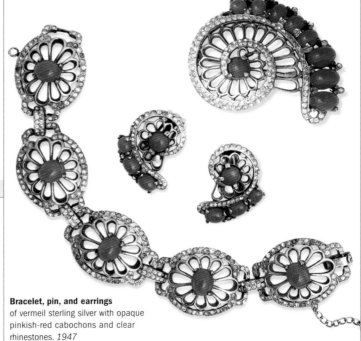

Bracelet, pin, and earrings of vermeil sterling silver with opaque pinkish-red cabochons and clear rhinestones. *1947*

B: 7½ in (19 cm) circ; P: 3½ in (9 cm) wide; E: 1½ in (3.75 cm) long

| $400–480 | RG |

Renoir–Matisse

Founded in Los Angeles in 1946 by Jerry Fels, Renoir of California specialized in solid copper jewelry. Although produced in the spirit of the late 19th- and early 20th-century Arts and Crafts movement—for which hand-worked copper was a favorite medium—most of its pieces display the geometric or abstract forms and patterns characteristic of mid-20th-century art and design.

In 1952, Fels established a subsidiary company, Matisse Ltd., which specialized in copper jewelry with colorful enamel decoration. Many pieces, especially the pins, employ more naturalistic imagery, notably artists' palettes and different types of leaves. Production at both companies ceased in 1964, leaving a very distinctive legacy: once seen, Renoir and Matisse jewelry becomes instantly recognizable thereafter.

Matisse copper twin-leaf pin with white and gunmetal gray enameled highlights. *Mid-1950s*

3⅛ in (8 cm) long

$70–80   **CRIS**

Renoir copper bangle with raised, round, geometric motifs, most commonly described as "Swiss Cheese" decoration. *Late 1940s*

1½ in (4 cm) wide

$110–160   **CRIS**

Matisse artist's palette and brushes pin with blue, yellow, brown, and red enameling on copper. *Mid-1950s*

2¾ in (7 cm) long

$105–130   **CRIS**

Renoir copper bangle with rope molding edges and hooped wire decoration. *Mid-1950s*

1 in (2.5 cm) wide

$120–145   **CRIS**

Matisse maple-leaf pin and earrings with blue and blue-black enameling on copper and copper berry highlights. *Mid-1950s*

P: 2½ in (6.5 cm) long; E: 1⅛ in (3 cm) long

$150–160   **CRIS**

Matisse maple-leaf pin and earrings with white and yellow ocher enameling on copper. *Mid-1950s*

P: 2½ in (6.5 cm) long; E: 1⅛ in (3 cm) long

$150–160   **CRIS**

Richelieu

The Richelieu mark was first used in 1911 by Joseph H. Meyer Bros., which was established in Brooklyn, New York in the early 1900s. The company, which merged with Lisner in the late 1970s (*see pp.88–89*), produced costume jewelry for both women and men, embracing many styles fashionable during the 20th century. It is, however, best-known for its use of faux pearls. The majority of Richelieu pieces that collectors will come across today date from the 1960s to the 1980s. Relatively inexpensive, they typically combine polished gold-tone metals with faux pearls, crystal rhinestones, or colorful cabochons, although antiqued metal pieces in various historical-revival styles can also be found, usually at slightly higher prices.

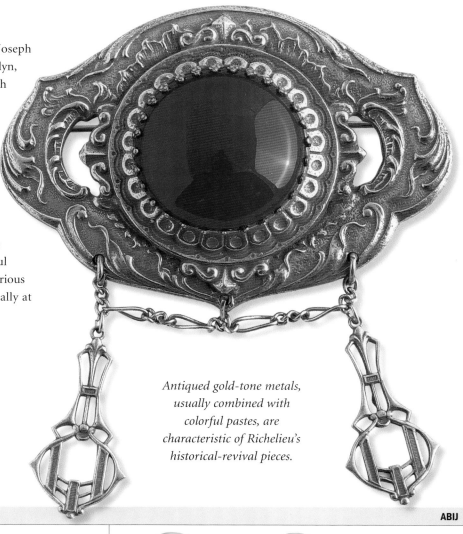

Antiqued gold-tone metals, usually combined with colorful pastes, are characteristic of Richelieu's historical-revival pieces.

Art Nouveau Revival cartouche pin with scrolled leaf decoration and pendants, in antiqued gold-tone metal with a faux cornelian cabochon. *1960s*

3 in (7.5 cm) wide

$65–70   ABIJ

Geometric form earrings of highly polished gold-tone metal and hinged pendants with three sections of pavé-set, round-cut, clear crystal rhinestones. *1980s*

1⅛ in (3 cm) long

$25–30   MILLB

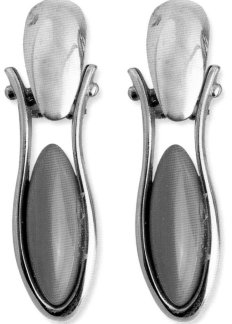

Drop earrings of highly polished gold-tone metal and navette-shaped faux coral inserts. *1980s*

2¼ in (5.75 cm) long

$20–25   MILLB

Oval faux pearl earrings of champagne color with a highly lustrous finish. *1970s*

¾ in (2 cm) long

$15–20   MILLB

Plastic Jewelry

First made in the mid-19th century, plastic jewelry gained popularity from the 1920s onward. Quick to produce and reasonably priced, it was readily available and appealed to customers in all income brackets.

Bathing belles pin in red, black, yellow, and flesh-colored celluloid. *Late 1920s 1¾ in (4.5 cm) long* **$40–50 JJ**

A TRULY MODERN MATERIAL

Celluloid, one of the first plastics, was invented by Alexander Parkes in 1855. It had the color and texture of ivory, but could be dyed to look like tortoiseshell or horn. Celluloid jewelry, popular during the late 1890s, was gradually eclipsed first by Galalith and later by Bakelite, more stable and less inflammable plastics. Lucite, a solid, clear plastic, was first introduced in 1937 and was soon used for costume jewelry. By the 1950s it had more or less replaced Bakelite, which was more expensive to produce.

Plastics are both malleable and versatile, qualities that have appealed to many jewelry designers. They can be molded, carved, tinted, laminated, and attached to other materials, allowing a designer greater creative freedom than traditional materials such as metal or glass. Plastics are also quick and easy to produce. Inevitably, much plastic jewelry was mass-produced, but interesting and well-preserved pieces from the 1920s, 30s, 40s, and 50s are much sought-after by collectors.

Art Deco pieces are worth looking out for, as are intricate floral pins, some of which are decorated with rhinestones, and novelty period pieces. Trifari's Jelly Belly figurals (*see p.127*) with a central Lucite "stone" are also highly collectible.

Art Deco stylized horse pin in blue acrylic with clear acrylic eyes. *1930s. 4¼ in (10.75 cm) long* **$30–50 JBC**

Floral motif necklace with clear Lucite links and drops, and clusters of crystal rhinestones. *1950s. 32 in (82 cm) long* **$640–800 CSAY**

Hinged bracelet and pendant hoop earrings in turquoise plastic. *1950s. B: 7 in (18 cm) circ; E: 2 in (5 cm) long* **$30–50 ECLEC**

Parrot pin in shades of red, black, yellow, and brown Lucite. *c.1940 3½ in (9 cm) long* **$140–160 TR**

American courting couple pin with revolving umbrella in colored plastic. *Late 1920s. 2¼ in (5.75 cm) long* **$70–80 JJ**

Basket-of-flowers pin with green and coral Lucite and clear crystal rhinestones. *Late 1930s. 2⅛ in (5.5 cm) long* **$130–160 CRIS**

American flower pin in yellow and green Lucite on a silver filigree backing. *Late 1950s 5 in (12.5 cm) wide* **$200–240 CRIS**

American flower pin in yellow, amber, and cream Lucite on a silver backing. *Late 1950s 5½ in (14 cm) wide* **$200–240 CRIS**

Italian flower pin with pale green-brown Lucite petals and faux jet Lucite beads. *1980s. 2½ in (6.5 cm) wide* **$80–110 CRIS**

Scottie dog head pins in black and yellow Lucite with chromed steel eyes. *Late 1930s 1⅛ in (3 cm) wide* **$250–350 ROX**

Bush pin and earrings with carved Lucite and prong-set *aurora borealis* rhinestones on gold-tone backs. *Late 1950s. P: 2¾ in (7 cm) long; E: 1⅜ in (3.5 cm) long* **$95–130 CRIS**

American elasticated "Mah Jong" bracelets of faux ivory and ebony plastic. *Late 1950s 7 in (17.75 cm) circ* **$200–240 CRIS**

American flower pin with petals and leaves of green, yellow, amber, and black Lucite on a silver filigree backing. *Late 1950s. 4¾ in (12 cm) wide* **$200–240 CRIS**

Robert

Robert is the trademark of the Fashioncraft Jewelry Company, founded in New York in 1942, which changed its name to Robert Originals, Inc. in 1960. Many Robert pieces use natural motifs reminiscent of Art Nouveau jewelry, with faux pearls, colored glass, and crystal rhinestones set into gilded filigree metalwork. The pieces are usually marked, although the trademarks vary. "Original by Robert" was used from 1942 to 1979, when the company ceased trading.

Floral motif pin of antiqued filigree gilt metal with prong-set pear-, round-, and oval-cut clear crystal rhinestones. *1950s*

2⅛ in (5.5 cm) long

$140–160   **MAC**

Art Nouveau pin with sapphire, ruby, pink, and clear crystal rhinestones, clear Lucite cabochons, and a black enamel crescent set in filigree gilt metal. *1950s*

3 in (7.5 cm) long

$950–1,000   **TR**

Butterfly pin of gilt metal with black poured glass body and blue and green enamel wings. *1960s*

1¾ in (4.5 cm) wide

$50–70   **JJ**

Figural pin of an Asian man with gilt metal casting and bands of red and blue enamel. *1950s*

2 in (5 cm) long

$220–230   **JJ**

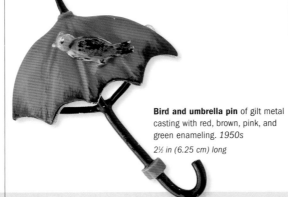

Bird and umbrella pin of gilt metal casting with red, brown, pink, and green enameling. *1950s*

2½ in (6.25 cm) long

$50–60   **JJ**

Horse pin with body and flowing mane and tail of silver gilt metal, the head set with polychrome crystal beads and rhinestones. *1950s*

5 in (12.5 cm) long

$250–300   **ROX**

Floral motif earrings with gilt wired clusters of faux pearls and faceted clear crystal beads. *1950s*

1½ in (3.75 cm) long

$45–50   **JJ**

Floral motif necklace with chain links of gilt metal set with clear crystal beads and rhinestones. *c.1960*

N: 20 in (51 cm) circ; Floral motif: 2¾ in (7 cm) wide

$250–270   **MAC**

Robert DeMario

The Robert DeMario Company was founded in New York in 1945 and continued trading until the early 1960s. DeMario pieces are distinctive for their bold designs, featuring clusters of colorful rhinestones and glass beads. Produced on a small scale, DeMario jewelry is rarer than most marked vintage costume jewelry.

Floral motif pin of gilt metal with large faceted emerald green crystal stones and small clear crystal rhinestone highlights. *1950s*

2¼ in (5.75 cm) wide

$120–130   **ROX**

Pin and earrings with pale blue crystal cabochons and rhinestones set in silver gilt metal. *Late 1950s*

P: 2½ in (6.5 cm) wide; E: 1⅜ in (3.5 cm) wide

$160–240   **CRIS**

Robert Goossens

Born in Paris, Robert Goossens was the chief jewelry designer for Coco Chanel from 1960 until her death in 1971, and worked with her to produce many hallmark pieces, such as her Byzantine crosses and "barbaric" jewels. Goossens's workshops have since created fabulous jewelry for many other couturiers, drawing much inspiration from the art of ancient civilizations.

> *"I take a pinch of Byzantine, a hint of Etruscan, a sprinkling of Celtic or Egyptian. And I make a Goossens cocktail."*
> Robert Goossens

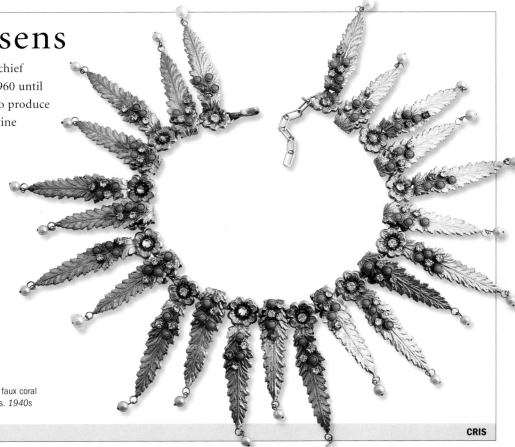

Flower and leaf motif necklace with stamped gilt metal, faux coral cabochons, clear crystal rhinestones, and faux pearl drops. *1940s*

N: 14 in (35.5 cm) circ

$640–800   **CRIS**

Sandor

Sandor was a small costume jewelry company founded by Sandor Goldberger in 1938. Innovative in approach, its signature pieces are delicate floral designs in sterling silver, beautifully decorated with enameling and rhinestones. It also produced attractive figural pieces that are much sought-after today. The company ceased operations in 1972.

Sandor jewelry is renowned for its artistry and craftsmanship. The fact that it is also rare makes it highly collectible. Most pieces are marked "Sandor," but those produced in 1939 and 1940 are marked "Sandor Goldberger."

Floral bouquets are characteristic of Sandor's jewelry. The sensitive blend of enamelwork and rhinestones shows fine attention to detail.

Floral bouquet pin of vermeil sterling silver with pale blue, pink, olivine, and peach enameling, and round-cut, prong-set rose pink crystal rhinestones. *Late 1930s*
3½ in (9 cm) long

$950–1,150   **TR**

Floral sprig pin of vermeil sterling silver with olivine and blue enameling, and aquamarine, blue, and clear crystal rhinestones. *Late 1930s*
4¼ in (10.75 cm) long

$950–1,150   **TR**

Flower pin of sterling silver with selected vermeil, clay-colored enameling, amethyst pastes, and crystal rhinestones. *Late 1930s*
4 in (10 cm) long

$1,100–1,200   **TR**

Pendant pin of filigree vermeil sterling silver with amber glass cabochons and jade green and clear crystal rhinestones. *Late 1930s*
3½ in (9 cm) long

$1,300–1,400   **TR**

Floral sprig pin of vermeil sterling silver with green and white enameling and citrine and clear crystal rhinestones. *Late 1930s*
3¼ in (8.25 cm) long

$450–500   **TR**

S & B Lederer & Co.

Founded in Providence, Rhode Island in 1878, and later also operating out of offices on Fifth Avenue in New York City, S & B Lederer Company remained on company listings until 1931. Its gold-plated and silver jewelry—the silver sometimes textured and contrasted with gilt or copper highlights—is of very good quality and unusual design. These increasingly valuable pieces bear a variety of company marks, including "S. B. & L.," sometimes accompanied by an inverted triangle and sometimes with a star.

Medal pin with a heraldic motif, of hand-beaten and textured sterling silver with copper and gold-plated dragon, and antiqued gold soldier's face. *c.1900*
1½ in (3.75 cm) wide

$1,400–1,600   CGPC

Sarah Coventry

From 1949 to 1984, Sarah Coventry was a successful company selling costume jewelry through parties in people's homes. The company did not design or make its own jewelry but purchased designs that were then manufactured by other jewelers. The pieces made in the 1950s and 60s were modestly priced but very attractive and beautifully executed. The better pieces and limited-production hostess sets are now especially prized.

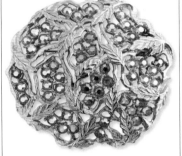

Leaves and berries medallion pin of antiqued brushed gold-tone metal with *aurora borealis* rhinestones. *1960s*
2½ in (6.25 cm) wide

$45–55   ABIJ

Floral motif earrings of latticework silver-tone metal with faceted silver-tone metal cabochon centers. *c.1980*
2¼ in (5.75 cm) wide

$25–35   MILLB

Cross pin of goldwashed base metal with embossed bead motif borders, red and white oval glass cabochons, and a central dark blue round glass cabochon. *1970s*
2½ in (6.25 cm) wide

$50–55   JJ

Bunny pin of polished and embossed gold-tone metal with one ruby glass cabochon eye and a garnet glass cabochon nose. *1960s*
2 in (5 cm) high

$25–35   ABIJ

Gold-tone metal pin with faux pearl highlights and an enameled "miniature" of the *Mona Lisa*. *1970s*
1½ in (3.75 cm) long

$25–35   JJ

Selro

Little is known about the Selro Corporation, owned by Paul Selinger, which was based in New York City and produced a distinctive range of colorful costume jewelry during the 1950s and 60s. Pieces by Selro are much prized by collectors for their dramatic designs. The company is best known for the brightly colored molded plastic faces, particularly devils' faces, which it incorporated in necklaces and earrings. However, Selro also produced many delicate and very feminine pieces.

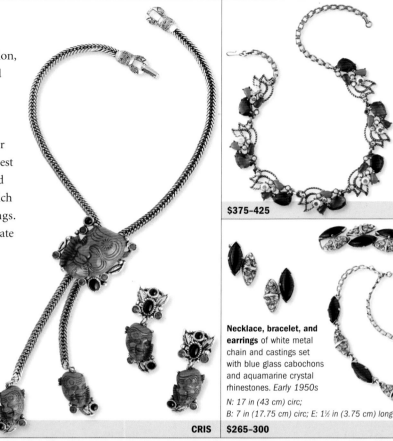

Devils' heads pendant necklace and earrings with silver-plated chain and castings, molded and incised red Lucite devils' heads, and round and oval black glass cabochons. *Late 1950s*

Large pd: 1¾ in (4.5 cm) long;
E: 1 in (2.5 cm) long

$200–240   **CRIS**

Necklace and earrings of gilt metal with prong-set red and emerald green glass stones, white beads, and *aurora borealis* rhinestones. *Early 1950s*

N: 17 in (43 cm) circ;
E: 1½ in (3.75 cm) long

$375–425   **JJ**

Necklace, bracelet, and earrings of white metal chain and castings set with blue glass cabochons and aquamarine crystal rhinestones. *Early 1950s*

N: 17 in (43 cm) circ;
B: 7 in (17.75 cm) circ; E: 1½ in (3.75 cm) long

$265–300   **JJ**

Shiebler

George W. Shiebler & Co. was a silver manufacturer based in New York City during the late 19th and early 20th centuries. Known for his creativity and high-quality craftsmanship, Shiebler was an Aesthetic Movement designer. His work featured beautiful and highly detailed naturalistic motifs, such as insects, animals, leaves, and flowers. Shiebler silver is now in very high demand.

Twin leaf pin of engraved sterling silver with applied insects, one in sterling silver, the other in a matte-finish copper alloy. *c.1903*

2¾ in (7 cm) long

$640–800   **CGPC**

Sterling silver belt pin with a frog, snakes, and wings encircling a gilded neoclassical-style bust of a female. *c.1903*

5 in (12.75 cm) wide

$1,900–2,300   **CGPC**

Cross pin of asymmetrical shape with a sterling silver casting and a large faceted sapphire blue crystal cabochon. *c.1903*

2¼ in (5.75 cm) wide

$800–960   **CGPC**

Open cuff bangle of sterling silver with applied, highly naturalistic floral and foliate imagery. *c.1903*

2½ in (6.25 cm) wide

$2,000–2,700   **CGPC**

Swarovski

The world's leading supplier of crystal stones to jewelry manufacturers since 1892, Swarovski launched its first line of fashion jewelry in 1985, featuring its clear crystal rhinestones. This high-quality jewelry is manufactured in limited editions and is only available initially through a collector's club.

Lyre pin in gilt metal with pavé-set Swarovski clear crystal rhinestones and faux pearl highlights. *1990s*
2¼ in (5.75 cm) long

$50–65   **RITZ**

CRYSTAL RHINESTONES

Born in 1862 in Bohemia, Daniel Swarovski became a gem cutter in his father's business. After experimenting with cutting glass stones, he managed to produce small, very high-quality, brilliant-cut crystal rhinestones. These were soon in such demand with jewelry manufacturers that Swarovski invented a mechanical stone-cutter that could shape and facet large quantities of equally perfect stones. Swarovski maintains its reputation for producing crystal rhinestones of unrivaled quality to this day.

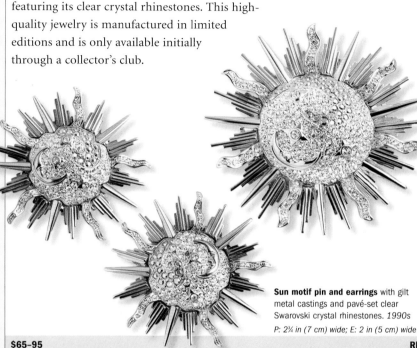

Sun motif pin and earrings with gilt metal castings and pavé-set clear Swarovski crystal rhinestones. *1990s*
P: 2¾ in (7 cm) wide; E: 2 in (5 cm) wide

$65–95   **RITZ**

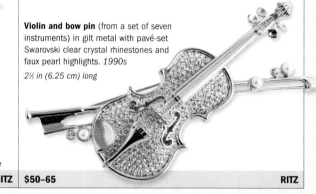

Violin and bow pin (from a set of seven instruments) in gilt metal with pavé-set Swarovski clear crystal rhinestones and faux pearl highlights. *1990s*
2½ in (6.25 cm) long

$50–65   **RITZ**

Swoboda

Founded in Los Angeles in 1956, Swoboda, Inc. produced fine pieces of semi-precious stones and cultured pearls in gold-plated settings. Pins were the most popular line, with motifs ranging from flowers to insects, animals, and crowns. None of its jewelry was marked before 1966, when the trademark "Swoboda" was first used.

Dragonfly pin of gilt metal wire and casting with green and ruby glass stones, and channel-set glass stones. *c.1980*
3 in (7.5 cm) long

$90–110   **JJ**

Tortolani

Italian-born Francisco Tortolani founded Tortolani Jewelry and, from 1950 to 1976, created an award-winning line of fine costume jewelry. Each piece was hand-cast in pewter, polished by hand, then finished in gold or silver plate and signed on the back. Original pieces of Tortolani jewelry are highly prized.

Cactus pin and earrings of stamped and soldered gold-plated base metal. *c.1960*
P: 2¼ in (5.75 cm) long;
E: 1⅛ in (3 cm) long

$140–160   **MG**

Unger Bros.

In business from 1872 to 1914, Unger Bros. produced fine silverware. From about 1890, the company made an impressive range of Art Nouveau sterling silver jewelry, mostly designed by Emma L. Dickinson, as well as dresser and desk sets, flatware, and smoking accessories. Unger pieces are often heavily chased with floral or foliate motifs. Cherubs and animals are also featured. The most collectible pieces are those with unusual shapes, or those featuring female or American Indian images.

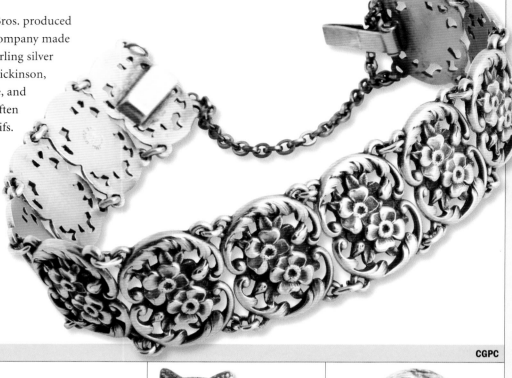

Goldwash over sterling silver bracelet comprising filigree scrolling leaf form cartouches with twin floral motif centers. *c.1900*

7½ in (19 cm) circ

$425–480  CGPC

Eagle-head cufflinks with goldwash over sterling silver castings and ruby red glass cabochon eyes. *c.1905*

¾ in (2 cm) long

$700–900 CGPC

Owl-head cufflinks of sterling silver with amber and brown glass cabochon eyes. *c.1905*

⅝ in (1.5 cm) wide

$700–800 CGPC

Bonneted lady's head belt pin in sterling silver with highly naturalistic detail and in exceptional condition. *c.1905*

3 in (7.5 cm) long

$850–1,200 CGPC

Classic Art Nouveau motif belt pin of a girl with flowing hair. In sterling silver with selected matte finish gold plating. *c.1905*

1¾ in (4.5 cm) wide

$640–855 CGPC

Belt pin with a goose head bursting out of an egg. In textured sterling silver with eyes of ruby red glass cabochons. *c.1905*

1¾ in (4.5 cm) wide

$800–1,100 CGPC

Vivienne Westwood

Celebrated fashion designer Vivienne Westwood started designing in 1971, using her shop on the King's Road, London, as a showcase for her ideas. Iconoclastic, she is perhaps best known for her association with late 1970s punk rock, bondage, and her witty reinterpretation of traditional British symbols. Most of her pieces are made of silver or gold-plated pewter decorated with clear Swarovski crystals and large faux pearls.

Bows, hearts, and emblems of royalty, such as crowns and orbs, are recurring motifs in Westwood's witty jewelry designs.

Royal orb necklace with gold-tone metal chain, faux pearls, and clear rhinestone highlights. *1980s*

N: 30½ in (78 cm) circ; Pd: 2¼ in (5.75 cm) long

$135–150 REL

Gold-tone metal royal orb earrings with round faux pearls and pendants, and clear rhinestone highlights. *1980s*

3 in (7.5 cm) long

Royal crown with velvet lining, fake fur trim, and gold-tone metal frame. The latter with fleur-de-lys, royal orb, and finial set with faux pearls, clear pastes, and crystal rhinestones. *1980s*

6¼ in (16 cm) long

$800–880 REL

$160–175 REL

Chain choker with four chains of gilt metal, three strands of faux pearls, and a gilt metal clasp with a royal orb motif. *1980s*

12½ in (32 cm) circ

$175–190 REL

Triple-strand faux pearl choker with a royal orb and clasp of silver-tone metal, the orb and cross finial studded with pavé-set clear crystal rhinestones. *1980s*

N: 13½ in (34.25 cm) circ

Bow and heart pendant earrings of silver-tone metal with black and pavé-set clear rhinestones. *1980s*

1½ in (3.75 cm) long

$135–145 REL

$105–110 REL

Scottish Agate Jewelry

During the second half of the 19th century, Queen Victoria's pride in her Scottish ancestry and the popularity of Sir Walter Scott's romantic novels made all things Scottish—including jewelry—highly fashionable.

HIGHLAND COLORS

Now highly sought-after, Scottish pebble jewelry – silver jewelry set with inlays of agate, granite, and other local stones – first became popular when Queen Victoria bought Balmoral Castle in 1848. The designs of the jewelry were based on those of traditional Celtic pieces, but were more elaborate and were often commissioned to suit individual tastes.

Agate, a banded and variegated form of chalcedony, has been used in jewelry since Roman times and is usually cut *en cabochon*, as ovals or other shapes. The rich, earthy colors of the different forms of agate—mossy greens, rusty reds, and ochres—combined with the gray of granite, were symbolic of the Scottish landscape and the tartans worn by different clans.

Scottish agate jewelry borrowed the forms of Celtic jewelry, such as the dirk or dagger pin, and the circular brooch with a long hinged pin known as a penannular. It also incorporated Scottish motifs such as the thistle, the harp, the Celtic cross, and heraldic coats of arms, by setting shaped pieces of polished agate into elaborate engraved silver.

Most of the jewelry is unmarked, but some of the pieces are signed by makers such as Sangster of Aberdeen or J.P. Hutton, which increases their value. Otherwise the value of a piece depends on its age—the earliest pieces date back to the late 18th century—or the sophistication of the motif or decoration.

Crowned paisley motif brooch inlaid with red, yellow, brown, black, and blue agate. *1850s. 2¾ in (7 cm) long* **$NPA LYNH**

Silver garter brooch with montrose blue agate and a topaz. *1880s 2½ in (6.5 cm) long* **$750–1,200 LYNH**

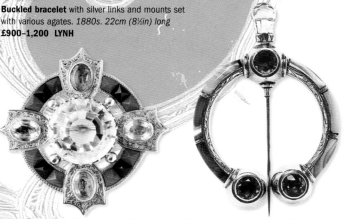

Buckled bracelet with silver links and mounts set with various agates. *1880s. 22cm (8½in) long* **£900–1,200 LYNH**

Shield motif brooch in silver with citrine stones and red and black agate. *1880s 2¾ in (7 cm) wide* **$1,100–2,200 LYNH**

Silver penannular brooch with Montrose blue agate and citrine and topaz stones. *1860. 2¾ in (7 cm) wide* **$825–975 JHB**

Silver shield brooch with a large citrine paste, inlaid with red, black, and blue agate. *1880s 2⅛ in (5.5 cm) wide* **$975–1,400 LYNH**

Engraved silver brooch with thistle motif and four panels of blue agate. *c.1870 2 in (5 cm) wide* **$750–825 RBRG**

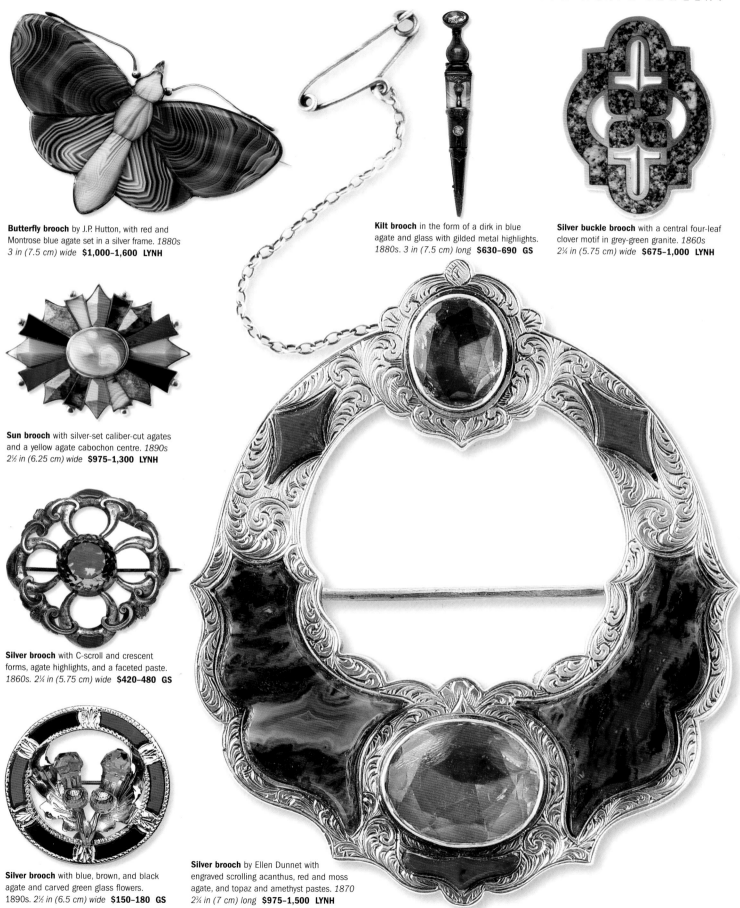

Butterfly brooch by J.P. Hutton, with red and Montrose blue agate set in a silver frame. *1880s 3 in (7.5 cm) wide* **$1,000–1,600 LYNH**

Kilt brooch in the form of a dirk in blue agate and glass with gilded metal highlights. *1880s. 3 in (7.5 cm) long* **$630–690 GS**

Silver buckle brooch with a central four-leaf clover motif in grey-green granite. *1860s 2¼ in (5.75 cm) wide* **$675–1,000 LYNH**

Sun brooch with silver-set caliber-cut agates and a yellow agate cabochon centre. *1890s 2½ in (6.25 cm) wide* **$975–1,300 LYNH**

Silver brooch with C-scroll and crescent forms, agate highlights, and a faceted paste. *1860s. 2¼ in (5.75 cm) wide* **$420–480 GS**

Silver brooch with blue, brown, and black agate and carved green glass flowers. *1890s. 2½ in (6.5 cm) wide* **$150–180 GS**

Silver brooch by Ellen Dunnet with engraved scrolling acanthus, red and moss agate, and topaz and amethyst pastes. *1870 2¾ in (7 cm) long* **$975–1,500 LYNH**

Silver harp motif brooch with engraved flowers and red and black agates. *1880s 2¼ in (5.75 cm) wide* **$1,200–1,500 LYNH**

Pendant brooch in gold with scrolling leaf and shell motifs and scalloped and bell-shaped panels of moss agate. *c.1900 2½ in (6.5 cm) long* **$825–1,300 JHB**

Silver brooch with scrolling leaf and crescent moon motifs, faceted topaz center, and agate highlights. *c.1860s. 2¼ in (5.75 cm) wide* **$525–675 GS**

Agate bar pin by Sangster of Aberdeen. *1880s 3¼ in (8.25 cm) long* **$675–1,000 LYNH**

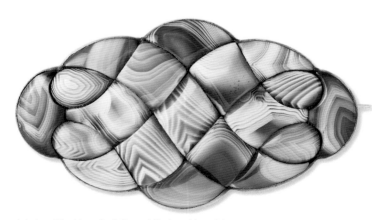

Interlaced knot brooch of silver-set Montrose blue agate. *1880s. 3 in (7.5 cm) wide* **$1,000–1,500 LYNH**

Engraved gold pendant-fob with a spinning disc mounted with agate. *c.1900 1½ in (3.75 cm) wide* **$150–225 JHB**

Silver link bracelet with geometric and heart-shaped mounts set with various agates. *c.1865. 8 in (20.25 cm) long* **$825–975 JHB**

Montrose blue agate bracelet with gold-capped links and a single pearl highlight. *1890s 9½ in (24 cm) long* **$600–675 CRIS**

Fleur-de-lys brooch with three Montrose blue agate feathers set in silver. *1880s 2½ in (6.25 cm) wide* **$1,000–1,500 LYNH**

Rosette brooch with carved and polished agate petals on a slate back. *1880s 2 in (5 cm) wide* **$525–675 LYNH**

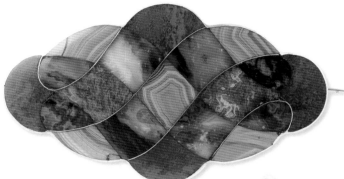

Knot motif brooch with interlaced bands of red, black, pink, and gray agate set in a silver mount. *1880s. 2½ in (6.5 cm) wide* **$900–1,200 LYNH**

Engraved silver crescent brooch set with panels of agate. *1880s. 2½ in (6.5 cm) wide* **$330–375 GS**

Cross brooch with a silver lattice pattern inlaid with red and black agate, set in a silver mount. *1870s. 2⅜ in (6.25 cm) long* **$525–825 LYNH**

Kilt pin in the form of a dirk in engraved silver with Montrose blue agate and three ruby red paste cabochons. *1880s 4 in (10.5 cm) long* **$225–270 LYNH**

Leaf motif brooch with panels of red, black, lavender, and moss agate set in a silver mount. *1880s. 2⅜ in (6 cm) long* **$600–1,000 LYNH**

Love knot brooch with interlaced bands of engraved silver-mounted Montrose blue agate. *1880s. 2½ in (6.25 cm) long* **$600–1,200 LYNH**

Vogue (Les Bernard)

Trading from the mid-1930s to the early 1970s (*see box, right*), Vogue is best known for its fine-quality, 1950s Austrian crystal bead rope necklaces, and for its 1940s patriotic flag and figural pins. The latter are now relatively scarce and highly desirable. Effectively an offshoot of Vogue, Les Bernard, Inc. has been making innovative and distinctive jewelry since the early 1960s, utilizing materials as diverse as marcasite, Austrian crystals, enamel, chromed steel, and various plastics and fabrics.

Vogue blackamoor pin and earrings of vermeil sterling silver with black enamel, glass cabochons, and a crystal rhinestone. *1940s*

P: 2¾ in (7 cm) long; E: 1 in (2.5 cm) long

$320–400   **RG**

HISTORY

1915 Vogue trademark first used by the Park Importing Company of New York City on its faux pearl and beaded costume jewelry

1936 Vogue company founded by Harold Shapiro, Jack Gilbert, and George Grant

1940s Produces highly successful patriotic and figural pins

1950s Becomes renowned for its bead rope necklaces

1962 The Shapiro family sells its interest in Vogue, which continues to trade until 1973

1963 onward Harold Shapiro's son Bernard and craftsman Lester Joy combine their names and found Les Bernard, Inc. Known especially for elaborate pieces with intricate combinations of marcasite and rhinestones.

Les Bernard interlaced scroll pendant earrings of marcasite and clear and pale green rectangular and pear-cut rhinestones. *1980s*

3¼ in (8.25 cm) long

$140–160   **JJ**

Les Bernard butterfly necklace with gold-tone metal chain and butterfly casting, and red enameled butterfly wings. *1970s*

Butterfly: 3 in (7.5 cm) wide

$25–30   **MILLB**

Les Bernard clown with umbrella pin of gold-tone metal casting with red, black, and white enameling. *c.1970*

2 in (5 cm) long

$35–40   **JJ**

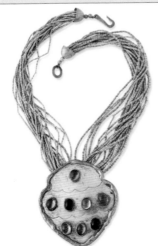

Les Bernard necklace with a pendant of clay-enameled, gold-tone metal with glass beads, hung from strands of shell beads. *1970s*

N: 20 in (51 cm) circ; Pd: 3¾ in (9.5 cm) long

$70–80   **JJ**

Les Bernard necklace with heart-shaped, relief-molded pendant of gold-tone metal hung from black cotton cord. *1980s*

N: 18 in (45.75 cm) circ; Pd: 2½ in (6.25 cm) long

$20–25   **MILLB**

Les Bernard bangles of black enameled plastic with round-cut, foil-backed clear rhinestones. *1970s*

8 in (20.5 cm) circ

$100–120   **JJ**

Volupté

From its foundation in 1926 in Elizabeth, New Jersey, until it ceased trading in the late 1950s, Volupté was best known for its elegant powder compacts, purses, and cigarette cases. However, it also produced a limited quantity of costume jewelry. Most pieces were intricate designs of oriental, Islamic, or Art Deco influence, usually worked in gold- or silver-tone metal and sometimes embellished with crystal rhinestones. Many have a soldered tag stamped "Volupté."

Intricately crafted designs of fine quality and exceptional beauty are a hallmark of all Volupté pieces. Their scarcity makes them all the more attractive to current collectors.

Open bangle of gold-tone metal, the inner band of wire mesh and the outer band pierced and chased with arabesque patterns. *1950s*
6½ in (16.5 cm) circ
$70–80   JJ

Warner

Founded by Joseph Warner in 1953, the Warner company produced costume jewelry under his direction until 1971. Usually executed in gold-tone or japanned metal, and often embellished with polychromatic crystal rhinestones, its pieces are mostly of floral or insect design, although novelty subjects, notably umbrella pins, were also produced. The most sought-after, however, are the intricately crafted open-and-shut mechanicals. Comparatively rare, they have been steadily increasing in price.

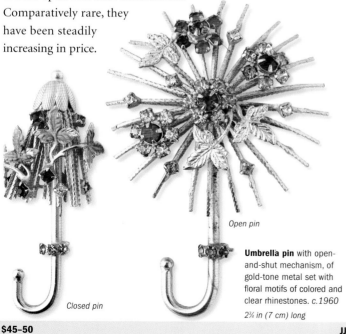

Closed pin

Open pin

Umbrella pin with open-and-shut mechanism, of gold-tone metal set with floral motifs of colored and clear rhinestones. *c.1960*
2¾ in (7 cm) long
$45–50   JJ

Open pin

Closed pin

Flower pin of naturalistic styling with "day and night" (open-and-shut) mechanism of gold-tone metal. *c.1960*
2⅛ in (5.5 cm) long
$130–160   LB

Whiting & Davis

Founded in Massachusetts in 1876, Whiting & Davis is primarily known for its beautiful, finely woven gold and silver mesh evening bags. In 1907, however, the company started creating a distinctive line of jewelry, using its expertise at making mesh to create silver and silver-plated metalwork as a basis for its pieces. Its jewelry ranges from delicate mesh chokers to dramatic bracelets and chunky earrings, many of which display Victorian or Art Nouveau influences. Its mesh spiral snake bracelets in particular are considered highly collectible.

Necktie earrings of gold-plated metal and mesh, the knot set with clear crystal rhinestones. *1970s*
2¾ in (7 cm) long

$50–65   **ABIJ**

Pendant snake-head earrings of silver-plated, punched, and engraved metal. *1960s*
1¾ in (4.5 cm) long

$25–30   **ABIJ**

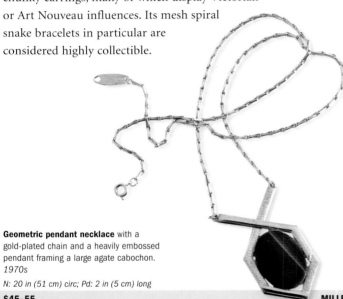

Geometric pendant necklace with a gold-plated chain and a heavily embossed pendant framing a large agate cabochon. *1970s*
N: 20 in (51 cm) circ; Pd: 2 in (5 cm) long

$45–55   **MILLB**

Gold-plated link bracelet with safety chain and ruby red glass cabochons. *Early 1960s*
7½ in (19 cm) circ

$50–65   **ABIJ**

Silver-plated coiled snake bangle with expandable mesh wrist band, and solid punched and engraved head. *1960s*
12 in (30.5 cm) circ

$45–50   **JJ**

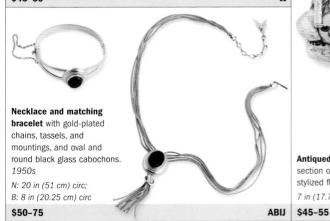

Necklace and matching bracelet with gold-plated chains, tassels, and mountings, and oval and round black glass cabochons. *1950s*
N: 20 in (51 cm) circ;
B: 8 in (20.25 cm) circ

$50–75   **ABIJ**

Antiqued gold-plated bracelet with safety chain, with section of engraved cross-hatching, and with applied stylized floral and foliate motifs. *1970s*
7 in (17.75 cm) circ

$45–55   **MILLB**

YSL

Christian Dior protégé Yves Saint Laurent established his own fashion house in 1961 and launched the first YSL collection the following year. His style has ranged from beatnik chic to the exotic and refined. His jewelry, introduced in the 1970s, is theatrical, colorful, and displays the same clarity of form inherent in his clothing.

Asymmetrical earrings with colored crystal rhinestones prong-set in gold-plated castings with turquoise and red enameling. *Late 1980s*
2 in (5 cm) long

$95–130   **CRIS**

Geometric motif necklace with gilt metal and twin strands of white faux pearls. *1980s*
18 in (45.5 cm) circ

$50–60   **MILLB**

Gold-plated earrings of oval form with suspended lozenge-shaped centers set with faceted sapphire blue glass stones. *c.1980*
1½ in (3.75 cm) long

$30–70   **LB**

Bar pin of gold-tone metal set with square- and rectangular-cut fuchsia and pale amber glass stones. *Late 1970s*
2½ in (6.25 cm) long

$70–80   **MILLB**

Zandra Rhodes

London fashion designer Zandra Rhodes launched her first eccentric fashion collection in 1969. Her costume jewelry, handcrafted by innovative designers such as Andrew Logan (*see p.138*) and Mick Milligan, displays a similar individualism, increasingly sought-after by collectors.

Bold, stylized, and unique, Zandra Rhodes's pieces are now hot property.

Stylized figural pin by Mick Milligan, of stamped, pierced, corrugated, and spiraling gold-tone metal with a small cluster of clear rhinestones. *1970s*
6 in (15 cm) long

$NPA   **LB**

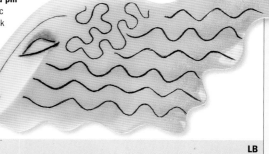

Stylized female head pin of skin-colored plastic with black and lipstick rouge highlights. *1970s*
3 in (7.5 cm) wide

$NPA   **LB**

Gallery of unsigned pieces

Collectible designs from around the world

Most costume jewelry is unsigned and these pieces constitute a veritable Aladdin's cave of treasures, with prices to suit all pockets. Because unsigned pieces have no marks to enhance their value, they cost less, yet they often share the same quality of design, materials, and craftsmanship as signed designer pieces. Without provenance, the best investment is in quality materials, such as sterling silver, vermeil, and Austrian crystal rhinestones, in sophisticated and innovative settings, and, above all, in pieces that are in excellent condition.

You may choose to collect pieces from a particular period that interests you, or themed pieces, featuring animals, bows, or flower baskets, for example. With a little background research, you may even be able to recognize an unsigned piece from a well-known maker.

Necklaces

There are necklaces to suit every taste, ranging in style from the long sautoirs of the 1920s flapper to the fantasy colored necklaces of the 1950s and the plastic pendant necklaces of the 1960s. As with all costume jewelry, seek out interesting and attractive pieces, made from good-quality materials. Innovative stone cuts and unusual color combinations are worth watching for, along with interesting period details. Always try necklaces on to make sure that they suit you and sit well on the neck, and check whether any stones are missing and that clasps fasten properly.

The streamlined geometric forms of the 1920s and 30s Art Deco style are now perennial favorites with collectors.

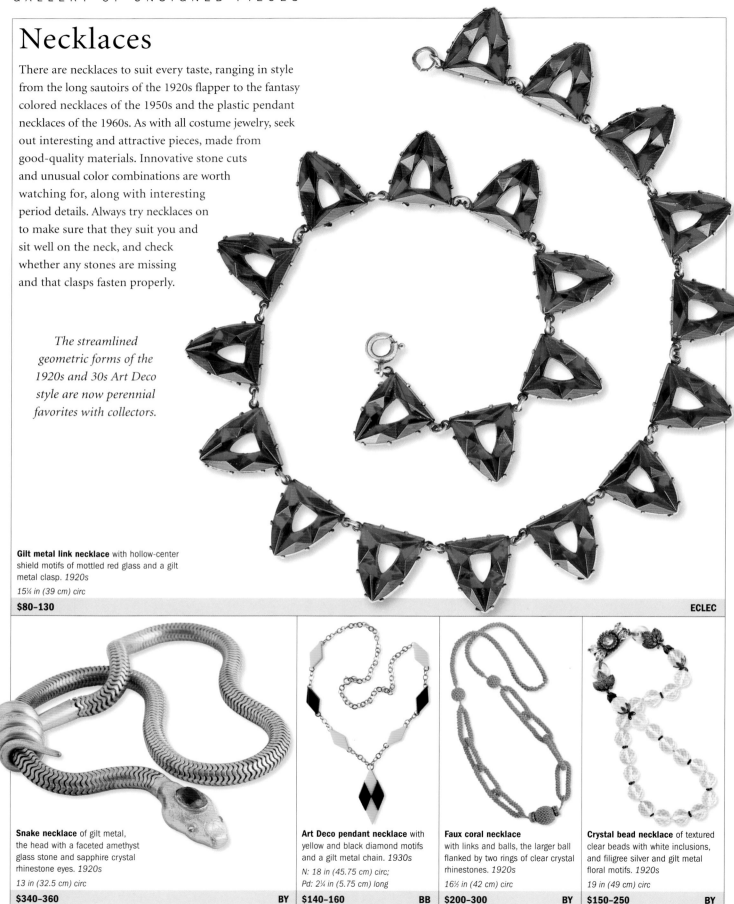

Gilt metal link necklace with hollow-center shield motifs of mottled red glass and a gilt metal clasp. *1920s*
15¼ in (39 cm) circ

$80–130   ECLEC

Snake necklace of gilt metal, the head with a faceted amethyst glass stone and sapphire crystal rhinestone eyes. *1920s*
13 in (32.5 cm) circ

$340–360   BY

Art Deco pendant necklace with yellow and black diamond motifs and a gilt metal chain. *1930s*
N: 18 in (45.75 cm) circ;
Pd: 2¼ in (5.75 cm) long

$140–160   BB

Faux coral necklace with links and balls, the larger ball flanked by two rings of clear crystal rhinestones. *1920s*
16½ in (42 cm) circ

$200–300   BY

Crystal bead necklace of textured clear beads with white inclusions, and filigree silver and gilt metal floral motifs. *1920s*
19 in (49 cm) circ

$150–250   BY

Pendant necklace with red plastic neckband and graduated, articulated discs of polished steel. *c.1970*

Pd: 6¼ in (16 cm) long

$1,600–2,400 LB

French necklace of gold-plated metal, green and clear glass beads, and clear crystal rhinestones. *c.1930*

16½ in (42 cm) circ

$300–400 BY

Murano glass necklace with green glass leaves and yellow and orange-red glass bead fruits. *c.1960*

16 in (41 cm) circ

$120–190 LB

Silver link necklace set with clear crystal rhinestones and faceted ruby glass shield motifs. *c.1930*

14 in (36 cm) circ

$110–160 ECLEC

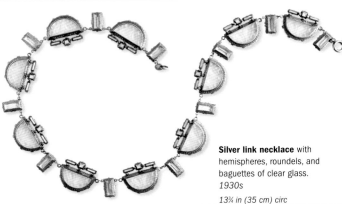

Silver link necklace with hemispheres, roundels, and baguettes of clear glass. *1930s*

13¾ in (35 cm) circ

$95–160 ECLEC

Fruit-and-berry-motif necklace of yellow and green frosted glass interspersed with faux pearls and clear and aqua rhinestones. *1950s*

22½ in (58 cm) circ

$130–160 CRIS

French Art Deco necklace of matte-finish, gold-plated metal with triangular sections of black enameling. *1930s*

17 in (43 cm) circ

$545–610 CRIS

Bunches-of-grapes necklace of ruby red glass beads alternated with hoops of clear glass. *1920s*

16½ in (42 cm) circ

$95–160   ECLEC

French necklace of gilt metal with faux pearls, ruby glass cabochons, and aquamarine and pink glass drops. *1920s*

17 in (43 cm) circ

$900–1,100   TR

Triple-strand faux pearl necklace with a pendant of gilt metal, clear crystal rhinestones, and faux pearl drops. *1950s*

N: 14 in (36 cm) circ; Pd: 3 in (8 cm) long

$225–255   CRIS

Glass necklace of faceted clear crystal stones and three emerald green poured glass stones. *1930s*

15¼ in (39 cm) circ

$150–200   BY

French necklace with gilt metal chain, faux pearls, and polychrome glass stones and beads. *1920s*

18 in (45.75 cm) circ

$900–1,100   TR

French necklace with silver links, clear crystal rhinestones, and red, blue, green, and black carved glass stones. *1920s*

14 in (35.5 cm) circ

$190–240   RG

Twin-strand necklace of faceted gray glass beads and a floral motif of gilt metal, pink glass, and faux pearls. *1960s*
17 in (44 cm) circ

$270–320   CRIS

Gilt metal link necklace with oval hoops of mottled amber-colored glass. *c.1930s*
15¼ in (39 cm) circ

$65–110   ECLEC

Rosette necklace of gilt metal with bead molding encircling turquoise glass cabochons. *1960s*
18¼ in (47 cm) circ

$105–120   CRIS

Attribution, albeit unsigned, to the prestigious French maker Rousselet enhances the value of this attractive necklace.

Floral motif necklace with silvered metal links and round- and navette-cut *aurora borealis* rhinestones. *1950s*
15½ in (40 cm) circ

$50–80   ECLEC

Pendant necklace, attributed to Rousselet, with cranberry-colored glass beads and clusters of small and larger faux pearls. *1930s*
N: 20 in (51 cm) circ; Pd: 3 in (7.5 cm) long

$500–600   BY

Necklace Sets

It is often assumed that necklaces were originally sold with other pieces in parures or demi-parures, but this was not always the case. One of the great pleasures of collecting costume jewelry, however, lies in tracking down the various components of a matching set. By acquiring a whole set, the collector not only adds to the interest of a necklace, but often increases its value as well.

Parures and demi-parures are highly desirable when they are of an attractive design and all the stones are intact.

Japanned metal link necklace and earrings with sapphire blue crystal stones in round, pear, and navette cuts. Made in West Germany. *Late 1940s*

N: 15½ in (39.5 cm) circ; E: 1 in (2.5 cm) wide

$650–750   **ROX**

Necklace, bracelet, and earrings of gilt metal with faux amethysts, faux coral glass beads, and green crystal rhinestones. *1960s*

N: 17 in (43 cm) circ; B: 8 in (21 cm) circ; E: 1½ in (3.75 cm) long

$230–270   **BY**

Choker, pin, and earrings of solid, woven, and filigree gilt metal set with pink, green, moonstone, and clear rhinestones. *1930s*

Choker: 12½ in (31.75 cm) circ;
P: 3½ in (9 cm) wide; E: 1 in (2.5 cm) wide

$800–1,500   **ROX**

Floral motif necklace and earrings of vermeil sterling silver set with faux pearls. *1940s*

N: 14 in (36 cm) circ; E: 1½ in (4 cm) long

$80–100   **RG**

Murano glass fruits and leaves necklace and bracelet with aquamarine cabochons, orange and red fruits, and unusual opaque green leaves. *1950s*

N: 16½ in (42 cm) circ;
B: 6½ in (16.5 cm) circ

$300–350   **BY**

Four-strand necklace and floral motif pendant earrings with carved frosted citrine, olivine, and gold glass beads, and a bow and hoops strung from tiny coral-colored beads. *1950s*

N: 17 in (44 cm) circ; E: 2 in (5 cm) long

$240–280   **CRIS**

Necklace and bracelet with strands of faux pearls and orange glass beads, *aurora borealis* rhinestone highlights, and green enameled leaves. *1950s*

N: 14 in (35.5 cm) circ; B: 6 in (15.25 cm) circ

$225–255   **CRIS**

Necklace and bracelet of gilt metal with peridot green rhinestones and glass cabochons and drops. *Mid-1950s*

N: 15 in (38 cm) circ; B: 6½ in (16.5 cm) circ

$145–160   **CRIS**

Necklace and pendant earrings with faceted rock crystal beads and drops and small rock crystal spacers. *1930s*

N: 16 in (41 cm) circ; E: 2 in (5 cm) long

$140–160   **BY**

Necklace and bracelet with cream celluloid chain links and tan-colored celluloid discs. *1930s*

N: 15½ in (40 cm) circ; B: 7 in (17.75 cm) circ

$350–450   **MAC**

Pendant necklace and earrings of gold-plated metal with mottled green glass cabochons. *c.1970*

N: 15 in (38 cm) circ;
Pd: 3½ in (9 cm) long;
E: 1⅛ in (3 cm) wide

$65–95   **ECLEC**

Bangles

A popular fashion accessory from the 1920s to the early 1940s, bangles are often made from unusual materials and have interesting features. Stylish Bakelite bangles are highly sought-after—particularly when handcarved or decorated with polka dots or zigzags—as are early Lucite bangles in desirable period colors.

Squirrel bangle of gold-tone metal with ruby crystal rhinestone eyes, probably made by Sphinx for Saks Fifth Avenue. *1980s*

6¾ in (17.5 cm) circ

$35–45   **CRIS**

Elasticated bangle with raised and chamfered squares of onyx and amber Bakelite. *1940s*

1¼ in (3 cm) wide

Tasseled bangle, possibly by Miriam Haskell, of gold-plated metal with white glass beads. *c.1940*

6½ in (16.5 cm) circ

$30–65   **ECLEC**

$60–70   **JJ**

Open copper bangle with motif commemorating the 1939 New York World's Fair. *1939*

2½ in (6.25 cm) wide

$40–50   **AIS**

Wooden bangle with copper clasp and carved wooden horse-head set on a disc of caned leather. *1940s*

Disc: 2 in (5 cm) wide

$130–160   **CRIS**

Plastic bangle with carved floral and foliate motifs in white, cream, gray, black, and shades of green. *1930s*

9 in (23 cm) circ

$15–30   ECLEC

Lucite bangle in "apple juice" color with reverse carved and colored flowers and foliage. *Late 1930s*

2¾ in (7 cm) wide

$500–600   BY

Cast phenolic hinged bangle in mottled green and yellow with two applied Scottie dogs. *Late 1930s*

2¾ in (7 cm) wide

$250–350   BY

Expandable bangle of gold-tone metal with emerald green, ruby red, and clear crystal rhinestones. *1950s*

6½ in (17 cm) circ

$120–135   CRIS

Cast phenolic bangle with laminated stripes in brown, red, and yellow. *Late 1930s*

3 in (7.5 cm) wide

$250–350   BY

Cast phenolic bangle with laminated stripes in yellow, mottled yellow-brown, and green. *Late 1930s*

3¼ in (8.25 cm) wide

$250–350   BY

Open copper bangle and cast phenolic scarab with selective gold painting and steel cabochons. *1920s*

2 in (5 cm) wide

$200–300   BY

Bracelets

Bracelets are an interesting collecting field in their own right, reflecting the changing styles of costume jewelry during the 20th century. A key Art Deco accessory, they were more popular than pins up until the 1940s. Look for good-quality 1940s vermeil retro-style bracelets and showy decorative pieces from the 1950s, resplendent with fantasy pastes in unexpected color combinations.

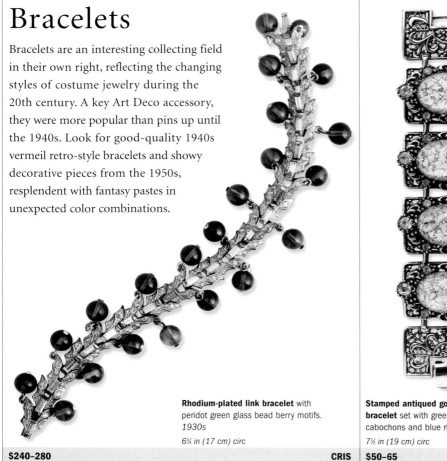

Rhodium-plated link bracelet with peridot green glass bead berry motifs. *1930s*

6¾ in (17 cm) circ

$240–280   **CRIS**

Stamped antiqued gold-tone metal bracelet set with green and gold glass cabochons and blue rhinestones. *1950s*

7½ in (19 cm) circ

$50–65   **ECLEC**

Faux amethyst bracelet of gilt metal, translucent plastic, crystal rhinestones, and faceted amethyst glass. *c.1930*

2½ in (6.5 cm) wide

$1,000–1,500   **BY**

Textured gold-tone metal link bracelet with alternating links of pavé-set clear crystal rhinestones. *Late 1950s*

7½ in (19 cm) long

$105–120   **CRIS**

French silver Art Deco bracelet with clear crystal rhinestones, emerald glass cabochons, and "fruit salad" stones. *1930s*

7¼ in (18.5 cm) circ

$1,600–1,900   **TR**

Wristwatch bracelet in gold-plated metal; the watch face encircled by clear crystal rhinestones. *1940s*

Face: 1⅜ in (3.5 cm) wide

$160–200   **CRIS**

Gold-plated metal bracelet with prong-set aquamarine blue, *aurora borealis*, and sapphire crystal rhinestones. *1950s*

6¾ in (17 cm) circ

$60–70   **BY**

Gilt metal bracelet with "butterfly wing" glass cabochons showing a tropical shoreline. *1950s*

7 in (18 cm) circ

$65–95   **ECLEC**

Gilt metal bracelet with red and green "fruit salad" glass stones, green baguettes, and clear crystal rhinestones. *1940s*

6¾ in (17 cm) circ

$325–375   **BY**

Solid silver bracelet with interlaced diamond motif of square-cut sapphire blue crystal rhinestones. *1950s*

7 in (17.75 cm) circ

$385–450   **CRIS**

Cocktail bracelet in vermeil sterling silver with scenes from *The Marriage of Figaro* in polychrome crystal rhinestones. *1940s*

8 in (20.25 cm) circ

$1,100–1,300   **CRIS**

Rose bracelet with gold-plated clasp and links, and round-cut rose pink crystal rhinestones. *1950s*

7½ in (19 cm) circ

$110–130   **CRIS**

Wristwatch bracelet of gilt metal set with polychrome glass beads, faux pearls, and round- and baguette-cut rhinestones. *1950s*

6¾ in (17 cm) long

$150–190   **CRIS**

Flower, Fruit, and Leaf Pins

The most common and traditional subject matters for pins, flowers, fruit, and leaves have always provided a wealth of inspiration for jewelry designers. The most valuable pieces are those that display complex and innovative designs, high-quality pastes in rich colors, and exquisite craftsmanship. Baskets or vases of flowers and fruit pins constitute worthwhile collecting fields in their own right.

Large rhinestones in flamboyant fantasy colors were popular features of flower pins during the 1950s and 60s.

Floral pin with lime green navettes and round aquamarine, emerald, clear, and *aurora borealis* rhinestones. Made in Canada in the style of the Regency company. *1960s*

3 in (7.5 cm) wide

$70–90   **CRIS**

Palm tree pin of sterling silver with channel-set emerald and clear crystal rhinestones. *1920s*

2 in (5 cm) long

$600–680   **CRIS**

Retro-style floral pin of sterling silver with sapphire glass cabochons and clear crystal rhinestones. *1940s*

2½ in (6.25 cm) long

$95–145   **RG**

Flower pin with open-and-shut mechanism, of gilt metal with blue enameling and clear crystal rhinestones. *1950s*

3½ in (9 cm) long

$250–350   **BY**

Bouquet-of-flowers pin with prong-set faux amethysts, polychrome enameled highlights, and clear crystal rhinestones. *1940s*

4 in (10 cm) long

$150–200   **BYA**

Vase-of-flowers pin of vermeil sterling silver with faceted ruby, emerald, and apple green glass stones, and clear crystal rhinestones. *1940s*
3¼ in (8.25 cm) long

$325–375 BY

Leaf and berry pin with faux pearl berries, emerald green glass leaves, and a mottled jade green glass drop. *1950s*
2 in (5 cm) long

$50–80 ECLEC

Triple flowerhead pin of white metal casting set with clear crystal rhinestones. *1940s*
2 in (5 cm) wide

$90–120 JJ

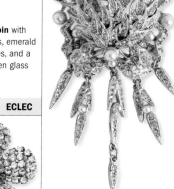

Byzantine-style floral pin of gilt metal casting set with clear crystal rhinestones and faux pearls. *1960s*
4 in (10 cm) long

$65–90 CRIS

Floral pin, possibly by Schreiner, with prong-set ruby red and clear crystal rhinestones on a gilt metal back. *1950s*
2 in (5 cm) wide

$150–190 CRIS

Floral-motif pin with gold-tone metal back and clusters of prong-set *aurora borealis* rhinestones. *1950s*
2½ in (6.25 cm) wide

$30–40 PC

Flower-and-leaf pin made in Canada with green navettes and carved blue glass stones in gold-plated settings. *c.1970*
3 in (7.5 cm) wide

$90–105 CRIS

Floral pin, possibly by Schreiner, with clear, lime green, and diamond-cut white crystal rhinestones, and a lime green glass cabochon. *1950s*
3¼ in (8.25 cm) long

$190–230 CRIS

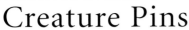

Creature Pins

Creature pins have become an extremely popular collecting field, and many collectors specialize in a particular species. From bird pins, with their romantic associations with departure, to butterfly brooches, to quirky pins featuring colorful creatures such as lobsters, there is a wealth of imagery to choose from. Both naturalistic and highly stylized designs are collectible, as are the much rarer and sometimes very expensive articulated creature pins.

Regardless of size, highly stylized creature pins create a far more dramatic visual impact than their more naturalistic or whimsical counterparts.

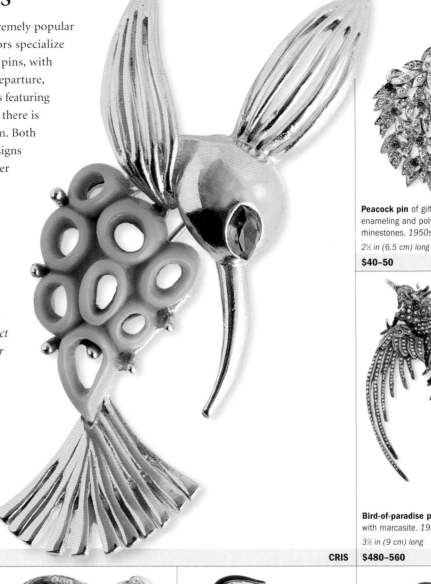

Peacock pin of gilt metal casting with black enameling and polychrome and clear crystal rhinestones. *1950s*

2½ in (6.5 cm) long

$40–50 CRIS

Bird-of-paradise pin in silver set with marcasite. *1920s*

3½ in (9 cm) long

$480–560 CRIS

Stylized hummingbird pin of gold-plated metal casting with turquoise Lucite rings and aquamarine crystal rhinestone eyes. *1960s*

3¼ in (8.25 cm) long

$55–65 CRIS

Hummingbird pin of gilt metal casting set with clear and ruby rhinestones and pavé-set turquoise crystal cabochons. *1950s*

2½ in (6.25 cm) long

$25–30 CRIS

Flamingo pin of vermeil sterling silver with faceted yellow glass body and pavé-set clear crystal rhinestones. *1940s*

3½ in (9 cm) long

$325–375 BY

Crested bird pin of gold-tone metal with black enameling and clear crystal rhinestones. *1950s*

3 in (7.5 cm) long

$15–25 CRIS

Toucan pin of gilt metal casting with blue, green, and red enameling and ruby glass cabochon eyes. *1950s*

2¼ in (5.75 cm) long

$15–25 CRIS

Bull pin of sterling and vermeil sterling silver with red enameling and sapphire, ruby, emerald, and clear crystal rhinestones. *1930s*

3½ in (9 cm) long

$560–640   **CRIS**

Violin-playing cricket pin of gold-plated metal with enameling and pavé-set clear crystal rhinestones. *1930s*

2⅜ in (6 cm) long

$130–170   **BY**

Poodle pin of gold-tone metal casting set with faux pearls. *1950s*

1¾ in (4.5 cm) wide

$15–25   **ECLEC**

Banjo-playing frog pin with articulated strumming arm, of green carved cast phenolic with painted banjo. Extremely rare. *1930s*

2¾ in (7 cm) long

$2,000–2,500   **BY**

Rare "catwalk" butterfly pin of French jet, pale blue glass beads, and variegated agate stones. *1990s*

7½ in (19 cm) wide

$430–480   **CRIS**

Butterfly pin with gilt wire frame set with pink, mauve, ruby red, and green rhinestones. *1950s*

2¼ in (5.75 cm) wide

$120–135   **CRIS**

Elephant watch pin in vermeil sterling silver with faux sapphire body and clear crystal rhinestones. *1940s*

2¾ in (7 cm) wide

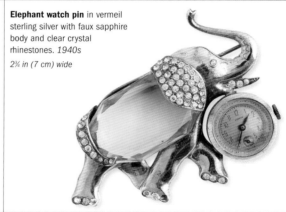

$140–160   **BY**

Lobster pin with *en tremblant* claws, of base metal with red and black enameling. *1930s*

3¼ in (8.25 cm) long

$70–80   **TR**

Tropical fish pin, possibly by Mazer Bros., of gilt metal casting with black and ivory enameling, clear crystal rhinestones, and "metallic" faux pearls. *1940s*

2¾ in (7 cm) wide

$225–255   **CRIS**

Miscellaneous Pins

This diverse category embraces pins of wide-ranging imagery, including abstract and geometric pieces. Favorite motifs are crosses, shields, masks, flowing fabric subjects such as bows and drapery, and the eye—a jewelry motif that extends right back to ancient times. Look for bold and original designs, good-quality materials, and pins that are characteristic of a particular period.

Maltese cross pin with scrolling forms of filigree gold wire set with faux baroque pearls and clear rhinestones. *1960s*

2½ in (6.5 cm) wide

$50–60   CRIS

Art Deco African mask pin of black and red Bakelite with chromed steel eyebrows and mouth. *1920s*

2½ in (6.5 cm) long

$255–305   RITZ

Pendant cross pin of vermeil sterling silver with polychrome rhinestones, faux pearls, and mottled turquoise glass cabochons. *1940s*

3 in (7.5 cm) long

$160–190   RG

Musical clef pin of vermeil sterling silver with a large aquamarine paste, and emerald, sapphire, ruby, and aquamarine crystal rhinestones. *1940s*

4 in (10 cm) long

$120–135   CRIS

Retro bow pin in sterling silver with clear crystal rhinestones and a large aquamarine glass stone. *1940s*

2¾ in (7 cm) wide

$145–160   CRIS

Eye pin of vermeil sterling silver with clear and sapphire crystal rhinestones, a black glass cabochon, and faux pearl drops. *1940*

2 in (5 cm) wide

$340–360   BY

Shield pin of sterling silver with faceted and baguette clear crystal rhinestones, and ruby, sapphire, and emerald glass stones. *1920s*

2 in (5 cm) long

$200–250   BY

Moorish-style pin of antiqued gilt metal with a large faux amethyst, turquoise and blue glass cabochons, and white, red, turquoise, and black enamel. *1920s*

2⅜ in (6 cm) wide

$180–220   BY

Zebra pin-pendant of vermeil sterling silver with black enameling, clear crystal rhinestones, and an emerald glass cabochon. *1940s*

2 in (5 cm) long

$150–180   ABIJ

Entwined snakes pin in brass with a large jade green plastic stone and four jade green drops. *c.1917*

2½ in (6.25 cm) long

$180–220   CGPC

Organic shape pin in gilt metal with a turquoise and gold ceramic cabochon and three similar ceramic drops. *c.1910*

1⅛ in (3 cm) wide

$120–140   CGPC

Bow pin, possibly by Coro, of rhodium-plated casting with round, baguette, and pavé-set clear crystal rhinestones. *1930s*

3¼ in (8.25 cm) long

$145–160   CRIS

Human Figurals

Human subjects lend themselves to whimsical designs and have provided the motifs for a witty, creative style of costume jewelry, especially during lean times, such as World War II. Pastiches of jazz musicians, clowns, ballerinas, and scarecrows abound, as do exaggerated portrayals of human faces. Articulated figures with movable arms and legs are particularly worth collecting.

African mask fur clip of cold enameled base metal with clear and ruby red crystal rhinestones. *1930s*
1¾ in (4.5 cm) wide

$80–95   PC

Novelty porter-and-suitcase pin in black, red, and blue Bakelite with plaited bow, chain, and highlights of gilt metal. *1930s*
3¼ in (8.25 cm) long

$450–500   TM

Green cast phenolic pin of a seated Asian man in profile playing a pipe.
1930s
2¼ in (5.75 cm) long

$150–200   BB

Caliph pin of gold-tone metal with black enameling, aquamarine and turquoise glass cabochons, clear rhinestones, and a faux pearl. *1960s*
2¾ in (7 cm) long

$70–95   CRIS

Caliph pin of vermeil sterling silver with black glass face, faux sapphire cabochons, and clear crystal rhinestones. *1940s*
2 in (5 cm) long

$95–130   RG

Ballroom dancer pin in vermeil sterling silver with black enameling and faux sapphires, ruby baguettes, and emeralds. *1940s*
3½ in (9 cm) long

$325–375   BY

Naturalistic detail with an extravagant sense of movement is invariably eye-catching.

Woman's torso and head pin of vermeil sterling silver with pavé-set clear crystal rhinestones. *1940s*
2¾ in (7 cm) long

$250–300   BY

Pins and Earrings

A pair of earrings, especially with a matching pin, has been the starting point of many a costume jewelry collection. As ever, well-crafted pieces made from high-quality materials command the highest prices. Most costume jewelry earrings are clips, so it is best to try them on before buying to make sure they don't pinch.

Scrolling bow pin and earrings of rose-vermeil sterling silver with large aquamarine glass stones. *1940s*

P: 3½ in (9 cm) long;
E: 1¼ in (3.5 cm) long

$230–265   CRIS

Ballerina pin and earrings in vermeil sterling silver with faceted aquamarine and sapphire glass stones and clear crystal rhinestones. *1940s*

P: 3½ in (9 cm) long; E: 1 in (2.5 cm) long

$325–375   BY

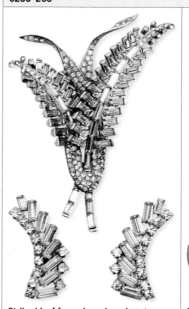

Stylized leaf form pin and earrings in sterling silver set with round- and baguette-cut clear crystal rhinestones. *1940s*

P: 2¾ in (7 cm) long; E: 1⅛ in (3 cm) long

$110–160   RG

Cat and goldfish pin and earrings of vermeil sterling silver with crystal rhinestones and Lucite bowls with carved goldfish. *1940s*

P: 2¼ in (5.75 cm) long; E: ¾ in (2 cm) long

$1,500–2,000   BY

Gilt metal pin and earrings set with hand-strung lacquered green and golden-corn-colored beads. *Early 1900s*

P: 2¾ in (7 cm) long;
E: ¾ in (2 cm) long

$300–500   ROX

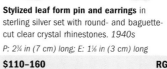

Floral motif pin and earrings with aquamarine crystal rhinestones and dark blue glass cabochons prong-set in gilt wire backs. *1950s*

P: 2¾ in (7 cm) long; E: 1⅜ in (3.5 cm) long

$120–135   CRIS

Fantasy colored stones, especially iridescent aurora borealis stones, have been popular with collectors since the mid-1950s.

Gilt metal earrings with prong-set topaz glass cabochons and *aurora borealis* rhinestones. *1950s*

1½ in (4 cm) long

$55–70   CRIS

Gilt wire frame earrings with prong-set topaz, olivine, clear, and *aurora borealis* rhinestones. *1950s*

1½ in (3.75 cm) long

$50–55   CRIS

French earrings in gold-tone metal with green and white enameling, clear crystal rhinestones, and French jet cabochons. *1960s*

1¼ in (3.25 cm) long

$40–50   CRIS

Silvered metal earrings with emerald green, turquoise, and coral glass cabochons, and faux baroque pearls. *1960s*

1¼ in (3.25 cm) wide

$40–50   CRIS

Faux precious earrings with citrine glass ovals and triangles, and clear crystal rhinestones. *1950s*

1¼ in (3.25 cm) wide

$50–60   CRIS

Oval earrings in textured gold-tone metal with a trellis pattern and turquoise glass cabochon centers. *1950s*

1 in (2.5 cm) long

$30–40   CRIS

Handbag earrings with gold-tone metal castings and patterned white enameling. *c.1970*

1½ in (3.75 cm) long

$135–160   LB

Ruthenium-plated bow and pendant hoop earrings with round- and baguette-cut clear crystal rhinestones. *1930s*

2½ in (6.5 cm) long

$240–320   CRIS

Oval earrings with filigree gilt metal castings and faux turquoise centers. *1960s*

1 in (2.5 cm) long

$25–30   CRIS

Shield-shape earrings with faceted citrine and ruby red glass prong-set in white metal. *1960s*

1 in (2.5 cm) long

$55–70   ROX

Floral motif earrings with textured gilt metal castings, rings of faux pearls, and larger faux pearl centers. *1950s*

1 in (2.5 cm) wide

$50–55   CRIS

Austrian earrings of antiqued filigree gilt metal with amethyst colored glass cabochon centers. *1930s*

1 in (2.5 cm) long

$40–50   JJ

Bow and pendant wreath earrings in silver with clear crystal rhinestones and faux sapphire pendant centers.
1920s
2⅛ in (5.5 cm) long

$2,500–3,200   **TR**

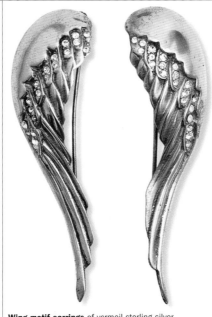

Wing-motif earrings of vermeil sterling silver set with clear crystal rhinestones.
1940s
2 in (5 cm) long

$190–240   **RG**

Art Deco multiple-pendant earrings of japanned metal with green glass cabochons and drops.
1930s
2¾ in (7 cm) long

$95–160   **ECLEC**

Pendant earrings in silver and marcasite with faux coral glass drops.
Early 1900s
2½ in (6.25 cm) long

$130–190   **RG**

Pendant earrings with prong-set amber and blue *aurora borealis* cabochons.
Mid-1950s
1½ in (4 cm) long

$50–55   **CRIS**

"Jewels of India" earrings of silver-tone metal set with faux lapis and faux coral cabochons, and clear crystal rhinestones. *1960s*
3 in (7.5 cm) long

$70–90   **CRIS**

Cluster earrings with prong-set aquamarine crystal rhinestones and prong-set amber and red glass cabochons. *1940s*
1¼ in (3.25 cm) long

$130–160   **PC**

Star motif earrings in silver set with bands of round-cut aquamarine crystal rhinestones.
1950s
1¼ in (3.25 cm) wide

$55–65   **CRIS**

Appendices and index

Further information and resources for collectors

This section of the book contains a wealth of essential, practical information for avid costume jewelry collectors. An extensive glossary of materials and techniques explains all the specialist terms used in the book, and this is followed by a comprehensive guide to designers' and makers' marks. There is also a key to the specialist dealer codes used in the price guides. The directory of other dealers, auction houses, and museums provides not only the addresses of useful specialists who may be able to help you in your search for particular pieces, but also lists museums that have good collections of costume jewelry, an invaluable source of further background information.

Glossary

Acrylics A type of plastic, which may be transparent or opaque and can be in varied colors. Lucite and Plexiglas are common acrylics.

Agate A common stone used in jewelry. It is found in a wide range of colors, including black, gray, brown, red, green, pink, blue, and yellow.

Alloy A metallic material that is a combination of two or more different metals.

Amber A semi-precious gemstone formed from the hardened resin of trees. Transparent or translucent, it is usually golden-orange, but can also be dark red.

Apple juice Golden-yellow plastic that is the color of apple juice.

Aquamarine A transparent, semi-precious gemstone that is light blue or pale sea-green in color.

Art Deco A style that originated in Paris and was popular from the mid-1920s until the late 1930s. Art Deco pieces are characterized by geometric lines and angles, with very few curves.

Articulated Connected with flexible joints or segments. The term is often used to describe pieces of jewelry that have moving parts.

Art Nouveau A style popular from the 1890s until World War I. Art Nouveau pieces are characterized by flowing, free-form imagery based on organic forms.

Arts and Crafts A late-19th-century movement that advocated simple craftsmanship, using the natural beauty and quality of materials to artistic effect.

Aurora Borealis Rhinestones, named after the Northern Lights, that have an iridescent fantasy finish, created with a polychrome metallic coating.

Baguette-cut A cut that makes a gemstone or paste into a long, rectangular shape.

Bakelite A robust and attractive plastic, often in strong colors, that was much used in costume jewelry from the 1920s to 40s.

Bangle A stiff bracelet. Some bangles have a hinge; others are solid and have to be slipped over the hand.

Baroque pearl A bumpy, irregularly shaped pearl. Baroque pearls can be either natural or artificial.

Bar pin A rectangular pin, usually worn horizontally.

Base metal A non-precious metal, sometimes also called pot metal. Brass, pinchbeck, and white metal are all base metals.

Berlin ironwork A style of cast iron jewelry, much suited to mourning wear, first made by the Royal Berlin Foundry in the first half of the 19th century.

Bib necklace A necklace with flowing pendants or chains at the front that resemble a bib.

Brilliant-cut A popular cut for gemstones. The standard brilliant has 57 facets, or 58 if the gem is cut with a flat face at the base.

Bristows (Bristol stones) Rock crystal stones found in rock near Bristol, England, which were brilliant-cut to imitate diamonds.

Bugle bead A long, thin, tube-shaped glass bead.

Cabochon A stone that has a rounded, domed surface with no facets, or a paste with a flat back.

Cairngorm A yellowish-brown type of smoky quartz often used in traditional Celtic jewelry.

Calibré-cut Individually cut to follow the exact outline of an irregularly shaped design.

Cameo A stone or shell with a design cut into it in relief, often in a naturally contrasting color.

Casting A process in which metal is shaped by melting it and pouring it into a mold.

Celluloid An early, highly flammable plastic introduced in 1869. It was used in costume jewelry and hair accessories until approximately the 1920s.

Chain mail Mesh of tiny plates or rings of metal woven together to form a metal fabric.

Chalcedony A decorative stone, part of the quartz family. Agate, cornelian, chrysoprase, and onyx are all forms of chalcedony.

Channel-set Setting in which stones or pastes are held in place in a metal channel by a slight rim around the edges of it.

Chasing A method of embossing or engraving metal, especially silver, using a hammer and a punch to create the desired effect.

Châtelaine A term used to describe a decorative pair of brooches connected by a chain.

Charm bracelet A bracelet hung with small ornaments known as charms, originally thought to bring the wearer good luck.

Choker A short necklace worn high on the neck.

Citrine A yellow or golden form of quartz. Natural citrine is pale yellow, but it is extremely rare.

Clasp A fastener that can open and close to attach two parts of a piece of jewelry together.

Cloisonné A method of applying enamel to metal. Metal wire is used to make a frame, which is then filled with enamel.

Cluster setting A setting in which small stones or pearls are set around a larger stone.

Coral A rock-like substance formed from skeletons of marine invertebrates. It can be pink, red, orange, white, or blue.

Cornelian A type of quartz that is usually translucent red in color.

Crystal Highest-quality, very clear glass that contains at least 10 percent lead oxide and looks like natural or rock crystal.

Cuff bracelet A stiff, wide bracelet.

Cultured pearls Pearls produced in controlled conditions to make them a regular size and shape.

Cut steel Tiny, faceted steel studs used in early costume jewelry.

Damascening The inlaying of a soft metal into a hard metal.

Demi-parure A partial matching set of two or three pieces of jewelry.

Diamanté Faceted, highly reflective crystal or glass stones cut to resemble gemstones. See *Rhinestone*.

Double clip See *Duette*.

Drop A small suspended stone or ornament.

Duette A pin or brooch that can be worn as two separate pins or clipped together as one.

Embossed A type of surface decoration in which a design is raised slightly above the surface.

Emerald A precious gemstone that is rich green in color. A variety of beryl, the finest gems are transparent and flawless.

Enamel A glassy substance that is fused to metal, porcelain, or other surfaces, using heat.

Engraving A type of decoration in which a design is etched into the surface with a sharp tool.

En tremblant A piece of jewelry with a motif that is mounted on a tiny spring so that it trembles when the wearer moves.

Essence d'orient A fish-scale coating that is used on glass or plastic beads to create faux pearls.

Faceting The cutting and polishing of the surface of a stone, to make it reflect light.

Faience Glazed colored earthenware that can be used to make beads.

Fantasy pastes Manufactured, unusually colored crystal stones that look deliberately false.

Faux False. A faux gem is an imitation of a real one.

Figural jewelry Commonly used to describe designs modeled on human, animal, bird, fish, or insect forms.

Filigree Intricate metal decoration created by twisting gold or silver wire into lacy patterns and soldering them into place. Imitation filigree is made of stamped metal.

Findings The functional parts of jewelry, such as clasps, hooks, links, and settings.

Foil back A reflective sheet of metal or foil placed behind a gem or paste to enhance its color and make it reflect more light.

Foliate Like a leaf.

French jet Shiny cut black glass designed to imitate real jet. It was frequently carved.

Fruit salads Costume jewelry set with red, green, and blue molded glass or plastic stones.

Fur clip A large decorative pin with a spring clasp designed to hold a fur stole in place around the wearer's shoulders or neck.

Galalith An early form of plastic used in some European costume jewelry up until the 1920s.

Gilding A process by which a base metal is plated with a very thin layer of gold.

Graduated strand A necklace of beads or pearls that increase in size from the back of the neck toward the center front.

Granulation A method of soldering tiny beads of metal to the surface of metal to form a pattern.

Hairwork jewelry Jewelry containing or made of locks of hair. It was popular in the mid-1800s as a way of remembering loved ones who had died.

Hallmark An official mark made in metal that indicates the fineness of the metal and the name or imprimatur of the manufacturer.

Hammered A term describing metal that has been shaped or decorated with a hammer.

Inlay Any material that is embedded in another contrasting material, so that their surfaces are level or flush.

Intaglio A design cut into a gem, a piece of glass, or plastic. Signet rings often have an intaglio.

Invisible setting Technique in which real or faux stones are fastened from the back, so it looks as if there is no metal mount.

Iridescent Term used to describe something that reflects many rainbow-like, changing colors.

Japanning A process that colors metal a dull black color.

Jelly Belly An animal pin that has a clear Lucite or glass stone in the center for the "belly."

Jet A fine-grained rock formed from fossilized wood. Black and opaque, it has a velvety luster and was popular for mourning jewelry during the 19th century.

Jonquil A pale yellow-colored rhinestone, named after the spring flower of the same color.

Lapis lazuli An opaque dark blue rock. It is usually cut as cabochons or beads and polished.

Lariat A style of long necklace, popular in the 1920s and 50s, that has no clasp and is knotted, looped, or held together by a ring.

Locket A pendant that can open up. Lockets can hold a charm, a photo, a lock of hair, or another precious keepsake.

Love token A piece of jewelry given as a gift to a loved one. It may be inscribed with a message or a name, or have a motif symbolizing love and affection.

Lucite A clear, strong plastic (acrylic resin) that was patented by the DuPont company in 1937.

Machine stamping A process in which sheet metal is cut and shaped by machine rather than by hand. Many medallions and jewelry findings are made in this way.

Maltese Cross A cross whose four arms of equal length increase in width the farther they get from the center.

Marcasite Iron pyrites cut to look like diamonds used extensively in the 1920s and 30s. They are often confused with cut steel.

Marquise-cut An oval-shaped gemstone or rhinestone that is pointed at both ends. (The same as a navette-cut).

Millefiori A glassmaking technique (meaning "a thousand flowers" in Italian) in which canes of different colored glass are fused together in bundles so that the cross-section creates a pattern when sliced. Millefiori glass can also be made into beads.

Modernism A 20th-century design movement that promoted simple, angular, geometric forms and repudiated excessive ornamentation.

Moonstone A semi-translucent, semi-precious stone that is milky blue with a white sheen, like moonshine. Some varieties are gray, yellow, pink, or green in color.

Mother-of-pearl The iridescent coating on the inside of oyster shells. Mother-of-pearl is often used to make buttons as well as jewelry.

Mourning jewelry Jewelry worn when people are in mourning for a deceased loved one. It is often made of jet or contains a memento of the deceased, such as a lock of hair or a portrait.

Murano glass Glass from the glass factories of Murano, near Venice, Italy, which have been making glass since the 14th century.

Nacre Another term (derived from French) for mother-of-pearl. Also used to describe the outer pearlized shell of a faux pearl.

Navette-cut An oval-shaped gemstone or rhinestone that is pointed at both ends. (The same as a marquise-cut.)

New Look A look created by Christian Dior in 1947, characterized by an exaggeratedly feminine hourglass silhouette and full skirts.

Niello A method of ornamenting metal by engraving and filling up the lines with a black compound. Can also be used to describe the compound used in niello-work.

Opalescence A milky blue-white type of iridescence, similar in color to opals.

Papier-mâché A material made from paper pulp or sheets of paper pasted together, which is painted and varnished so it resembles wood.

Parure A complete matching set of four or five pieces of jewelry, usually containing a necklace, earrings, a brooch or pin, and a bracelet (or two bracelets). See *Demi-parure*.

Paste Crystal or ordinary glass with a high lead content, which has been cut and faceted to look like a gemstone. Also known as diamanté and rhinestone.

Pâte-de-verre (also known as poured glass). A paste of crushed glass that has been colored with metal oxides, then molded and fired.

Patina A subtle sheen or change in color that some metals acquire when they are exposed to the air over a period of time. Patina can be an aid to dating jewelry.

Pavé-set Setting in which stones are set so close together (literally "paved") that the backing is not visible and the effect is one of a continuous jewelled surface.

Pear-cut A teardrop-shaped cut for stones.

Pectoral An ornament worn on the chest.

Pendant An ornament hanging from a necklace, pins, or earrings.

Perspex A colorless and transparent form of plastic much used in 1960s jewelry.

Pewter A blueish-gray metal alloy that is composed mostly of tin combined with lead, antimony, bismuth, copper, or silver.

Pin An ornament that can be pinned to a garment (also called a brooch).

Pinchbeck An alloy of copper (also known as "false gold") that looks like gold, invented by the British watchmaker Christopher Pinchbeck in the early 18th century.

Plating A process in which one metal is coated with another. In costume jewelry, inexpensive base metals are often plated with more expensive ones, such as gold.

Plique-à-jour Translucent enamel with no backing in a wire framework, which creates an effect like that of stained glass.

Pop art An art movement of the 1960s that drew its inspiration from popular culture and everyday materials.

Porcelain Fine, white earthenware (china) that is thin and semi-transparent. Most commonly used for fine tableware, porcelain is also made into beads.

Pot metal A grayish base metal, made from an alloy of tin and lead, which was widely used in early 20th-century costume jewelry.

Poured glass See *Pâte de verre*.

Prong-set A setting in which stones are held in position by claw-like metal prongs.

Repoussé A metal design formed in relief. Special punches are used to form the designs on the surface of the metal.

Resin A substance obtained from the sap of certain trees, or its synthetic counterpart, used in the production of plastics.

Retro jewelry A bold, chunky style of jewelry popular in the late 1930s and 40s, influenced by Art Deco machine-age forms. Retro costume jewelry was often made in vermeil and featured geometric shapes.

Rhinestones Faceted, highly reflective crystal or glass stones cut to resemble gemstones. The original rhinestones were quartz stones (rock crystal) dug out of the Rhine River. See *Diamonté*

Rhodium A silvery gray metal in the platinum family that is often mistaken for silver. It is used for plating in costume jewelry because it is unusually hard and resistant to rust.

Rock crystal A naturally occurring colorless, transparent form of quartz from which brilliants were frequently cut at one time, as imitation diamonds.

Rondelle A small disc that is used as a spacer between beads in necklaces or bracelets.

Rope of pearls A string of pearls that is over 40 in (1 m) long.

Rose montée A faceted, flat-backed rhinestone, often mounted in a pierced metal cup, so that it can be wired onto clothes or jewelry. Rose montée was not used much in jewelry, but was frequently used in embroidery for *haute couture* clothes.

Ruby One of the most prized gemstones, the classic ruby is rich red in color.

Russian gold plating A coppery gold matte finish first used on costume jewelry in movies in the 1940s because it reduced the glare produced by studio lights.

Ruthenium A metal in the platinum group that is used for plating in costume jewelry.

Safety catch A secondary fastening on a fine chain or necklace that is used as a backup, to make sure that the piece is not lost if the primary clasp opens.

Sapphire A precious gemstone that ranges in color from light to deep blue. Sapphires can also be yellow, green, pink, or colorless.

Scatter pins Small pins or brooches, popular in the 1950s, that are worn in a group.

Seed pearls Tiny pearls, either real or artificial, that are less than $\frac{1}{16}$ in (2 mm) in diameter and weigh less than 0.25 g.

Setting The method of securing a stone in a piece of jewelry. There are many different types of setting, such as prong-setting and pavé-setting. Some settings are closed, meaning that there is metal behind the stone. Open settings have no metal behind the stone, allowing light to shine through the stone.

Spacer A decorative bead that is used between larger beads or pearls in a necklace, to separate them and set them off.

SS An abbreviation for sterling silver.

Star-setting A setting in which a stone is set within an engraved star. The stone is held in place by a small grain of metal soldered to the base of each ray of the star.

Step-cut A rectangular or square-shaped gemstone cut with several facets parallel to the edges of the stone.

Sterling silver An alloy that is 925 parts pure silver and 75 parts base metal, such as copper, which increases the silver's hardness.

Surrealism An early-20th-century movement in art and literature that sought to obscure the boundaries between dream and reality by portraying things that didn't make sense in a hyper-realistic manner.

Swarovski crystals Top-quality, brilliant-cut crystal rhinestones produced by the Swarovski company and much used by costume jewelry designers and couturiers.

Teardrop-cut A gemstone cut that is the shape of a teardrop.

Topaz A semi-precious, transparent gemstone that ranges in color from deep golden yellow and pink to blue and green.

Tortoiseshell A mottled brown and yellow horn-like material originally made from the shell of the rare hawksbill turtle, now a protected species. The tortoiseshell used in jewelry nowadays is made from plastic.

Translucent A term used to describe stones that allow some diffused (scattered) light to pass through them.

Transparent A term used to describe materials that allow light to pass straight through them.

Trembler A piece of jewelry that has a motif or parts of it set on a spring or springs; these parts appear to tremble whenever the wearer of the jewelry moves.

Trifanium A very shiny metal alloy patented by the Trifari company, which looked just like real gold but did not tarnish.

Turquoise An opaque semi-precious stone that varies in color from an intense blue-green to bright blue. It is usually cut and polished into rounded beads or cabochons.

Vauxhall glass Named after early mirror glass made at a glassworks in London, Vauxhall glass was workable shiny glass, often black or a deep burgundy red, that was popular for use in trinkets and other jewelry in the late 18th and 19th centuries.

Vermeil Sterling silver plated with gold. Also called silver gilt or gold wash. During the 1940s, most American costume jewelry was made of vermeil sterling silver.

Designers' and Makers' Marks

Identification marks and signatures are usually found on the clasp of necklaces, bracelets, and earrings, and on the back of pins. They may be stamped directly onto the piece, or onto a small tag which is soldered to the jewelry. Examine pieces closely as marks are sometimes in unexpected locations or are only clearly visible thorgh a jeweler's eyeglass. The following is a selection of some of the stamps and copyright marks of the designers and makers featured in this book.

Alice Caviness
1945–present

CHANEL

Chanel
1920s–present

Art
1940s–late 1960s

Christian Dior
c.1947–present

AVON

Avon
1871–present

CINER

Ciner
c.1931–present

BEAUJEWELS

Beaujewels
Late 1940s–early 1970s

Coppola e Toppo
Late 1940s–1986

B.S.K.©

B.S.K.
c.1950–early 1980s

Coro

Coro
1919–1979

Corocraft
1933–1979

FLORENZA©

Florenza
Late 1940s–1981

DeRosa
1935–c.1970

FREDA.
BLOCK

Fred A. Block
1930s–1950s

De Nicola
Late 1950s–1973

Carnegie

Hattie Carnegie
1918–1980s

EISENBERG
ICE©

Eisenberg
1940s–present

SCHREINER
NEW YORK

Henry Schreiner
1951–1970s

Eisenberg
ORIGINAL

Eisenberg
c.1930–1945

Hobé

Hobé
1920s–present

Fahrner
1855–1979

HOLLYCRAFT
COPR. 1953

Hollycraft
1948–mid 1970s

 **JJ**
c.1935–present

©BOUCHER **Marcel Boucher**
1937–1972

JOMAZ **Jomaz**
1946–1981

MARVELLA **Marvella**
1911–1982

 **Joseff**
1930s–present

Matisse **Matisse**
1952–1964

©KJL **Kenneth Jay Lane**
1963–present

MAZER BROS. **Mazer Brothers**
1927–1981

KRAMER **Kramer**
1943–late 1970s

 **Miriam Haskell**
1926–present

©**LISNER** **Lisner**
c.1938–1979

©PANETTA **Panetta**
1945–early 1980s

REBAJES

Rebajes
1934–1967

SANDOR

Sandor
1938–1972

REGENCY

Regency
1950s–1970s

©**SARAH COV.**

Sarah Coventry
1949–1984

Réja

Réja
1941–1952

Schiaparelli

Schiaparelli
1920s–late 1950s

Renoir

Renoir
1946–1964

TRIFARI©

Trifari
1918–present

Robert
1942–1979

©**VENDOME**

Vendome
1944–1979

**ROBERT
deMARIO
N.Y.C.**

Robert DeMario
1945–early 1960s

WEISS

Weiss
1942–1971

Key to Dealer Codes

Each piece of jewelry shown in this book has an accompanying letter code that identifies the dealer or auction house that is either selling or has sold it. The following list is the key to these codes. It should be noted that inclusion in this book in no way constitutes or implies a contract or a binding offer on the part of any contributing dealer or auction house to supply or sell the pieces illustrated, or similar items, at the prices stated. It should also be noted that the code PC, and any code ending in PC, denotes the piece comes from an anonymous or named private collection.

ABAA
Abacus Antiques
Grays Antiques Market
58 Davies Street
London W1Y 2LP
UK
Tel: 011 44 20 7629 9681

ABIJ
Aurora Bijoux
Jenny Stephens
E-mail: aurora@aurorabijoux.com
www.aurorabijoux.com

AIS
Arthur Ivan Spike
South Street Antiques Center
615 South 6th Street
Philadelphia, PA 19147–2128
Tel: (215) 592 0256

ANA
Ancient Art
85 The Vale, Southgate
London N14 6AT
UK
Tel: 011 44 20 8882 1509
Fax: 011 44 20 8886 5235

BB
Barbara Blau
South Street Antiques Center
615 South 6th Street
Philadelphia, PA 19147-2128
Tel: (215) 592 0256

BBG
Baubles
Bunny Brooks Goldberger
South Street Antiques Center
615 South 6th Street
Philadelphia, PA 19147–2128
Tel: (215) 487 0207

BONBAY
Bonhams, Bayswater
10 Salem Road
London W2 4DL
UK
Tel: 011 44 20 7313 2727
Fax: 011 44 20 7313 2701
www.bonhams.com

BY
Bonny Yankauer
bonnyy@aol.com

CAA
Contemporary Applied Arts
2 Percy Street
London W1T 1DD
UK
Tel: 011 44 20 7436 2344
Fax: 011 44 20 7436 2446

CBU
Chéz Burnette
South Street Antiques Center
615 South 6th Street
Philadelphia, PA 19147-2128
Tel: (215) 592 0256

EC
Chris & Eddie's Collectibles
South Street Antiques Center
615 South 6th Street
Philadelphia, PA 19147–2128
Tel: (215) 592 0256

CGPC
Cheryl Grandfield Private Collection

CRIS
Cristobal
26 Church Street
London NW8 8EP
UK
Tel/Fax: 011 44 20 7724 7230
E-mail: steven@cristobal.co.uk
www.cristobal.co.uk

CSAY
Charlotte Sayers F.G.A.
Stand 360, Grays Antique Market
58 Davies Street
London W1K 5LP
UK
Tel: 011 44 20 7499 5478

CVS
**Cad Van Swankster at
"The Girl Can't Help It"**
Stands G100 & G116
Alfies Antique Market
13-25 Church Street
London NW8 8DT
UK
Tel: 011 44 20 7724 8984
Fax: 011 44 20 8809 3923

DN
Dreweatt Neate
Donnington Priory Salerooms
Donnington
Newbury
Berkshire RG14 2JE
UK
Tel: 011 44 1635 553553
Fax: 011 44 1635 553599
E-mail: fineart@dreweatt-neate.co.uk
www.auctions.dreweatt-neate.co.uk

DO
DODO
Liz Farrow
Alfies Antique Market
Stands F071, 072 & 073
13-25 Church Street
London NW8 8DT
UK
Tel: 011 44 20 7706 1545

ECLEC
Eclectica
2 Charlton Place
London N1 8AJ
UK
Tel/Fax: 011 44 20 7226 5625
E-mail: eclecticaliz@yahoo.co.uk

EL
Elms Lesters
Painting Rooms
Flitcroft Street
London WC2H 8DH
UK
Tel: 011 44 20 7836 6747
Fax: 011 44 20 7379 0789
E-mail: gallery@elms-lesters.demon.co.uk

FM
Francesca Martire
Stands 131–137
Alfies Antique Market
13–25 Church Street
London NW8 0RH
UK
Tel: 011 44 20 7724 4802
www.francesamartire.com

GCA
Griffin & Cooper Antiques
Dale W. Griffin & Joseph P. Cooper
South Street Antiques Center
615 South 6th Street
Philadelphia, PA 19147-2128
Tel: (215) 582 0418/3594

GS
Goodwin's Antiques Ltd
15 & 16 Queensferry Street
Edinburgh EH2 4QW
UK
Tel: 011 44 131 225 4717
Fax: 011 44 131 220 1412

JBC
James Bridges Private Collection

JHB
Joseph H Bonnar
72 Thistle Street
Edinburgh EH2 1EN
UK
Tel: 011 44 131 226 2811
Fax: 011 44 131 225 9438

JJ
The Junkyard Jeweler
E-mail: thejunkyardjeweler@tias.com
www.tias.com/stores/thejunkyardjeweler

L&T
Lyon and Turnbull Ltd.
33 Broughton Place
Edinburgh EH1 3RR
UK
Tel: 011 44 131 557 8844
Fax: 011 44 131 557 8668
E-mail: info@lyonandturnbull.com
www.lyonandturnbull.com

LB
Linda Bee
Grays Antique Market, Stands R18–19
1-7 Davies Mews
London W1K 5AB
UK
Tel/Fax: 011 44 20 7629 5921

LCG
Lesley Craze Gallery
34 Clerkenwell Green
London EC1R 0DU
UK
Tel: 011 44 20 7608 0393
Fax: 011 44 20 7251 5655
E-mail: gallery@lesleycraze.demon.co.uk
www.lesleycrazegallery.co.uk

LH
Lucy's Hat
South Street Antiques Center
615 South 6th Street
Philadelphia, PA 19147-2128
Tel: (215) 592 0256
E-mail: shak06@aol.com

LYNH
Brian & Lynn Holmes
Stands 304–306, Grays Antique Market
58 Davies Street
London W1K 5LP
UK
Tel/Fax: 011 44 20 7629 7327

LNXG
Lennox Gallery Ltd
Grays Antique Market
4 Davies Mews
London W1Y 2LP
UK
Tel: 011 44 20 7491 0091
E-mail: lengal4@aol.com

MAC
Mary Ann's Collectibles
South Street Antiques Center
615 South 6th Street
Philadelphia, PA 19147-2128
Tel: (215) 923 3247

MARA
Marie Antiques
Stands G136-138, Alfies Antique Market
13-25 Church Street
London NW8 8DT
UK
Tel: 011 44 20 7706 3727
www.marieantiques.co.uk

Key to Dealer Codes cont.

MG
Mod-Girl
  South Street Antiques Center
  615 South 6th Street
  Philadelphia, PA 19147-2128
  Tel: (215) 413 0434

MILLB
Million Dollar Babies
  Marian Barba
  BY APPOINTMENT ONLY
  47 Hyde Blvd
  Ballston Spa, NY 12020
  Tel: (518) 885 7397

NBLM
N Bloom & Son Ltd
  12 Piccadilly Arcade
  London SW1Y 6NH
  UK
  Tel: 011 44 20 7629 5060
  Fax: 011 44 20 7493 2528
  www.nbloom.com

RBRG
RBR Group at Grays
  Stand 175
  Grays Antique Market
  58 Davies Street
  London W1Y 2LP
  UK
  Tel/Fax: 011 44 20 7629 4769

REL
Relick
  8 Golborne Road
  London W10 5NW
  UK
  Tel/Fax: 011 44 20 8962 0089

RITZ
Ritzy
  Christopher St. James
  7 The Mall
  Camden Passage
  London N1 0PD
  UK
  Tel: 011 44 20 7704 0127

RG
Richard Gibbon
  34/34a Islington Green
  London N1 8DU
  UK
  Tel: 011 44 20 7354 2852
  E-mail: neljeweluk@aol.com

ROX
Roxanne Stuart
  E-mail: gemfairy@aol.com

SM
Sparkle Moore at
"The Girl Can't Help It"
  Stands G100 & G116
  Alfies Antique Market
  13-25 Church Street
  London NW8 8DT
  UK
  Tel: 011 44 20 7724 8984
  Fax: 011 44 20 8809 3923
  www.sparklemoore.com

SUM
Sue Mautner
  Stands A18-19
  Antiquarius
  135 King's Road
  London SW3 4PW
  UK
  Tel: 011 44 7743 546744

TM
Tony Moran
  South Street Antiques Center
  615 South 6th Street
  Philadelphia, PA 19147-2128
  Tel: (215) 592 0256

TR
Terry Rodgers & Melody
  30 Manhattan Art and Antique Center
  1050 2nd Avenue
  New York, NY 10022
  Tel: (212) 758 3164
  Fax: (212) 935 6365
  E-mail: melodyjewelnyc@aol.com

WAIN
William Wain
  Stand J6
  Antiquarius
  135 King's Road
  London SW3 4PW
  UK
  Tel: 011 44 20 7351 4905

Directory of Other Dealers, Auction Houses, and Museums

Below is a comprehensive list of additional specialist costume jewelry dealers and leading auction houses, plus a selection of international museums that hold collections of costume jewelry.

US AND CANADA

Absolutely Vintage
Joan Vogel Elias
www.absolutelyvintage.net

Agnes Lee at the New Pagoda Specialty Company
International Antique Center Building
30 West 26th Street
New York, NY 10010
Tel: (212) 645 1964
Fax: (212) 732 1452
E-mail: newpagoda@aol.com

Alice's Vintage Costume Jewelry
E-mail: alice@alicejewels.com
www.alicejewels.com

Annie Sherman
P.O. Box 9036
Kailua-Kona, HI 96745
E-mail: annie96740@yahoo.com
www.AnnieSherman.com

Antique Designer Costumer Jewelry
Valerie Gedzuin
www.valerieg.com

Antiquing On Line— The Jewelry Box
www.antiquingonline.com

Azillion SPARKLZ
www.sparklz.com

Bobbie's Baubles
www.bobbiesbaubles.com

Broadwater Rose Jewels
The Blue Crow Antique Mall
32124 Lankford Hwy
Route 13
Keller, VA 23401
Tel: (757) 442 4150
www.broadwaterrosejewels.com

Christie's East
219 East 67th Street
New York, NY 10021
Tel: (212) 606 0400
Fax: (212) 452 2063
www.christies.com

Collectible Costume Jewelry
Suzanne Smith
Web site: www.costumejewelry.com

Deco Jewels
131 Thompson Street
New York, NY 10012
Tel: (212) 253 1222

Doyle New York
Auction House
175 East 87th Street
New York, NY 10128
Tel: (212) 427 2730
Fax: (212) 369 0892
E-mail: info@DoyleNewYork.com
www.doylenewyork.com

Eclectica Vintage Jewelry and Collectibles
Laurel Ladd Ciotti
P.O. Box 671
McIntosh, FL 32664
www.eclecticala.com

Eileen Chesner
Victorian Silver, New York
BY APPOINTMENT ONLY
Tel: (212) 254 5564

Fantasy Jewels
P.O. Box 5697
Baltimore, MD 21210
Tel: (410) 435 5599
E-mail: Bobbi@FantasyJewels.com
www.fantasyjewels.com

For Your Ears Only
Karen & Gary Foggin
Wilmington, DE
Tel: (302) 764 2954
E-mail: foggin@earthlink.net
www.oldjewels.com

Illusion Jewels
E-mail: jewels@illusionjewels.com
www.illusionjewels.com

Ira Scheck
984 S. Kenosha Court
Pueblo West, CO 81007
Tel: (719) 647 1568
E-mail: irascheck@aol.com

Jewel Diva
Chris and Connie DeNave
www.jeweldiva.com

Joseff of Hollywood
Janice Widdowes
E-mail: Bobana1950@aol.com
www.joseffofhollywood.com

Directory of Other Dealers, Auction Houses, and Museums cont.

Katie Atikian Antiques
E-mail: katerooa@aol.com
www.kateroo.com

Manhattan Art & Antique Center
1050 Second Ave
New York, NY 10022
Tel: (212) 355 4400
Fax: (212) 355 4403
www. the-macc.com

Morning Glory Antiques & Jewelry
Jane H. Clarke
12815 Central NE
Albuquerque, NM 87123
www.morninggloryantiques.com

Naomee Vintage and Contemporary Costume Jewels
www.naomee15.com

Past Perfection
Cheryl Kilmer
www.pastperfection.com

Plastic Fantastic
Karima Parry
Pennsylvania
E-mail: info@plasticfantastic.com
www.plasticfantastic.com

Rago Modern Auctions
333 North Main Street
Lambertville, NJ 08530
Tel: (609) 397 9374
Fax: (609) 397 9377
www.ragoarts.com

Remember When
www.tias.com/stores/rewhen

Sassy Classics
Sassy Classics
P.O. Box 2140
Pine, AZ 85544
Tel: (928) 476 2112

Sandot's Costume Jewelry
Sandy Butterfield
www.sandot.com

Sotheby's Chicago
215 West Ohio Street
Chicago, IL 60610
Tel: (312) 396 9599
Fax: (312) 396 9598
www.sothebys.com

Sotheby's New York
1334 York Avenue, New York
NY 10021
Tel: (212) 606 7000
Fax: (212) 606 7016
www.sothebys.com

South Texas Trading Company
Bee Gee McBride and John Borgstrom
P.O. Box 857 Port Aransas, TX 78373A
Tel: (800) 484 9293, enter 3474
www.southtexastrading.com

The Glitter Box
Sheila Pamfiloff
P.O. Box 35 Walnut Creek, CA 94597
Tel: (925) 937 7554
E-mail: pamfil@glitterbox.com
www.glitterbox.com

The Poet's Wares
E-mail: poetswares@tias.com
www.tias.com/stores/poetswares

This 'n' That
124 West 25th Street
New York, NY 10001
Tel: (212) 255 0727
E-mail: Anita613@aol.com

Three Jacks Vintage Costume Jewelry & Collectables
1121 W. Sherman Ave
Fort Atkinson, WI 53538
www.tias.com/stores/threejacks

Yesterjewels
Bonni Mancini
www.yesterjewels.bigstop.com

Zelda's Jewels
Merry Rae Kaufman
www.zeldasjewels.com

UK

Beauty and the Beast
Joel Rothman Unit Q9, Antiquarius
131–141 King's Road
UK
London SW3 8DT
Tel: 011 44 20 7351 5149

Christie's South Kensington
85 Old Brompton Road
London SW7 3LD
UK
Tel: 011 44 20 7581 7611
Fax: 011 44 20 7321 3321
www.christies.com

Diana Antique Jewellery
Stands G104–105, Alfies Antique Market
13–25 Church Street
London NW8 8DT
UK
Tel: 011 44 20 7724 2229
E-mail: dijewellery@aol.com
www.dianaantiques.co.uk

Hallmark Antiques
Stands 319 & 356, Grays Antique Market
1–7 Davies Street, London W1K 5LP
UK
Tel: 011 44 20 7629 8757
Fax: 011 44 20 7266 3587

Jezebel
14 Prince Albert Street
Brighton, East Sussex BN1 1HE
UK
Tel 01273 206091
Fax 01273 206091

Ian Lieber

29 Craven Terrace

London W2 3EL

UK

Tel: 011 44 20 7262 5505

Steinberg & Tolkein

193 King's Road

London SW3 5EB,

UK

Tel: 011 44 20 7376 3660

Fax: 011 44 20 7376 3630

Stevie Pearce

Stand G144

Alfies Antique Market

13–25 Church Street

London NW8 8D

UK

Tel: 011 44 20 7723 2526

E-mail: stevie@steviepearce.co.uk

Sylvie Spectrum

Stand 372, Grays Antiques Market

58 Davies Street

London W1Y 2LB

UK

Tel: 011 44 20 7629 3501

Fax: 011 44 20 8883 5030

Tadema Gallery

10 Charlton Place

Camden Passage

London N1 8AJ

UK

Tel: 011 44 20 7359 1055

The Gilded Lily

Stands 145–146, Grays Antique Market

58 Davies Street

London W1K 5LP

UK

Tel: 011 44 20 7499 6260

E-mail: jewellery@gilded-lily.co.uk

www.graysantiques.com

MUSEUMS:

Ashmolean Museum

Beaumont Street

Oxford, OX1 2PH UK

Tel: 011 44 1865 278000

Fax: 011 44 1865 278018

www.ashmol.ox.ac.uk

Birmingham Museum and Art Gallery

Chamberlain Square

Birmingham B3 3DH UK

Tel: 011 44 121 303 2834

Fax: 011 44 121 303 1394

www.birmingham.gov.uk/mag

Cheltenham Art Gallery & Museum

Clarence Street

Cheltenham

Gloucestershire GL50 3JT UK

Tel: 011 44 1242 237 431

Fax: 011 44 1242 262 334

E-mail: ArtGallery@cheltenham.gov.uk

www.cheltenhammuseum.org.uk

Egyptian Museum

Midan El Tahrir

Cairo, Egypt 11557

Tel: 011 20 2 5782 448/452

Fax: 011 20 2 579697

www.egyptianmuseum.gov.eg

Il Museo del Bijoux di Casalmaggiore

Via A. Porzio, 9, 26041

Casalmaggiore, Italy

Tel: 011 39 375 42309

Le Musée de la Mode et du Textile

Union Centrale des Arts Décoratifs

107-111 rue de Rivoli, 75001

Paris, France

Tel: 011 33 1 44 55 57 50

www.ucad.fr

Liverpool Museum

William Brown Street

Liverpool, L3 8EN UK

Tel: 011 44 151 478 4399

E-mail: themuseum@liverpoolmuseums.org.uk

www.liverpoolmuseums.org.uk

The British Museum

Great Russell Street

London WC1B 3DG UK

Tel: 011 44 20 7323 8000

email: information@thebritishmuseum.ac.uk

www.thebritishmuseum.ac.uk

The Kremlin Museum

The Kremlin

Moscow

Russia

Tel: 011 7 95 202 4256 / 202 3776

Fax: 011 7 95 921 6323

www.kreml.ru/

The Metropolitan Museum of Art

1000 Fifth Avenue

New York, NY 10028-0198

Tel: (212) 535 7710

www.metmuseum.org

Victoria & Albert Museum

Cromwell Road

London SW7 2RL UK

Tel: 011 44 20 7942 2000

www.vam.ac.uk

Index (Page numbers in *italics* refer to illustrations)

Acknowledgements

AUTHORS' ACKNOWLEDGEMENTS

The authors would like to thank the following people for their substantial contibutions to the production of this book:

Photographer Graham Rae for his unflagging humor and consistently wonderful pictures. Also Mike Malloy for additional photography.

All of the dealers, auction houses, and private collectors for kindly allowing us to photograph their jewelry, and for taking the time to provide a wealth of information about it.

The team at DK for all the long hours, dedication, and skill they have committed to the project, including Mandy Earey and Kelly Meyer for tackling a vast array of images and turning them into a visual treat, Paula Regan for her unflagging patience and encouragement, Angela Wilkes and Amber Tokeley for their editorial research and generation of copy, and finally, Julie Oughton and Heather McCarry for expertly overseeing the development of the text and design.

Also special thanks to Mark Hill, Meg Watson, Sara Sturgess, Cara Miller and, especially, Julie Brooke at the Price Guide Company (UK) Ltd for sourcing a wealth of oral, written, and visual information.

And finally, special thanks to Stephen Miners, Yai Thammachote, and Kevin Miners at Cristobal, without whom this project would never have gotten off the ground.

PUBLISHER'S ACKNOWLEDGEMENTS

Dorling Kindersley would like to thank Juliet Duff for picture research, Scott Stickland and Jonathan Brookes for digital image coordination, Philip Gilderdale and Martin Dieguez for design contribution, Caroline Hunt for proofreading, and Dorothy Frame for compiling the index.

PICTURE CREDITS

The publisher would like to thank the following for their kind permission to reproduce their photographs. (Abbreviations key: t=top, b=bottom, r=right, l=left, c=centre).

11: Kobal Collection; 14: Bridgeman Art Library, London/New York/Egyptian National Museum, Cairo, Egypt (t and bcl), Werner Forman Archive/The Egyptian Museum, Cairo (bl); 15: Heritage Image Partnership/The British Museum (cbl, ctl, t); 16: Michael Holford (bl, br, t); 18 Bridgeman Art Library, London/New York/Ashmolean Museum, Oxford (bc), Bridgeman Art Library, London/New York/British Museum, London (t), Bridgeman Art Library, London/NewYork/City of Liverpool Museum, Merseyside (br), Bridgeman Art Library,London/NewYork/Kremlin Museums, Moscow, Russia (bl); 19: Bridgeman Art Library, London/New York/S.J.Philips, London (c); 19: Corbis /Elio Ciol (bl); 19: Michael Holford (br); 55: Corbis; 56: Corbis/Hulton-Deutsch Collection; 57: Bridgeman Art Library, London/New York/Private Collection (b); 57: The Picture Desk/The Art Archive/Dagli Orti (tr); 57: Topham Picturepoint (tl); 60: Corbis (b), Corbis/Bettmann (t); 61 Corbis/Bettmann (b); 61 Vin Mag Archive (t); 69: The Picture Desk/Advertising Archives; 72: Mary Evans Picture Library (br); 74: Corbis (tl), Vin Mag Archive (br); 76: Hulton Archive/Getty Images (br); 78: Corbis/Bettmann (tl), Corbis/Arte & Immagini srl (bc); 79: Ronald Grant Archive (br); 79: Photos 12 (bl); 84: Corbis/Stephanie Colasanti (br); 84:Kenneth Jay Lane (tl); 86: Corbis/Bettmann (br); 90: Corbis/Bettmann (tl); 91:Corbis/Bettmann (tr); 94: The Picture Desk/Advertising Archives (br); 96: The Picture Desk/Advertising Archives (bc). 98: Vin Mag Archive (br); 99: Camera Press (tr); 99: Corbis/Horace Bristol (bl); 108: Hulton Archive/Getty Images (tl); 108: Topham Picturepoint (bl); 109: Mary Evans Picture Library (tr); 109:Corbis/Hulton-Deutsch Collection (bl); 112: Corbis/Bettmann (tl), Corbis/Gail Mooney (br); 113: Corbis (tr), Corbis/Kelly-Mooney Photograhy (bl); 118: The Picture Desk/Advertising Archives (br); 119: Corbis/Bettmann (tr), Corbis/Sygma (br); 130: Vin Mag Archive (br); 135: Hulton Archive/Getty Images; 215: Corbis/Hulton-Deutsch Collection; 237: Corbis/Bettmann.

Scottish Agate Jewellery p.209